Merry Christmas 2017!

—Paul

The

Blue Apron

Cookbook

The
Blue Apron
Cookbook

---

165 Essential Recipes & Lessons for
a Lifetime of Home Cooking

FROM THE BLUE APRON CULINARY TEAM

HARPER WAVE
An Imprint of HarperCollinsPublishers

HarperCollins books may be purchased for educational,
business, or sales promotional use. For information, please e-mail
the Special Markets Department at SPsales@harpercollins.com.

FIRST EDITION

Cover and interior design by Laura Palese
Photography by John Kernick

Library of Congress Cataloging-in-Publication Data
Names: Kernick, John, photographer. | Blue Apron Culinary Team.
Title: The Blue Apron cookbook : 165 essential recipes and
lessons for a lifetime of home cooking / from the Blue Apron
Culinary Team ; photography by John Kernick.
Description: First edition. | New York, NY : HarperCollins Publishers, [2017] |
Includes index. | Identifiers: LCCN 2017018933 (print) | LCCN 2017020421 (ebook) |
ISBN 9780062562777 (eBook) | ISBN 9780062562760
Subjects: LCSH: Cooking. | Cooking (Natural foods) | LCGFT: Cookbooks.
Classification: LCC TX714 (ebook) | LCC TX714 .B5768 2017 (print) | DDC 641.5—dc23
LC record available at https://lccn.loc.gov/2017018933

ISBN: 978-0-06-256276-0

ISBN: 978-0-06-283594-9 (Costco Edition)

ISBN: 978-0-06-282429-5 (Target Edition)

17 18 19 20 21   DES/LSC   10 9 8 7 6 5 4 3 2 1

Contents

Techniques, Recipes & Meals

Preface

It is common for executive chefs in France to wear a black-and-white-striped apron, but the cooks working under the executive chef traditionally wear a blue apron when they are learning their trade. This is a time-honored tradition that has been part of the kitchen hierarchy for generations. Cooks aspire to donning the black-and-white apron themselves as a symbol of their top status in the kitchen. Many American chefs who apprenticed in Europe continued to wear the blue apron, forgoing the black-and-white apron as a sign of respect to their mentors, a deferential gesture to indicate that they are never done learning in the kitchen. The Blue Apron was, and still is, a constant and humbling reminder that there's always more to learn from each other and ourselves, whether in the kitchen or beyond. This dedication to lifelong learning formed the foundation of our careers as chefs and was in the very DNA of the company. It ties directly into Blue Apron's mission as a company, because the first step toward building a better food system in America is developing the confidence and knowledge to cook at home more.

This foundation of continued learning is built into everything that we do at Blue Apron and extends to relationships with our farm partners, to learning and teaching new techniques through the study of historical food cultures, and to reinventing and building a better food system. The book works as a collection of immersion-based lessons based on a lifetime of learning from the Blue Apron culinary team. In the kitchens of the world-renowned restaurants we've worked in, we learned the skills that remain essential for us to this day: work neat, stay organized, don't mess with the food too much—and that great food always starts with great ingredients.

Once available only to restaurant chefs, fresh and sustainable ingredients are now available to many. Yet, knowing how to turn those ingredients into something spectacular may seem out of reach for novice cooks. *The Blue Apron Cookbook* will show you how easily you can learn how to cook at home with the right fundamentals. The lessons are fail-safe, because we've made all the mistakes so you don't have to.

Once you start cooking, it becomes an essential and meaningful part of your life, and you may find that it's difficult to live without it. Even today, after a long day of work or traveling, the first place many of us head to is to our own kitchens to make a simple, satisfying meal. We continue to cook, and never stop learning, in honor of what the blue apron represents. We hope you'll feel the same way.

Happy cooking from our kitchen to yours,
The Blue Apron Culinary Team

Introduction

This book is organized around cooking essential meals that will teach you how to apply the same fundamental techniques and lessons to a whole range of culinary possibilities. Learning the very basics, for even the simplest of techniques (how to season a chicken before roasting, how to perfectly sear a fillet of fish, how to sauté spinach so it's not watery), sets you up for success when those lessons are tried and true. We show you that if you know how to roast one chicken, you know how to roast any chicken, whether it's spatchcocked, stuffed with lemon and herbs, slathered with spices, or cut into pieces on a bed of root vegetables. If you can braise beef with red wine, you can braise chicken with red curry paste and coconut milk, or lamb with *ras el hanout* and dried apricots, or pork belly with soy sauce and star anise. If you can whisk together a vinaigrette, you can make an aioli and a mayonnaise from scratch.

You've learned how to make a beautiful roasted kabocha soup, but now it's spring and that soup can be asparagus, or you can use zucchini or corn in summer. We explain the principles behind every important step because knowing the "why" is what will empower you to take these recipes, explore, experiment, and run wild with your newfound freedom and instincts to make them your own. Once you have this foundation, you'll have the confidence and ability to cook almost anything.

Most important, you learn by doing, by being immersed in the work at hand (think of how you'd learn Italian much more easily living in Italy than by sitting in a classroom). To learn how to cook, you must get in the kitchen and start—the more you do it, the easier it is. It's like learning an instrument: When you first pick up a guitar, your fingers don't know what to do, but with practice, the movements come instinctively. World-renowned chef Charlie Trotter used to compare cooking to jazz. Once you learn the basics, then you can improvise. With cooking, you'll experience the same process. All that repetition slowly becomes intuition, like muscle memory. Even a task like prepping vegetables may seem tedious now, but it gets easier and faster over time.

We don't think of this book as a collection of recipes—rather, these pages represent the meals you'll create throughout your endless culinary journey. They'll act as a guide that sets you up for a lifetime of unforgettable experiences in the kitchen with the people and ingredients you cherish most.

GETTING STARTED

In this section, we offer an overview
of the basic tools and ingredients you'll need to
prepare the recipes in this book.

That doesn't mean you need to run out and purchase each and every item on our list before you start cooking—instead, consider this a starting point and handy reference for your developing pantry and arsenal of kitchen equipment. In fact, we believe the best-stocked kitchens have fewer, but smartly chosen, pieces of equipment—more is not better in this case. We focus on fundamental items that we reach for every day (not gimmicky items to impress your friends) because they will help you cook more efficiently—there's a sense of confidence that comes from being able to reach for what you need.

We all have that drawer of kitchen tools we haven't touched in years. Start by taking stock of the tools and equipment you already have; donate or give away things that you never use because they weren't built to last (such as anything with a plastic handle or that isn't heat-resistant) or don't have a useful purpose (like that garlic press). It might help to imagine yourself standing in front of the blank canvas of an empty kitchen counter. The following tools and ingredients will gradually occupy that space, and the growing collection (whisks, knives, strainers, and more) will give you a sense of what you're going to learn in this book and provide a map of where we'll take you. Then we'll stock your pantry with our favorite kitchen staples, and touch on basic techniques to help you navigate and visualize how recipes will come together. Finally, just before you dig in, we share our Kitchen Mantras that we return to again and again. Keep in mind that this is our initial overview to get you fired up—countless more specific tips appear throughout the book. In other words, we'll be with you every step of the way.

Stocking Your Kitchen

You don't need fancy gadgets to create an extraordinary meal—in fact, the most commonplace tools are often the most useful. Sure, it's nice to have a metal fish spatula for flipping a fillet, but in a pinch you can also do it with a metal spoon. (Don't forget that spoons were one of the first tools invented, for a reason—they're endlessly versatile.) We think the following "bare essentials" are indispensable for getting dinner on the table.

ESSENTIAL TOOLS

Apron: Aprons do more than just protect your clothes; they're like a uniform that helps put you in the mind-set of all the cooking to come. We're particularly fond of ones that are a linen-cotton blend in a nice, crisp shade of blue, of course.

Bench scraper: Metal or plastic bench scrapers are a versatile tool that helps transfer and cut dough, clean surfaces, or transfer chopped vegetables to a skillet.

Box grater: The classic for grating cheeses and root vegetables such as potatoes and carrots. Look for a sturdy, stainless steel grater with both fine and coarse options and a comfortable grip.

Butcher's twine: A ball of chef-grade (16- to 24-ply) twine is essential for securing a bouquet garni and tying large cuts of meat or trussing poultry. Choose 100 percent cotton professional chef–grade twine that's meant for oven use. Don't confuse it with baker's twine, which is much thinner and meant for crafts and food packaging and presentation.

Colander: A large colander that fits in the sink is perfect for draining, washing, or rinsing everything from noodles to fruit and salted vegetables.

Cutting boards: Thick, high-quality **wooden cutting boards** create a durable surface that won't warp and is resistant to scoring. Wooden boards also help keep blades sharper than other materials do. Choose a large size (18 by 12 inches) that will give you a generous surface area for prepping. Thick cutting boards may be a little more cumbersome to clean and move around, but the stability they provide is well worth it. Before using, put a wet paper towel underneath the board to prevent slipping. To clean, wash it thoroughly by hand and stand it up to dry; never put it in the dishwasher. Once a month, lightly oil with mineral or walnut oil to maintain the supple wood.

Fine-mesh strainer (large and small): Choose a strainer with a comfortable handle and use for straining and removing solids from sauces and soups or draining cooked greens or blanched vegetables.

Glass or stainless steel mixing bowls: Have a range of sizes that you can use for prep (your *mise en place*) and mixing. Sturdy, large mixing bowls are great for seasoning or marinating meat or vegetables, tossing salads, and mixing sauces. Also, never underestimate the importance of *mise en place*, French for "set in place." Keeping prepped ingredients (for example, chopped celery, snipped chives) organized and close at hand gives you the confidence to proceed with a recipe in a relaxed mind-set and avoid last-minute scrambling—and there's something Zen-like in the process of preparing each ingredient. Having several smaller bowls for prep will help you keep things under control while you cook, and ensure you're ready every step of the way.

Instant-read thermometer: To ensure that meats and poultry are cooked to a safe internal temperature and the desired doneness, use an instant-read thermometer for the most accurate gauge. Digital-display versions tend to be the easiest to read.

Knives: The first two knives we reach for in any kitchen are a **chef's knife** (for chopping just about anything) and its smaller, more precise relative, the **utility (or petty) knife**. A small **paring knife** (counterintuitively, the cheaper ones are the way to go) is super handy for coring and slicing fruit, and a **serrated bread knife** makes quick work of slicing large rustic loaves.

Oven thermometer: Essential for making sure your oven isn't running too hot or too cool. Place the oven thermometer on the center rack while preheating and adjust the oven temperature if needed.

Pepper grinder: It's rare to find yourself in the kitchen without using pepper, so a high-quality, large grinder is a worthy investment for your pantry. Use the dial to choose how fine or coarse you'd like your grind to be, depending on what you're making.

Salad spinner: A salad spinner efficiently cleans and dries leafy greens and herbs. The spinner basket allows you to lift them up and out of the water, leaving grit behind. The spinning removes excess moisture from greens without bruising them. Drier greens result in crisper, less watery salads, as vinaigrettes cling best to greens that are dry. Spinners are also handy for rinsing off berries and herbs and cleaning leeks.

Salt cellar: Keep a salt cellar (made of wood, ceramic, or stone) filled with kosher salt on the kitchen counter for easy-to-access seasoning. Adding salt to food by pinching the salt between your fingers will give you a better feel for how much seasoning you're using.

Sturdy tongs (not auto-locking): A key instrument for handling hot ingredients, whether vegetables, pan-seared meats, or flatbreads out of the oven, tongs ease flipping and turning in high temperatures. Choose a metal set with insulated handles.

Spatulas: A thin, slotted, **metal spatula** (sometimes called a "fish spatula") easily slips under pan-seared fish without ruining the nicely browned skin you've just worked to create. With a flexible slotted design and a wide, thin edge, a fish spatula is an essential tool for mastering pan-seared fish and ideal for flipping all sorts of foods (such as burgers or seared scallops). A heatproof **silicone spatula** (with a solid, single-piece construction) is needed for folding and stirring ingredients.

Sharp vegetable peeler: An everyday essential for peeling vegetables or shaving aged cheese. Choose one with a comfortable grip. Our favorite is a Y-peeler with a carbon steel blade.

Wooden spoon: The sturdy tool you'll use for almost every recipe, a wooden spoon is essential for scraping up flavorful fond from the bottom of the skillet, sautéing vegetables, combining batters, and much more.

Wire whisk: The most effective way to whisk together Dijon mustard, acid (citrus juice or vinegar), and oil into an emulsified vinaigrette, or whip cream and egg whites into billowy peaks. Choose stainless steel whisks, not silicone.

Zester/grater (such as a Microplane): This is based on woodworking rasps and is one of the most-used tools in the Blue Apron kitchen—we use ours to grate Parmigiano-Reggiano into a fluffy pile, create aromatic zest from citrus peel, and grate garlic into a fine paste. It's also handy for grating fresh ginger or nutmeg.

Essential Cookware & Bakeware

FOR THE STOVETOP

Heavier materials (for example, stainless steel, enamel-coated cast iron) maintain a steady temperature.

Cast-iron skillet (12 inches): A cast-iron skillet is the workhorse of the kitchen. Thick and durable, these skillets retain heat well and maintain a steady temperature for searing thicker cuts of meat and fish and shallow frying. When well-seasoned and cared for, cast-iron pans are nonstick and will only get better with age—you'll pass them on for generations.

Dutch oven (enamel-coated cast iron; 10 or 12 quarts): These heavy pots moderate temperature and hold heat, so they're perfect for slow, steady braises and long-simmered stews.

Saucepans: Choose a small saucepan (1 to 2 quarts) for browning butter, melting chocolate, and more; a medium saucepan (2 to 4 quarts) for making sweet and savory sauces; and a large saucepan (4 quarts) for cooking soups, stews, and beans and grains.

Sauté pans: Sauté pans and skillets provide a wide cooking surface that allows for even cooking and fast evaporation of cooking liquid. Have both a large (12 to 14 inches) and a medium (10 to 12 inches) stainless steel sauté pan at the ready.

Stockpot (10 or 12 quarts): Pots made of heavier materials like stainless steel will help maintain an even temperature and a slow, steady simmer.

COOK'S *tip*

CARING FOR CAST-IRON PANS: *After cooking, immediately rinse to clean, but never use soap as that will hurt the pan's "seasoning." Dry the pan immediately and lightly oil, if needed, before storing. If the pan needs more than a rinse, heat it on the stove, put in a generous amount of kosher salt, and scrub with a dish towel or thick wad of paper towels. The kosher salt will rub off the bits of food without affecting the seasoning.*

FOR THE OVEN

Baking pans: Glass or ceramic **baking dishes (9 by 13 inches; 8 by 8 inches)** are essential for baked goods, gratins, casseroles, and baked pastas. **Cake pans (9-inch rounds and 9-inch springform), loaf pans (9 by 5 inches),** and **pie dishes (9 inches, shallow)** are needed for cakes, quick breads, and pies. Choose high-quality pans for the most even results.

Oven-safe wire racks: These are among the most essential items in the kitchen. We use oven-safe, metal wire racks primarily for roasting large cuts of meats and whole chickens. Made to fit snugly in rimmed sheet pans, the racks elevate the meat, allowing hot air to circulate around the food for even cooking. Rendered fat collects on the bottom of the pan, not against the roast. The racks are also useful for cooling baked goods.

Rimmed sheet pans (13 by 18 inches, half sheets): Possibly one of the most essential bakeware items, aluminum and/or stainless steel sheet pans (with 1-inch rolled edges) will be necessary to have on hand for all of your roasting needs. They're also useful for resting meats and doughs and *mise en place*.

Roasting pan with elevated rack: In some cases, we call for a roasting rack (V-shaped) set in a deep roasting pan when the meat renders a high volume of fat. Choose a model made of a heavy, durable material (such as stainless steel) that won't react with foods; the pan should also have upright handles to make it easier to transfer into and out of the oven. The roasting rack keeps the meat from sitting in the accumulating fat.

SPECIALTY TOOLS AND EQUIPMENT

Our ancestors got by without them, but these items make modern life in the kitchen much easier.

Cake tester: When inserted into the middle of a cake, thin wire testers help ensure doneness (or a dry crumb). (You can also use a toothpick or paring knife for this task.) Cake testers are also useful for testing the doneness of fish—if the wire is warm, the fish is cooked.

Deep-fry/candy thermometer: They're adjustable and they attach to the pot (without touching the bottom) to ensure that the oil is at the proper temperature for frying. Look for one with an insulated handle that reads temperatures up to 400°F.

Food mill: Part strainer and part processer, hand-cranked food mills are useful for applications such as puréed potatoes or puréed soup and tomato sauce. The metal plates purée the ingredients while removing seeds and skins.

Kitchen shears: A sturdy pair of kitchen shears can be used for everything from snipping herbs to spatchcocking a chicken.

Mortar and pestle: A hefty mortar and pestle made from stone will serve you well in crushing toasted spices, pounding garlic into a paste, and making pesto the traditional way.

Pasta machine: Choose a high-quality, stainless steel model for cranking out your homemade tagliatelle and thin sheets of lasagna noodles.

Pizza stone: The satisfaction that comes with biting into a perfectly crispy slice of pizza is one that can be achieved only by using a pizza stone. The thick stone allows the heat to concentrate and then spread evenly under the dough, reaching higher temperatures than a sheet pan and producing a crispier crust.

Plastic Japanese mandoline: Inexpensive and less cumbersome than the heavy metal versions, plastic Japanese mandolines are a quick way to create paper-thin slices of vegetables. The blade is very sharp, so be very careful with your fingertips!

Spider strainer: A traditional Asian-style strainer with a shallow, coarse wire mesh basket and an extended handle is helpful for turning, scooping, and lifting foods in or from hot oil or boiling water. The wider basket weave allows for the hot oil (or hot water) to quickly drain from the food when you lift it.

SPECIALTY APPLIANCES

Blender: A stand blender is useful for puréeing soups and emulsifying dressings; high-speed models create the silkiest results. An immersion (or stick) blender is handy for blending smaller amounts.

Food processor: Food processors are perfect for making quick and easy work of pestos, sauces, coarse purées, and pastry crust.

Stand mixer: Stand mixers are a heavy-duty, workhorse appliance for kneading pizza dough, whipping egg whites, mixing batters, and more.

Stocking Your Pantry

SALTS

Most salts contain iodine and anticaking agents—always look for all-natural varieties with no preservatives.

Kosher: Kosher salt is our kitchen staple. The salt is a coarser grain than common table salt (and isn't iodized), and its texture makes it easier to handle when you're sprinkling with your fingertips.

Sea salts: All-natural salts are made through the ancient process of slowly evaporating seawater. Delicate flaky sea salts (such as Maldon) enhance flavor and add a faint crunchy texture. They create the perfect finish and "top layer" of seasoning for salads, fish, vegetables, chocolate desserts—just about anything. Coarser French gray salt, favored by many chefs especially as a finishing salt for meats, is formed as seawater flows into the Guérande marshes in France; it obtains a natural gray coloring from crystallizing on clay. Even sea salts can include preservatives, so make sure to check the label to ensure yours doesn't.

OILS

Extra virgin olive oil: Our go-to oil for most of the recipes in this book is extra virgin olive oil. Look for cold-extracted olive oil, preferably of single origin. Take a look at the label for the date of production—you always want to use olive oils within 1 year of that date. We prefer extra virgin olive oil over basic "olive oil" as extra virgin comes from the first extraction of the olives, is unrefined, and is of the highest quality, so that it has the best taste. (Although some labels may refer to olives being "pressed," olives today are processed by other methods, such as being ground into a paste that's then decanted in a centrifuge.) Regular olive oil is a refined product made from a blend of lower-quality olive oils. Choose a good-quality extra virgin olive oil for your everyday cooking needs, and have a very high-quality one on hand that you use only for finishing dishes right before serving.

Neutral vegetable oils: For sautéing and frying at high heat, choose canola, grapeseed, peanut, or safflower oil for their high smoking points.

Toasted sesame oil: Nutty and rich. We use it for cooking and finishing in Asian-inspired vinaigrettes, marinades, and other preparations.

VINEGARS

For everyday cooking, we rely on good-quality **red wine, white wine, cider, and aged sherry wine vinegars.** Some of the best quality vinegars are unfiltered, so some cloudiness is a good sign. **Seasoned rice vinegar,** made from fermented rice, adds a mild tartness to Asian-inspired preparations.

SPICES, HERBS, CONDIMENTS, AND OTHER FLAVORINGS

Mustards: For vinaigrettes, sauces, and sandwiches, have Dijon mustard (smooth and whole-grain) and dried Colman's mustard powder on hand.

Pickled, brined, and fermented vegetables: Capers, olives (the buttery green Castelvetrano variety is a Blue Apron favorite), cornichons, kimchi, sour dills—consider them flavor bombs and a quick way to add a burst of bright, tart flavor to a range of dishes.

Soy sauce: This classic Asian condiment is much more versatile than one may think—use it for marinades, stir-fries, vinaigrettes, and more. Depending on the brand and age, soy sauces can vary in flavor and thickness, adding both salty and savory touches that will round out the dish.

COOKING WITH WINE

In general, cook with dry white wines (such as pinot grigio or an unoaked chardonnay) and dry, full-bodied red wines (such as Côtes du Rhône or non-oaky pinot noir). Although you may have been warned against cooking with wines you wouldn't drink, there's no need to splurge on expensive, premium wines for cooking purposes only. Wines in the $10 per bottle price range will suffice, as well as leftover wine that you may have in your refrigerator (sealed, for up 2 weeks; you don't want to add anything overly astringent and undrinkable to your dish either). In general, avoid over-oaked wines—they leave an off-taste in your dish. Stick with simple wines that express their varietals. When in doubt, talk to the staff at the wineshop about what you'll be cooking.

Vanilla beans: Look for pods from Madagascar that are soft and leathery, not dry and brittle, so you can split the pod with a paring knife and scrape out the fragrant seeds.

Whole, ground, and dried spices and chiles: Buy in small amounts as they lose their potency over time. Store in tightly sealed containers in a cool, dry place away from direct sunlight.

FLOURS

All-purpose flour: "A.P. flour" is our go-to choice for pizza dough, breading, and baking.

Whole grain flours: Add texture and flavor to bread and baked goods with whole grain flours. These flours use grains that include the germ and bran (making them "whole"). Whole wheat and rye flours are two that are great to have on hand to make whole wheat focaccia or rye pizza dough. Blend whole grain and all-purpose flours together to achieve your desired texture (whole grain flours provide a coarser result).

SWEETENERS

Various sugars: Have granulated white sugar, light and dark brown sugars, confectioners' sugar, and natural or raw turbinado sugar on hand.

Honey: Honey adds both sweetness and nuanced flavor to a dish. The flowers that honeys are made from play a big role in their flavor, so we recommend you explore a range of varieties, from wildflower to buckwheat or clover, to find what you like best.

Maple syrup: When working with high-quality maple syrup, you're able to add to your dish a buttery sweetness that you cannot get from pure sugar. Although Grade A syrup is often recommended, we actually like cooking with Grade B dark amber syrup, ideally single origin, best. Grade B syrup is darker and richer, and has a more buttery flavor.

DRIED GRAINS AND BEANS

A variety of dried beans, including lentils (black beluga, French green, and quick-cooking red lentils) and chickpeas, as well as grains such as quinoa, barley, farro, millet, and kamut, set you up for soups, stews, pilafs, and pantry dinners. We love the flavor and texture of heirloom Italian bean varieties, such as borlotti, cranberry, corona, and cannellini beans (available online and at specialty markets). Except for lentils, dried beans should always be soaked overnight before being used. When soaking, use a nonreactive container and cold water, and place in the refrigerator. Warm water or a warm environment could cause the beans to ferment.

NUTS AND SEEDS

Have a variety of nuts and seeds on hand (almonds, walnuts, pistachios, pecans, hazelnuts, sesame seeds) to help add interest and texture to salads, sandwiches, and noodle dishes. Store in a sealed container in the refrigerator or freezer for a longer shelf life.

SEASONING TO TASTE

This phrase is kicked around a lot, but what does it really mean? For us, seasoning to taste means cooking with your senses, seasoning a dish in layers throughout the process, and tasting as you go. The easiest way to understand how this plays out in any dish is something we call our "Carrot Test."

When you have the time for a bit of kitchen experimentation, cook a small bunch of carrots in boiling, unsalted water. Once cooked, drain thoroughly and blend until smooth in a high-powered blender. Transfer to a bowl and taste the carrots with no salt added. They will most probably taste like bland baby food. Add salt a little at a time and taste the difference with each addition. The salt brings out the natural flavor of the carrots. After the first addition, the carrot blend will begin to have a fuller, richer taste. You'll reach a point where it will taste very flavorful, but not assertively salty. At this point, add more salt to experience what oversalting tastes like as well.

Basic
Knife Skills

Remember to keep your blades sharp. Dull knives are more dangerous than sharp knives because you need to put more pressure on them to perform (raising the risk of slipping). For the safest results, sharpen your knives on a regular basis, whether on your own or professionally. When cutting, position your body square to the cutting board (not at an angle). Using a wooden cutting board or butcher block (versus flimsy, pliant plastic varieties) for most of your cutting needs will be much easier on your knife. While your cutting hand grips the knife, use your other hand in a "bear claw" position to stabilize the ingredient being cut.

BASIC CUTS

Basic knife skills are essential because they directly affect how the ingredients cook in the dish. Ingredients that are cut in a uniform size and shape will cook evenly and at the same rate. Without consistent cuts, you could end up with some ingredients that are cooked perfectly, while others are still raw. While it might take some practice, learning basic knife cuts is the first thing you need to do to set yourself up for success in the kitchen. Remember that the more you practice, the faster and better you'll get.

utility knife

chef's knife

paring knife

bread knife

large dice
(¾ inch)

medium dice
(½ inch)

small dice
(¼ inch)

picked leaves

coarsely chopped

finely chopped

GARLIC PREP

paste

chopped

crushed

whole

HOW TO DICE AN ONION

1 While holding the onion steady with your nondominant hand, trim off and discard the stem and root ends of the onion. **2** Halve the onion lengthwise. **3** Peel away and discard the papery outer layers and the first tough, pale layer. **4** Place each half, cut side down, on the cutting board. While holding the top of the onion steady, carefully make horizontal cuts toward the root end without going all the way through. **5** Using your knuckles as a guide, make a series of vertical cuts with the same spacing as the horizontal cuts. **6** Finish by cutting crosswise or perpendicular to the vertical cuts, creating square dice.

HOW TO JULIENNE A VEGETABLE

1 Peel the vegetable. Trim off and discard the ends. Cut the vegetable crosswise into 2- to 3-inch-long pieces. **2** Carefully cut a thin slice off each piece, so it sits flat against the cutting board. Thinly slice lengthwise into planks. **3** Cut each plank into matchsticks.

HOW TO MAKE GARLIC PASTE

1 Peel and mince the garlic cloves. Sprinkle with salt. **2** Position the knife at a low angle to the board; repeatedly drag and scrape the knife over the garlic against the board until it resembles a paste.

HOW TO CHIFFONADE LEAFY HERBS OR VEGETABLES

1 Pick the leaves off the stems. Stack the leaves one on top of another. **2** Roll the leaves into a tight cylinder or cigar shape. **3** Thinly slice the roll crosswise into thin ribbons. Fluff the ribbons to separate the strands.

COOK'S
tip

MEASURING FRESH HERBS: *When a recipe calls for an herb and does not specify the leaves only, utilize the leaves in addition to the tender stems that extend just below the leaves. If a recipe calls for a chopped herb, a good rule of thumb is to measure the whole leaves (and tender stems) as double the amount called for in the recipe and you'll end up with the correct amount chopped. For example, for 1 tablespoon chopped parsley, start off with chopping 2 tablespoons whole leaves.*

medium-well

medium

medium-rare

rare

CHECKING MEAT FOR DONENESS

Instant-read thermometers are indispensable. To use one, insert the probe in the center of the thickest part of the meat, making sure not to touch bone. The meat will continue to cook as it rests, raising the internal temperature by 5 to 15 degrees depending on the size of the meat and the cooking method (smaller cuts, such as steak, will have less "carryover cooking").

For beef, lamb, or pork, check for the following temperatures **before resting**. Cook to 115°F for rare, 120° to 130°F for medium-rare, 135° to 140°F for medium, 145° to 150°F for medium-well, and 155° to 160°F for well-done. The USDA recomments that ground meat be cooked to 160°F, but you may use your judgment for dishes like hamburgers that you want to cook to a lower temperature, such as medium-rare. (Note that pork should be cooked to at least medium.)

For roasted chicken, we like to take the internal thigh temperature to 170°F, which is higher than the typical 165°F that you most often see as a guideline (165°F is recommended by the USDA as it's the temperature at which harmful bacteria are destroyed). At 170°F, the connective tissue in the thigh meat begins to break down, giving you a more tender result (and remember to always let your meat rest). Ground chicken should be cooked to 165°F.

Two exceptions to these temperatures are braising and slow-roasting meats. These methods cook meat to a point beyond well-done, until the connective tissue in the meat breaks down. For these applications, the meat is done when it is tender enough to pull with a fork or falls off the bone.

SEASONALITY AND SOURCING

We believe that for every ingredient, there's a right time and place to buy it. It could be a succulent Georgia peach that can barely contain its own juices, or grass-fed cattle that's harvested at the right time of year so its meat has fat and flavor, or grapes picked on the perfect day for the best wine possible—foods should be cooked at the right time and should come from the right places. We believe in cooking in season and we think you should too. Supporting farms and their growing cycles will help create the best food system for this country. Seeking out those ingredients and learning how to prepare them well are the first steps in building a better food system.

Always remember that even the most basic preparations—a green salad or a bowl of spaghetti and tomato sauce, for instance—won't shine unless the components (such as fresh young greens, flavorful canned tomatoes, high-quality extra virgin olive oil, and freshly grated authentic Italian cheeses) are great. When the ingredients are top-notch, you don't have to do much to them—you could say that the food almost cooks itself.

KITCHEN MANTRAS

Get organized.

Before you start any recipe, prepare your cooking area—a clean and empty sink is part of a happy kitchen. Prepare the ingredients for your *mise en place* and have all the tools and equipment you'll need at the ready.

Clean as you go.

This also plays to the principle of staying organized. If you clean as you go (discard scraps, place unneeded tools in the dishwasher), then you'll keep your workspace neat and make the end-of-night cleanup much easier.

Cook with your senses.

For the best results and the most enjoyable process, use your senses to see how the dish is coming together. Feel the salt with your fingertips. Smell meat roasting as the scent fills your kitchen. You will soon develop an intuition or sixth sense—a hallmark of a great cook.

Season and taste throughout cooking.

Build flavor slowly and in layers by seasoning and tasting your food throughout the process. It may take practice, but learning to season your food properly is a skill that can be mastered and is one of the most important things you'll learn.

Perfection is not required.

There should never be a reason to throw your food away, because even a "mess up" creates something to eat. There are clever ways to look at a less-than-perfect result and transform it into something else that makes a perfectly suitable meal. For instance, if your risotto gets too soft and mushy? Chill it, form it into balls with cheese in the middle, bread it, and fry it the next day for delicious arancini.

Do it your way.

Adapting a recipe to your preferences is always encouraged. Getting these techniques down means having the freedom to explore and experiment with your own recipes. We want you to take ownership of your food, to find out firsthand what your cooking style is.

Have fun.

The most important message in this book. We're passionate about cooking, not because we're perfectionists, but because we love the process of cooking itself. We're grateful we get to do what we love while cooking for the people we care about. This is your cooking journey to enjoy and share.

1
Roast Chicken

You're about to master what might be the
most valuable and satisfying recipe you'll ever prepare:
simple, perfectly roasted chicken.

The preparation reminds us that only a handful of ingredients are needed to create something that's timeless, nourishing, and deeply satisfying. We truly believe that a meal of roast chicken, herb-roasted potatoes, and a simple salad might be the best meal around. For us, the ultimate roast chicken has crispy, golden-brown skin and juicy, tender meat. The challenge lies in creating that beautiful, burnished skin without overcooking or undercooking the meat. Rest assured, our technique—tried, true, and tested over decades of cooking—follows just a few basic rules to help you achieve these results every time.

Once you've roasted one chicken, it's like having roasted them all—master the basic method, then adjust the elements (such as fresh herbs, spices, citrus, vegetables) to your preferences. One of the best things about roast chicken is that its flavor possibilities are seemingly endless. While a whole roast chicken is a show-stopping sight to behold, learning to break down and cook chicken butterflied or in individual pieces has its own unique merits.

No matter how you slice it, a chicken dinner isn't complete without a vegetable (whether roasted, mashed, or puréed) or starch to soak up the flavorful juices. That's why in this chapter we'll also share a master method for roasting vegetables that will enable you to cook virtually any seasonal accompaniment that catches your eye. And, of course, we can't forget about gravy—we'll teach you how to transform those flavorful pan drippings into a lush gravy that turns a roasted bird into a comforting feast.

Tools to Have on Hand

- Heavy-duty rimmed sheet pan
- Oven-safe wire rack
- Instant-read thermometer
- Butcher's twine

Keys to Success

1. Start with the best-quality chicken. As with any dish that relies on only a few ingredients, quality is key. Seek out the best, freshest chicken you can find; don't be shy about enlisting your butcher's recommendations. Look for birds that have a clean, fresh smell and are pasture raised.

2. Allow the chicken to come to room temperature. Meat that's roasted from room temperature will cook more evenly and yield more consistent results. Take the chicken out of the refrigerator, season it, and let it stand at room temperature for a full hour. Preheat the oven while the chicken is tempering.

3. Dry the chicken really well. Use paper towels to pat the skin and cavity dry, until all visible moisture is absorbed. Excess moisture turns to steam in the hot oven, while less moisture means a much better chance of creating crispy, golden-brown chicken skin.

4. Season generously. After tempering and drying, lightly drizzle the chicken with olive oil and rub all over. Coating the bird with olive oil helps the seasonings adhere to the skin and promotes browning, ensuring full-flavored results. After oiling, season the chicken again, showering the chicken inside and out with salt and pepper—don't be shy about the amount. The seasonings enhance the flavor of the meat, of course, but the salt serves an additional function by helping to dehydrate the skin—another way to boost its chances of rendering its fat and becoming crispy and richly colored.

5. Remember that the legs take longest to cook. To ensure even cooking, slide the legs of the chicken in first, so they're toward the warmer part of the oven.

6. Let the chicken rest before carving. Allowing chicken to rest before carving lets the juices settle and be reabsorbed by the meat. If you slice the meat when it comes straight out of the oven, those juices will spill out onto the cutting board and turn to steam against your once-crispy chicken. Since a whole chicken holds heat very well, it's hard to over-rest it; aim for at least 20 to 30 minutes.

COOK'S tip

AIR-DRYING: *Another way to remove moisture from a chicken is to air-dry it in the refrigerator. After you rinse the bird and pat it dry inside and out, salt it well and place it on a plate. Transfer to the refrigerator and chill uncovered for at least 2 hours or up to overnight. Let it stand at room temperature before cooking, as directed in the recipes.*

Simple Roast Chicken

Among all of the chefs here at Blue Apron, we've roasted thousands of chickens in our lifetimes. For this cookbook, we roasted countless more (a lot of chicken sandwiches and salads were eaten too). We basted chicken, we buttered it, we stuffed it. We turned the heat up, we turned the heat down. But we kept coming back to the basics: The technique we arrived at combines high heat, a well-tempered and trussed bird, generous resting time, and just a trio of staple seasonings (olive oil, salt, and pepper)—the ultimate proof that simple is often best.

1 whole chicken (3½ to 4 pounds)

Kosher salt and freshly ground black pepper

Extra virgin olive oil

1 lemon, cut into wedges, for serving

❶ Prepare the chicken. Pat the chicken dry with paper towels inside and out. Season with 1 tablespoon salt and ½ teaspoon pepper. Use butcher's twine (see page 2) to truss the chicken (see opposite page). Transfer to a wire rack set on a sheet pan and let stand at room temperature for 1 hour. While the chicken is tempering, put the oven rack in the middle position and preheat the oven to 475°F.

❷ Roast the chicken and serve. Rub 1 tablespoon olive oil all over the chicken. Season with 1 teaspoon salt and a generous amount of pepper. Roast for 1 hour 5 minutes to 1 hour 10 minutes, until the chicken is well browned and the juices run clear when the skin is pierced between the thigh and leg; an instant-read thermometer inserted into the thigh (without touching the bone) should register 170°F. Remove from the oven. Let the chicken rest for 35 minutes. Transfer to a cutting board, leaving any fat and browned bits (fond) in the pan to make the Pan Gravy (page 40). Transfer to a serving dish or, if desired, carve the chicken (see opposite page). Serve with the lemon wedges.

COOK'S
tip

OVEN RACK POSITION: *Since you're roasting at very high heat in this case, it's essential to place the oven rack in the middle of the oven. If the rack is too high, the oil coating can splatter and smoke; if it's too low and close to the heat source, the chicken might burn.*

How to TRUSS A CHICKEN

Trussing the chicken helps it cook more evenly—you'll want to use butcher's twine for this.

❶ Cut a long piece of butcher's twine (about 24 inches). With the chicken legs facing you, cross the legs and tie tightly with the twine. ❷ Wrap the twine around the outside of the legs to the top of the chicken. ❸ Tie tightly in a knot at the top of the breast and trim off the excess twine.

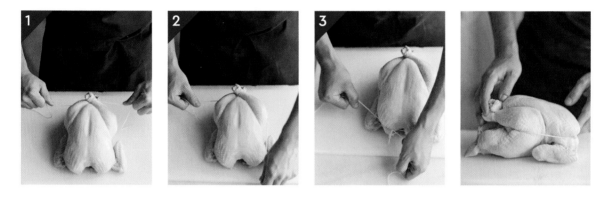

How to CARVE A CHICKEN

❶ To remove the legs, cut along the thigh, next to the breast. Carefully pull the leg away while using the tip of the knife to find the joint inside; cut through to remove the leg. ❷ Cut through the joint connecting the drumstick to the thigh. Repeat with the other leg. ❸ To remove the breast, cut along the breastbone and down along the ribs. Repeat with the other breast. If desired, cut the breasts in half on an angle.

Pan Gravy
(page 40)

Herb-Roasted Potatoes
(page 41)

PAN GRAVY

Makes 1 cup

Mastering the art of pan gravy is an essential and lifelong skill for elevating simple roasted meats into homey, deeply satisfying meals. Like making pasta, making pie crust, and other timeless procedures, this process is somewhat intuitive. Use your senses: As you whisk in the flour, you'll be able to smell when the aroma changes from "raw flour" to something more toasted and nutty. Of course, the more flavorful the liquid, the richer the gravy, so homemade stock (page 174) is ideal. As with almost everything else you'll do in the kitchen, a last-minute taste for seasonings is key.

Reserved fond from Simple Roast Chicken (page 36)

2 teaspoons olive oil (if needed)

2 tablespoons all-purpose flour

1 cup chicken stock (page 174) or water

2 tablespoons unsalted butter

Kosher salt and freshly ground black pepper

❶ **Start the roux.** Place the sheet pan with the fond on the stovetop and heat on medium-high until hot. If the sheet pan seems dry, with very little or no fat, add the olive oil. Add the flour and cook, whisking constantly, for 1 to 2 minutes, until golden-brown and fragrant. Add ½ cup of the chicken stock and cook, whisking frequently, for 30 seconds, until all of the browned bits are scraped up. Transfer the mixture to a small saucepan and heat on medium-high. Add the remaining ½ cup chicken stock, and cook, whisking frequently, for 3 to 5 minutes, until thickened and thoroughly combined.

❷ **Finish the gravy.** Add the butter and cook, whisking constantly, for 1 to 2 minutes, until melted and thoroughly combined. Remove from the heat. Season with salt and pepper and serve.

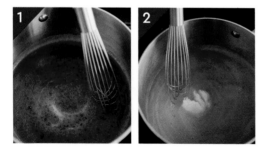

WHAT IS FOND?

In cooking, "fond" refers to the caramelized, browned bits that form on the bottom of a pan after pan-searing or roasting meat or fish. Fond, which comes from the French word for "bottom" or "foundation," equates with flavor and is the culinary equivalent of gold. To incorporate the fond into your dish, whether as a pan sauce or the base of a braise, "deglaze" by adding liquid to it or sautéing vegetables in it, then scrape it up with a wooden spoon. The moisture from the liquid or vegetables will help release the fond from the bottom of the pan and into your dish.

Variations

Just as with everything else in this book, feel free to experiment with your gravy seasoning. Once you've got your gravy technique down, there are many ways to brighten and vary the flavors of the finished sauce. Our favorite ways include adding finely chopped fresh rosemary and sage and replacing half of the chicken stock with white wine; incorporating grated lemon zest, capers, and chopped fresh parsley; or starting with chopped garlic and finishing with a hit of chopped fresh basil and parsley.

HERB-ROASTED POTATOES

Serves 2 to 4

A crispy, salty sidekick that goes with just about everything. There are few dishes these potatoes won't benefit, and they're essential alongside roasted meats, pan-seared fish, or steak. We'd be happy to make a meal of them on their own too, topped with Herb Vinaigrette (page 48), Aioli (page 272), or a crispy fried egg. Keeping the aromatics—in this case, rosemary and garlic—whole rather than chopping them ensures that they won't burn while the potatoes roast. Other hearty herbs such as thyme, oregano, and sage can be roasted along with the potatoes, but softer herbs such as parsley, mint, or chives are best incorporated after roasting. Spreading the sweet, roasted garlic on bread to eat alongside the chicken and potatoes is never a bad idea, either.

1 pound fingerling or other small potatoes

3 tablespoons extra virgin olive oil

1½ teaspoons kosher salt

4 large sprigs rosemary

2 cloves garlic, unpeeled

❶ Prepare the potatoes. Preheat the oven to 475°F. Halve any large potatoes lengthwise on an angle; keep smaller potatoes whole. Place the potatoes in a large bowl and add the olive oil, salt, rosemary, and garlic. Toss to combine. Transfer to a sheet pan and arrange cut side down in a single, even layer.

❷ Roast and serve the potatoes. Roast for 25 to 30 minutes, until the potatoes are golden brown and tender when pierced with a knife. Discard the rosemary and serve.

COOK'S
tip

PREPARING ROASTED VEGETABLES: *Roasting vegetables cut side down allows more surface area to develop a deeply golden crust. When you're preparing the potatoes (or other vegetables), tossing them in a large bowl really makes a difference because it's much easier to distribute the oil and seasoning evenly.*

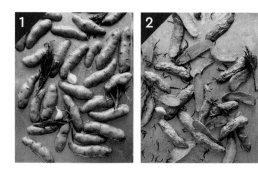

HOW TO ROAST
Any VEGETABLE

Once you've mastered the art of perfectly
roasted potatoes, you'll understand how easy it is to
apply the same technique to virtually any in-season
vegetable that strikes your fancy.

Roasting is an intuitive approach that comes down to grouping vegetables in categories based on their shape, texture, and density. Starchy winter root vegetables take longer, while summer vegetables with a higher moisture content roast more quickly. With other varieties, you'll want to achieve slightly different results: crisped browned edges on cauliflower and brussels sprouts; sweet, melting, caramelization with leeks and shallots.

Keys to Success

1. Roast by category and keep the pieces the same size. Roasting vegetables of the same category in the same pan (green vegetables together, root vegetables together) allows all the vegetables to finish at the same time. Whether cooking smaller pieces or larger wedges, cut vegetables into a uniform shape and size and toss once or twice during cooking to ensure even browning.

2. Season well. To season, place the vegetables in a large bowl and season generously with salt and pepper and a thin coating of good-quality oil or fat. Seasoning in the bowl, not on the sheet pan, allows you to evenly distribute the seasoning and oil. If there's too much oil on the sheet pan, it will start smoking; if there's too little on the vegetables, they won't brown.

3. Choose the right cooking vessel, and don't overcrowd it. Use a pan with shallow sides so that the moisture doesn't get trapped and steam the vegetables. Arrange the vegetables in a single, even layer in the pan and don't overcrowd—again, if they're crowded they'll steam rather than brown.

4. Roast at a high temperature. Roasting at a high temperature allows a deep, caramelized crust to form. Compared with green vegetables with a higher moisture content (like asparagus or broccoli), denser, starchier vegetables (like root vegetables) will roast at slightly lower temperatures and for longer.

5. Test for doneness with the tip of a knife. No matter the vegetable, it's done (tender) when you can insert the tip of a knife into it with no resistance.

STICKING VEGETABLES: *If the roasted vegetables are sticking to the pan when you remove them from the oven, try letting them stand for 3 to 5 minutes and they might release.*

ROASTED CAULIFLOWER

More vegetables that love a little roasted char:
broccoli, brussels sprouts, carrots, turnips, and celery root

Core 1 head of cauliflower and cut into small florets. In a large bowl, lightly drizzle with olive oil and season with salt and pepper. Spread on a sheet pan in a single, even layer. Roast at 475°F for 30 to 35 minutes, stirring halfway through, until browned. Transfer to a bowl and toss with lemon zest, freshly squeezed lemon juice, and chopped parsley.

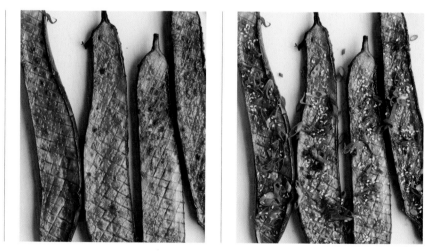

MISO-ROASTED EGGPLANT

More vegetables that could use a savory-sweet miso glaze:
summer squash and carrots

Cut 2 Japanese eggplants in half lengthwise. Using the tip of your knife, score a shallow, diagonal crosshatch pattern into the cut sides. In a small bowl, whisk together ¼ cup mirin, ¼ cup white miso paste, 2 tablespoons sesame oil, and 2 tablespoons water. Spread the mirin-miso mixture on the cut sides of the eggplants. Place on a sheet pan, cut side up. Roast at 450°F for 18 to 20 minutes, until golden brown and tender. Top with thinly sliced scallion tops and white sesame seeds.

ROASTED WINTER SQUASH *with Maple Butter*

More vegetables that can be roasted whole or halved with the skin on: *any winter squash and root vegetables (such as rutabagas or sunchokes)*

Halve 2 acorn squash; scoop out and discard the seeds. Drizzle the cut sides with olive oil and season with salt and pepper; turn to thoroughly coat. Place the seasoned squash, cut side down, on a sheet pan. Roast at 450°F for 20 minutes. Combine 6 tablespoons softened butter with 1 tablespoon maple syrup. Remove the pan from the oven and flip the squash, cut side up. Divide the maple butter among the squash cavities. Return to the oven and roast for 10 to 15 minutes more, until browned and tender when pierced with a knife. Top with chopped chives and serve.

ROASTED ASPARAGUS

More tender green vegetables that roast quickly: *scallions, spring onions, summer squash, and whole pole beans*

In a large bowl, lightly drizzle 1 pound asparagus (bottoms trimmed off) with olive oil and season with salt and pepper. Spread on a sheet pan in a single, even layer. Roast at 475°F for 8 to 10 minutes, until slightly browned and tender. Just before serving, drizzle with freshly squeezed lemon juice and top with chopped fresh herbs (tarragon, chervil, and chives). Best suited for "later season" asparagus that is tougher and thicker.

Spice-Rubbed Roast Chicken

with Spicy Cilantro Cream Sauce

Spice rubs go a long way on any roasted meat, but chicken in particular is the perfect blank canvas for robust flavors, such as the marinade in this recipe. It was inspired by the sultry, savory flavors of Latin America. We've found that the best way to evenly spread any marinade on chicken (or any meat) is in a large mixing bowl. It allows you to efficiently roll the chicken in the seasonings because you won't have to scrape them up from a flat surface. And don't skip serving this with the sauce. It's cool, creamy, and easy to whip together and it packs a fiery kick all its own.

4 cloves garlic, finely grated into a paste

2 tablespoons ground cumin

2 tablespoons sweet paprika

2 tablespoons white wine vinegar

3 tablespoons extra virgin olive oil, plus more for drizzling

Kosher salt and freshly ground black pepper

1 whole chicken (3½ to 4 pounds)

1 lemon, cut into wedges

SPICY CILANTRO CREAM SAUCE

1 jalapeño pepper, stemmed, seeded, and finely chopped

½ cup sour cream

2 tablespoons freshly squeezed lemon juice

¼ cup finely chopped cilantro, plus whole leaves for garnish

❶ Prepare the spice rub. In a small bowl, stir together the garlic paste, cumin, paprika, vinegar, the 3 tablespoons olive oil, 1 tablespoon salt, and ½ teaspoon pepper.

❷ Prepare the chicken. Place the chicken in a large bowl lined with paper towels and pat it dry inside and out. Discard the paper towels. Rub the spices all over the chicken and inside the cavity. Let stand at room temperature for 1 hour, turning and rubbing halfway through to thoroughly coat again. While the chicken is marinating, preheat the oven to 425°F.

❸ Truss and roast the chicken. Lightly season the chicken with salt. Rub the chicken one more time, inside and out, with any remaining spices left in the bowl. Use butcher's twine to truss the chicken (see page 37). Place the chicken breast side up on a wire rack set on a sheet pan.

Drizzle with 2 teaspoons olive oil. Roast for 50 to 55 minutes, until well browned and the juices run clear when the skin is pierced between the thigh and leg; an instant-read thermometer inserted into the thigh (without touching the bone) should register 170°F. Remove from the oven and let rest for 30 minutes.

❹ Make the sauce. While the chicken rests, stir together the jalapeño, sour cream, lemon juice, and chopped cilantro in a bowl. Season with salt to taste.

❺ Carve and serve the chicken. Transfer the chicken to a cutting board and carve as desired (see page 37). Transfer to a serving dish. Garnish with the cilantro leaves and serve with the sauce and lemon wedges on the side.

COOK'S *tip*

HANDLING HOT PEPPERS: *When using fresh hot peppers, for a less spicy result, cut out the ribs and membrane of the pepper where the spicy oils come from. Wash your hands thoroughly after handling any hot peppers and avoid touching your face or eyes.*

Roasted Butterflied Chicken

with Herb Vinaigrette

Spatchcocking poultry, a term believed to come from "dispatching" the bird, is a traditional technique that may date back to eighteenth-century Ireland. To spatchcock, we use kitchen shears to remove the backbone of a chicken and split it in half so it lies flat before roasting or grilling. When it's opened like a book, more surface area comes into contact with the heat, so it will end up with more seasoned, crispy skin. Better yet, this also allows the chicken to cook faster. Pouring some of the vinaigrette over the chicken once it's roasted allows the meat to absorb the fresh flavors of chives, parsley, basil, and oregano.

1 whole chicken (3½ to 4 pounds)

Kosher salt and freshly ground black pepper

Extra virgin olive oil

Coarse sea salt, for serving

1 lemon, cut into wedges, for serving

HERB VINAIGRETTE

Juice of 4 lemons

½ cup coarsely chopped fresh basil leaves

¼ cup thinly sliced fresh chives

2 tablespoons finely chopped fresh flat-leaf parsley leaves

1 tablespoon finely chopped fresh oregano or marjoram

½ cup extra virgin olive oil

Kosher salt and freshly ground black pepper

❶ **Prepare the chicken.** Use kitchen shears to spatchcock the chicken (see below). Pat the chicken dry with paper towels. Season all over with 2 tablespoons kosher salt and ½ teaspoon pepper. Transfer to a wire rack set on a sheet pan, skin side up. Let stand at room temperature for 1 hour. While the chicken is tempering, preheat the oven to 475°F.

❷ **Roast the chicken.** Drizzle both sides of the chicken with 1 tablespoon olive oil and season lightly with salt. Roast for 45 to 55 minutes, until the juices run clear when the skin is pierced between the thigh and leg; an instant-read thermometer inserted into the thigh (without touching the bone) should register 170°F.

❸ **Make the vinaigrette.** While the chicken roasts, in a bowl, whisk together the lemon juice, basil, chives, parsley, oregano, and olive oil. Season with salt and pepper.

❹ **Dress the chicken.** Remove the chicken from the oven. Transfer to a serving platter and immediately spoon half of the vinaigrette over it. Let rest for 20 minutes.

❺ **Carve and serve the chicken.** Transfer the chicken to a cutting board and carve as desired (see page 37). Return to the serving platter and serve the remaining vinaigrette on the side. Sprinkle with sea salt and serve with the lemon wedges.

How to SPATCHCOCK A CHICKEN

❶ Use kitchen shears to cut along both sides of the backbone; discard. ❷ Lay the chicken flat, breast side up, and use the heel of your hand to press down forcefully on the breastbone until it cracks. ❸ Flip the chicken and cut out the rib bones on either side.

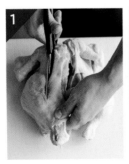
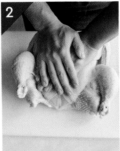

Tandoori-Style Roast Chicken

with Spicy Yogurt Marinade

Traditional tandoori chicken is made in a tandoor oven, a clay oven shaped like a cylinder with a fire at the bottom. Pieces of marinated chicken are skewered, placed in the oven, and roasted until cooked through and perfectly juicy. Here, we've taken those flavors and made the dish accessible for home cooks with any oven. This bold, Indian-style chicken is made with a marinade of yogurt, lime, ginger, garlic, and warm spices. Roasting the chicken in pieces is a nod to the traditional method, but it also allows you to season the entire surface area of each cut. The chicken needs to marinate for at least an hour to pick up the most flavor, but it can easily be done up to a day in advance. Complete the meal by serving it with traditional sides, such as warm basmati rice, grilled naan bread, raita (see below), or plain yogurt.

Juice of 2 limes

1 cup finely chopped cilantro, plus more for garnish

1 (2-inch) piece ginger, peeled and minced

4 cloves garlic, minced

1 tablespoon hot curry powder (Madras or Indian)

1 tablespoon garam masala

2 tablespoons tomato paste

1 cup full-fat Greek yogurt

Kosher salt

2 pounds bone-in, skinless chicken thighs

Freshly ground black pepper

Extra virgin olive oil, for drizzling

1 lime, cut into wedges, for serving

❶ Make the marinade. In a large bowl, combine the lime juice, the 1 cup chopped cilantro, ginger, garlic, curry powder, garam masala, tomato paste, yogurt, and 1 tablespoon salt.

❷ Marinate the chicken. Pat the chicken dry with papers towels. Add the chicken to the marinade and toss to coat. Cover the bowl with plastic wrap and let the chicken marinate at room temperature for 1 hour. While the chicken is marinating, preheat the oven to 425°F.

❸ Roast the chicken. Place the chicken in a single layer, skinned side up, in a 9 by 13-inch baking dish. Lightly season with salt and pepper. Pour any marinade left in the bowl over and around the chicken. Roast for 50 to 60 minutes, until browned and cooked through; an instant-read thermometer inserted in the chicken (not touching the bone) should register 170°F. Remove from the oven and let rest for 30 minutes.

❹ Serve the chicken. Transfer to a serving dish, discarding any marinade left in the baking dish. Drizzle with olive oil and garnish with chopped cilantro. Serve with lime wedges on the side.

RAITA

Raita is an Indian condiment typically served alongside spicy foods to cool the palate. To make a simple raita, combine ½ cup plain full-fat Greek yogurt, 1 small cucumber (cut lengthwise into 8 wedges and thinly sliced), 1 tablespoon lime juice, 1½ teaspoons salt, and freshly ground black pepper.

Roast Chicken & Vegetables in a Pot

Serves 4

Chicken that roasts alongside potatoes, carrots, and onions creates the quintessential Sunday dinner. This time-honored technique is ideal for cooking chicken pieces because they're easy to brown, and the covered pot keeps everything moist. It's even better for the vegetables. They're sautéed in the rendered chicken fat, so they pick up all the flavor of the browned bits (or fond) left from the chicken. We all know that fat and fond equal flavor—they add to any dish an immeasurable layer of richness that's hard to achieve with just olive oil or butter.

1 whole chicken (3½ to 4 pounds), cut into 6 pieces (2 breasts, 2 thighs, 2 drumsticks)

Kosher salt and freshly ground black pepper

Extra virgin olive oil

¾ pound red potatoes, quartered if small, large diced if bigger

2 carrots, peeled and large diced

1½ cups pearl onions, peeled

4 cloves garlic, peeled and lightly crushed

4 sprigs thyme

2 sprigs sage

3 dried bay leaves

1 cup dry white wine (such as sauvignon blanc or pinot grigio)

1 teaspoon white wine vinegar

2 tablespoons unsalted butter

¼ cup chopped fresh flat-leaf parsley

Coarse sea salt, for garnish

❶ Prepare the chicken. Pat the chicken pieces dry with paper towels. Season with 1 tablespoon salt and ¾ teaspoon pepper. Let stand at room temperature for 1 hour.

❷ Sear the chicken. In a large Dutch oven, heat 2 tablespoons olive oil on medium until hot. Add the chicken, skin side down. Cook for 13 to 14 minutes, flipping halfway through and being careful not to break the skin as you flip, until browned on both sides. Transfer the chicken pieces to a plate. While you're browning the chicken, preheat the oven to 425°F.

❸ Roast the vegetables and chicken. Add the potatoes, carrots, onions, and garlic to the pot. Season with salt and pepper. Cook, stirring occasionally, for 4 to 5 minutes, until lightly browned. Stir in the thyme, sage, and bay leaves. Return the chicken to the pot, nestling the pieces in the vegetables, skin side up. Add the wine. Bring to a simmer and cook for 30 seconds. Cover the pan and transfer to the oven. Roast for 25 to 30 minutes, until the vegetables are tender and the chicken is cooked through; an instant-read thermometer inserted into the thigh (without touching the bone) should register 170°F. Remove from the oven.

❹ Make the sauce and serve. Use a slotted spoon to transfer the chicken pieces to a plate. Remove and discard the herb sprigs and bay leaves. Heat the vegetables and juices over medium until simmering. Cook for 1½ to 2 minutes, until the liquid is reduced in volume by half. Reduce the heat to medium-low. Stir in the vinegar and butter. Cook, stirring constantly, for 30 seconds to 1 minute, until thoroughly combined. Stir in the parsley and remove from the heat. Transfer the vegetables to a serving dish and top with the chicken pieces. Pour any accumulated juices from the plate over the chicken. Spoon the sauce over the chicken and vegetables. Sprinkle with sea salt and serve.

COOK'S
tip

BETTER BROWNING: *Anytime you're adding several items to a pan, wait 5 seconds between pieces. This allows the pan to recover and regain its temperature, which ensures that the next thing you add doesn't stick. You'll know that ingredients (like the chicken in this recipe) are ready to flip when they quit sizzling and "quiet down."*

2
Sunday Roasts

Weeknights call for recipes that are quick and simple,
but there are occasions like holidays and family get-togethers
that warrant something more special.

This chapter is devoted to the latter—the weekly tradition of gathering your nearest and dearest for leisurely, generous feasts like prime rib au jus, an Italian-style pork loin, or rosy pink slices of roasted leg of lamb.

A Sunday roast is such a classic dish around the globe, it's no wonder every culture has its own unique version. Whether the meat was spit-roasted in the radiant heat of a wood-burning hearth or prepared in one of the first iron stoves (the original "closed hearth"), there have been many ways to make a delicious recipe. So what does that mean when it comes to Blue Apron? For us, a Sunday roast translates to splurges: bone-in, tender cuts of meat, such as a rack of lamb or a prime rib roast, that are at their best when roasted at moderate to high temperatures to ensure even cooking and a juicy texture throughout. The roasting time is shorter and the texture of cooked meat is firmer than with a "slow roast," such as pork or lamb shoulder (which you'll read about in the next chapter), and a Sunday roast is also easier to slice, so you can expect a beautiful presentation.

Typically, the biggest challenge with these roasts, particularly with larger cuts of meat, is achieving that perfect balance of a browned exterior with a juicy, moist interior. We've focused on a few key details below to achieve that. To round out the meal, we'll teach you how to sauté vegetables of all kinds—the perfect side to your roasted masterpiece. Read on to develop your own weekly tradition.

Tools to Have on Hand

- Heavy-duty rimmed sheet pan
- Oven-safe wire rack
- Instant-read thermometer
- Butcher's twine

Keys to Success

1. Start with the highest-quality meat or fish.
From prime rib to a rack of lamb, cuts that benefit from moderate-to-high-temperature cooking tend to be more tender and expensive. Since you're investing in a special meal, it's important to seek out a quality source, such as a butcher or well-attended supermarket meat department that sells high-grade meat (preferably pasture raised). In general, you want to choose cuts with a rich color, minimal gamy smell, a nice creamy fat cap (when appropriate), and light marbling. Make sure there are no nicks to the meat, and that the bones don't have a strange odor.

2. Season early and generously, and let the roast come to room temperature. Massaging a roast with salt, pepper, and other seasonings early on allows the flavors to better permeate the entire cut. Bringing the roast to room temperature ("tempering") before roasting will allow it to cook more evenly.

3. Account for carryover cooking. Large roasts hold a lot of heat, and they'll continue to cook for a period of time after you remove them from the oven. To avoid overcooking, remove them at the lower end of the suggested temperature range; carryover cooking will bring the roast to your preferred doneness.

4. Is it done yet? Resist the temptation to sneak peeks and check on a roast too often. Opening the oven door will cause temperature fluctuations that result in uneven cooking and will also increase total cooking time.

5. Rest meat for half its cook time. For the best results, allow roasted meat to rest for at least half of the time it was cooked (for example, 2 hours cooking time = 1 hour resting time).

OVEN RACK POSITION: *The oven's main source of heat comes from the bottom. For the most even, effective roasting, always position the oven rack at the bottom third of the oven when cooking large roasts.*

DRIPPINGS: *For any roast, if you're too short on time to make a jus or a gravy, transfer drippings to a measuring cup and skim off any excess fat. Pour the remaining juices over your sliced meat. Even better, roast thinly sliced potatoes or other root vegetables in the drippings while the roast rests and serve as a side.*

LEFTOVER BONES: *After carving the bones from a roast before serving, don't throw the bones away. If they're not fated to be gnawed on by the luckiest dog, simmer them as a base for soup or in a pot of beans served with a poached egg.*

Roasted Rack of Lamb

with Herbs & Breadcrumbs

With a crunchy, golden-brown crust and an enticing garlicky aroma, a roasted rack of lamb is an impressive centerpiece and one of the most satisfying but simplest ways to enjoy the meat's rich flavor. Cut perpendicularly to the spine, a rack typically offers seven or eight chops. (Two or three racks tied into a circle create a crown roast.) An herb-and-breadcrumb coating made with garlic, Dijon mustard, and tarragon—although you can use any herb—creates a flavorful outer crust. After the meat has rested, carve single chops (one bone) for thinner servings or double chops (two bones) for thicker servings.

1 rack of lamb, frenched (7 or 8 bones, about 1½ pounds)

1 tablespoon extra virgin olive oil, plus 2 teaspoons for drizzling

Kosher salt and freshly ground black pepper

1 clove garlic, finely grated into a paste

¼ cup Dijon mustard

1½ tablespoons finely chopped fresh tarragon leaves

½ cup panko breadcrumbs

1 large egg white, beaten

Sautéed Sugar Snap Peas (page 60), for serving (optional)

KNOW YOUR LAMB

Seek out grass-fed and grass-finished lamb grown in New Zealand, in Australia, or domestically. Lambs from New Zealand tend to be smaller as they're raised for wool, while in Australia they're raised for both wool and meat production. American lambs are larger as they're raised only for their meat and usually grain-fed.

❶ Season the lamb and prepare the breadcrumbs. Remove the lamb from the refrigerator and pat dry with paper towels. Drizzle with 2 teaspoons olive oil. Season with 1 tablespoon salt and ¼ teaspoon pepper. Let stand for 30 minutes to temper. Meanwhile, preheat the oven to 450°F. In a bowl, combine the garlic paste, mustard, 1 tablespoon olive oil, tarragon, breadcrumbs, ½ teaspoon salt, and ¼ teaspoon pepper.

❷ Coat the lamb. Use a pastry brush to lightly brush the outer side of the lamb with the egg white. Coat with the mustard-breadcrumb mixture, pressing to adhere.

❸ Roast the lamb. Transfer the lamb, breadcrumb side up, to a wire rack set on a sheet pan. Roast for 28 to 30 minutes, until the breadcrumbs have browned and an instant-read thermometer inserted into the center of the meat (not touching the bone) registers 140°F (for medium doneness). Remove from the oven; let rest for 15 to 20 minutes.

❹ Serve the lamb. Transfer the lamb to a cutting board and carve by cutting straight down between the bones. Transfer to a serving dish and serve with the snap peas on the side.

COOK'S *tip*

FRENCHED BONES: *A rack of lamb is traditionally prepared with the bones "frenched" or trimmed clean of fat, so that they're exposed. These days you can usually find frenched racks in the meat case of good markets, or you can ask the butcher to do the frenching for you. Before roasting, season the bones as well as the meat to develop even more flavor as the rack cooks. Avoid putting the breading on the inner curve (the bone side) of the rack because it will insulate the bones (you want them to heat up faster to cook the rack).*

SAUTÉED SUGAR SNAP PEAS

Serves 2 to 4 as a side

With their sweet springtime flavor and crisp texture, sautéed sugar snap peas brighten the plate and balance the richness of roasted meats. When it comes to sautéing snap peas or other young vegetables, make sure you allow the cooking oil to get very hot and avoid overcrowding the pan. They'll cook quickly—just long enough to take on a few blistered spots while retaining their crispness. A squeeze of fresh lemon juice at the end adds a touch of brightness that elevates any sautéed vegetable.

½ **pound sugar snap peas**

Extra virgin olive oil

Juice of 1 lemon

1 teaspoon kosher salt

❶ Prepare the snap peas. Snap off the stem end of each snap pea; pull off and discard the tough string that runs the length of each pod.

❷ Cook the snap peas. In a large sauté pan, heat 2 teaspoons olive oil on high until hot. Add the snap peas and cook, stirring occasionally, for 3 to 5 minutes, until tender and lightly browned. Remove from the heat. Drizzle with the lemon juice and season with salt. Transfer to a serving dish and serve.

COOK'S *tip*

TOUGHER VEGETABLES: *As the season progresses, snap peas can become a little tougher. If this is the case with your snap peas, add a few tablespoons of water at a time as the peas cook so the exterior will become tender. This works well with asparagus and other sautéed vegetables that need a little more moisture to cook through in the pan.*

SAUTÉED SPINACH

with Garlic & Lemon

Serves 4 to 6 as a side

Garlicky sautéed spinach comes together in minutes and makes a savory, nourishing side dish for virtually any roasted or pan-seared meat or fish. Everyone has had a plate of spinach that sits sadly in a pool of its own water. Leafy greens like spinach release a fair amount of liquid when they're cooked, so they need to essentially be cooked twice: first, to wilt and drain the greens to extract excess moisture; and second, to finish with the seasoning.

Extra virgin olive oil

2 pounds spinach

4 cloves garlic, coarsely chopped

Kosher salt and freshly ground black pepper

Juice of 1 lemon

❶ Wilt and drain the spinach. In a large, high-sided sauté pan or pot, heat 2 teaspoons olive oil on medium-high until hot. Working in batches, if needed, add the spinach and cook, stirring frequently, for 3 to 5 minutes, until wilted. Transfer to a fine-mesh strainer. Use a wooden spoon to press down on the spinach to release as much liquid as possible. When cool enough to handle, transfer to the cutting board and coarsely chop. Wipe out the pan.

❷ Finish the spinach. In the same pan, heat 1 tablespoon olive oil on medium-high until hot. Add the garlic and cook, stirring frequently, for 30 seconds to 1 minute, until fragrant and golden brown. Add the spinach and season with salt and pepper. Cook, stirring frequently, for 1 to 2 minutes, until well combined. Remove from the heat and add the lemon juice. Transfer to a serving dish and serve.

CLEANING GREENS

Greens such as spinach and escarole are excellent at harboring grit. To clean them, first wash the sink and fill it with cold water. Soak the greens in the water. Use your hands to gently agitate the greens, and then lift them out of the water, leaving any grit behind, and drain in a colander. If you have a salad spinner, you can use it for the entire cleaning process. Place the greens in the basket, fill the spinner with water, and agitate to clean the greens. Lift out the basket to drain the greens, leaving the dirty water behind.

HOW TO SAUTÉ
Any VEGETABLE

Whether you're preparing snap peas,
pole beans, or parsnips, sautéing them will
create big flavor fast.

Unlike panfrying, sautéing relies on just a small amount of fat. Cooked over moderately high heat, the vegetables take on a caramelized depth, while retaining their fresh, vibrant flavor. Sautéing is also a method that fits any season. Once you choose your vegetable, it's simply a matter of determining the timing, the specific result you want to achieve (crispy leaves on brussels sprouts, or charred, tender eggplant), and the flavorings (aromatics, seasonings, liquids) that pair best with what you're serving.

Keys to Success

1. Arrange vegetables in a single layer. This will expose more surface area to the direct heat of the sauté pan and ensure quick, even cooking. Sauté in batches, if needed.

2. Choose the right fat. Most sautéed vegetables call for moderately high heat, so olive oil is our fat of choice. For extra-high heat (in stir-frying, for example), you'll want to use an oil with a high smoking point, such as grapeseed, safflower, or peanut oil. Use a light hand (you want just enough oil to lightly coat the vegetables), and watch the heat or you'll wind up producing a burned flavor. Sautés are typically finished with butter to create a richer result.

3. Let the pan get hot. To gauge the temperature of the oil, place a vegetable in the pan: it should sizzle, but not crackle. You'll know your oil is hot enough when it shimmers and slides easily in the pan. If the oil begins to smoke, it's too hot—remove the pan from the heat and let cool slightly.

4. Add liquid if needed. If the vegetables are sticking to the pan once browned, but not cooked through, add a splash of water (or wine) to create additional steam. This will help cook the vegetables until they're tender.

5. Add vegetables in the right sequence. If you're cooking a medley, start with the largest, sturdiest vegetables, or the ones that you want to fade into the background (for example, onions or celery). Finish with tender, quick-cooking vegetables that deliver the brightest color (like snow peas or asparagus spears).

6. Finish with flavor. A last-minute hit of flaky sea salt, a squeeze of lemon juice, or a swirl of butter creates a fuller or brighter flavor.

WATERY VEGETABLES: *For leafy vegetables that can expel a lot of water, like bok choy, add a tiny bit of cornstarch slurry (1 teaspoon cornstarch mixed with 1 teaspoon water) to the sauté to help thicken the liquid and create a flavorful glaze.*

More green vegetables great for a very quick, Asian-inspired sauté: *bok choy, gai lan, and watercress*

In a large pan, heat 1 tablespoon grapeseed or canola oil on medium until hot. Add 1 teaspoon minced ginger and 1 teaspoon chopped garlic. Cook, stirring frequently, for 30 to 45 seconds, until softened and fragrant. Add 1 pound trimmed snow pea leaves. Cook, stirring occasionally, for 30 seconds to 1 minute, until wilted. Remove from the heat and season with salt and pepper.

SUMMER VEGETABLES

More quick-cooking summer vegetable medleys: *corn, lima beans, and tomatoes (succotash); and peppers, scallions, and eggplant*

In a large pan, heat 1 tablespoon olive oil on medium-high until hot. Add ½ pound green beans cut into ½-inch pieces; season with salt and pepper. Cook, stirring occasionally, for 2 to 4 minutes, until softened. Add 1½ cups corn kernels (about 2 ears corn), 1 minced shallot, and 2 minced garlic cloves; season with salt and pepper. Cook, stirring occasionally, for 2 to 4 minutes, until slightly softened and fragrant. Add 2 cups cherry tomatoes, halved; season with salt and pepper. Cook for 1 to 2 minutes, until slightly softened. Season with salt and pepper.

HONEY-GLAZED CARROTS

More vegetables perfect for a glaze:
pearl or cipollini onions, root vegetables (such as parsnips), and radishes

Peel 1 pound carrots; quarter lengthwise (or halve, if thinner) and cut into 2-inch-long pieces on an angle. In a large pan, heat 1 tablespoon olive oil on medium-high until hot. Add the carrots; season with salt and pepper. Cook, stirring occasionally, for 5 to 7 minutes, until slightly softened. Add ½ cup water; cook, stirring occasionally, for 2 to 4 minutes, until the water has evaporated. Add 2 tablespoons butter, 2 tablespoons honey, and 2 teaspoons water. Cook, stirring occasionally, for 1 to 2 minutes, until the carrots are tender and thoroughly coated.

PAN-SEARED BRUSSELS SPROUTS *with Bacon*

More vegetables that love to be pan-seared and cooked with bacon:
cabbage, butternut squash, and cherry tomatoes

Trim 1 pound brussels sprouts; quarter lengthwise. Small dice 2 slices thick-cut bacon. In a large pan, cook the bacon for 4 to 5 minutes on medium, until browned and crispy. Transfer to a paper towel–lined plate, leaving any fat in the pan. Add the brussels sprouts; season with salt and pepper. Cook on medium-high, stirring occasionally, for 8 to 10 minutes, until browned and slightly softened. Remove from the heat. Stir in the crispy bacon and 2 teaspoons apple cider vinegar.

Tuscan Roast Pork Loin

This crowd-pleasing pork roast is known in Italy as *arista Toscana*. The culinary legend is that the dish dates back to the fifteenth century, when representatives of the Greek church came to Florence. Upon tasting the pork, the Greek cardinal exclaimed, *"Aristos!"* meaning "the best." The rest of his clergymen began chanting the same and the name stuck.

COOK'S tips

BUYING THE PORK: *When you buy the pork roast, tell the butcher to leave the fat cap (the thick layer of fat) on, but remove the chine bone (part of the backbone). The fat provides flavor, and removing the chine bone makes the pork easier to slice after roasting.*

MARINATING: *Scoring the fat and partially separating the meat from the bones will allow you to coat more of the pork with the herb mixture, while still giving you the delicious benefit of roasting bone-in meat. Marinating the roast with the aromatics for several hours deepens the flavor of every bite.*

¼ cup finely chopped fresh rosemary leaves

¼ cup finely chopped fresh sage leaves

4 cloves garlic, minced

Grated zest of 2 lemons

½ teaspoon ground fennel seed

2 teaspoons fennel pollen or ½ teaspoon ground coriander

Extra virgin olive oil

Kosher salt and freshly ground black pepper

1 bone-in pork loin roast (about 4 pounds; see Cook's Tip)

Sautéed Spinach with Garlic and Lemon (page 61), for serving (optional)

❶ Make the marinade. In a small bowl, combine the rosemary, sage, garlic, lemon zest, ground fennel seed, fennel pollen, and 2 tablespoons olive oil. Season with salt and pepper.

❷ Prepare the pork. Use a sharp knife to score the fat about ¼ inch deep in a crosshatch pattern. Holding the knife parallel to the row of bones, cut the meat away from the bones without cutting all the way through; leave about 2 inches attached at the bottom.

❸ Stuff the pork. Lightly drizzle inside the cut area with olive oil. Spread half of the herb mixture inside and season generously with salt and pepper. Use butcher's twine to close the roast by tying around the loin and between each two bones.

❹ Marinate the pork. Lightly drizzle the outside of the pork with olive oil. Rub the remaining herb mixture on all sides. Season generously with salt and pepper. Tightly wrap the pork with several layers of plastic wrap. Let stand at room temperature for 3 hours to marinate.

❺ Roast the pork and serve. Preheat the oven to 325°F. Unwrap the pork and discard the plastic wrap. Transfer the pork, fat side up, to a wire rack set on a sheet pan. Roast for 1 hour 45 minutes to 2 hours, until an instant-read thermometer inserted into the center of the meat (not touching the bone) registers 135°F (for medium). Remove from the oven and let rest for 45 minutes. Transfer the pork to a cutting board; cut off and discard the twine. Carve the meat from the bones and thinly slice. Transfer the pork to a serving dish and serve with the spinach on the side.

Roasted Salmon

with Fresh Herbs

Meatier varieties of fish like salmon, wild striped bass, and line-caught swordfish benefit from high-heat roasting, and cook in much less time than other roasts. In this recipe, a side of salmon is roasted on a bed of lemon slices that perfumes the fish and serves as a buffer to the heat of the sheet pan. Note that salmon varieties come in different thicknesses and levels of fat. Wild sockeye and coho, with a deep copper color, for instance, will be smaller and leaner than Atlantic salmon—so you'll need to adjust cooking times accordingly.

A fresh herb salad with tarragon and chervil balances the rich flavor and silky texture of the fish.

2 lemons, thinly sliced into rounds

Extra virgin olive oil

1 skin-on side of salmon (preferably king salmon), belly flap removed (about 3 pounds)

Kosher salt and freshly ground black pepper

¼ cup coarsely chopped fresh flat-leaf parsley leaves

¼ cup sliced fresh chives (½-inch pieces)

¼ cup fresh chervil leaves

2 tablespoons fresh tarragon leaves

High-quality extra virgin olive oil, for garnish

Flaky sea salt, for garnish

❶ Prepare the salmon. Preheat the oven to 450°F. Arrange half of the lemon slices on a sheet pan roughly the size of the fish and drizzle with olive oil. Pat the fish dry with paper towels. Drizzle the flesh side of the fish with olive oil and rub to evenly distribute. Season with salt and pepper. Place the salmon, skin side down, on top of the lemon slices. Let stand for 15 minutes.

❷ Roast the salmon. Roast the fish for 8 to 10 minutes, until an instant-read thermometer inserted into the center of the fish registers 120° to 125°F (for medium-rare). Remove from the oven and let rest for at least 5 minutes.

❸ Make the herb salad and serve the salmon. In a small bowl, combine the parsley, chives, chervil, and tarragon. Add a drizzle of olive oil and toss gently to combine. Season with salt and pepper. Use a wide spatula to carefully transfer the salmon and lemon to a serving dish; drizzle with high-quality olive oil and sprinkle with sea salt. Scatter the herb salad on top, garnish with the remaining lemon slices, and serve.

COOK'S
tip

SERVING: *Instead of using a sheet pan, you can roast the salmon in an oven-safe serving dish or a beautiful baking dish, so you can bring it straight to the table to serve.*

Herb-Stuffed Boneless Leg of Lamb

Serves 6 to 8

A quick bit of mincing is all that's required to create a flavorful rub made with lamb's best allies—rosemary and garlic. The great thing about a boneless leg of lamb is that it's easy to massage both sides of the meat with seasonings, allowing the flavors to permeate every bite. However, you can achieve similar results with a bone-in leg (see variation) by studding the meat with the aromatics instead. The secret to the best result (less chew) is letting the leg rest before slicing very thinly. The best part of this recipe is that the leftovers make one of the best sandwiches (page 268).

1 boneless leg of lamb (about 4 pounds)

Kosher salt and freshly ground black pepper

¼ cup finely chopped fresh rosemary leaves

4 cloves garlic, finely grated into a paste

Extra virgin olive oil

❶ Season the lamb. Generously season all sides of the lamb with 2 tablespoons salt and 1½ teaspoons pepper. Let stand at room temperature for 2 hours. In a small bowl, combine the rosemary, garlic paste, and ¼ cup olive oil. Rub half of the herb paste on the inside of the lamb. Season with salt and pepper.

❷ Tie the lamb. Preheat the oven to 325°F. Cut 8 to 10 long pieces (about 12 inches) of butcher's twine. Roll the leg into a cylinder. Season with salt and pepper. Place the center of the lamb on a length of twine. Tie tightly with a knot and trim off any excess. Continue tying the roast at 1-inch intervals. Cut one more piece of twine (about 24 inches) to tie around the length of the roast. The tied roast should be a tight cylinder. Trim off any excess twine. Rub the outside of the lamb with the remaining herb paste. Season generously with salt and pepper.

❸ Sear the lamb. Heat a large, heavy-bottomed sauté pan on high. Add 1 tablespoon olive oil and heat until hot. Add the lamb and sear for 2 to 4 minutes, until browned. Flip the lamb and continue searing until well browned on all sides.

❹ Roast the lamb. Transfer the lamb to a wire rack set on a sheet pan. Roast for 1 hour 40 minutes to 1 hour 50 minutes, until an instant-read thermometer inserted into the thickest part of the meat registers 130°F (for medium). Remove from the oven and let rest for 1 hour.

❺ Slice and serve the lamb. Transfer the lamb to a cutting board. Cut off and discard the twine. Thinly slice the lamb. Transfer to a serving dish, pour any accumulated juices over it, and serve.

COOK'S tip

AT THE BUTCHER'S: *The interior of a lamb leg has a large vein structure that should be removed before cooking. You can ask the butcher to do this for you when deboning the leg.*

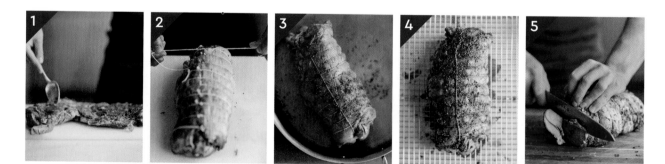

70   The Blue Apron Cookbook

Variation: Roasted Bone-In Leg of Lamb
Roasting a bone-in leg of lamb with the shank attached is just as easy and impressive. Use the tip of your knife to cut small slits equally spaced on all sides of a bone-in leg of lamb (about 6 pounds). Cut 3 cloves garlic into small slivers. Finely chop the leaves from 3 to 5 large rosemary sprigs. Push a sliver of garlic into each slit. Drizzle with 2 tablespoons olive oil. Sprinkle with the rosemary and season with 2 tablespoons salt and 1½ teaspoons pepper. Rub the seasoning into the lamb. Let stand at room temperature for 2 hours. Proceed to searing the lamb in step 3 (no need to tie) and roast as directed (the oven temperature and cooking time remain the same).

Prime Rib au Jus

A grand prime rib roast—served with a rich, meaty jus made from its flavorful juices—is the ultimate special-occasion meal, perfect for holidays and other celebratory occasions. It's a splurge cut that no one wants to see poorly prepared—especially when the stakes are as high as a holiday meal. Not to worry—we've made the process foolproof so you'll feel confident and proud when you carve into that first rib.

For the best results, start by seasoning your beef a day in advance to allow the salt to fully permeate the meat. Then roast the meat with the fat side up, so the fat renders and you can baste the meat while it cooks. Basting helps create the flavorful browned crust and keeps the meat juicy. Elevating the meat on a wire rack makes sure the bottom of the roast actually crisps and prevents it from stewing in excess moisture.

1 (6-rib) prime rib roast (preferably dry-aged; about 12 pounds), fat trimmed to ½ inch and chine bone removed

Kosher salt

Extra virgin olive oil

Freshly ground black pepper

3 cups beef stock (page 176)

Coarse sea salt, for garnish

Sautéed Mushrooms with Thyme (page 74), for serving (optional)

❶ Prepare the beef. The day before cooking, pat the beef dry with paper towels. Season all sides with 4 tablespoons kosher salt. Tightly wrap the beef in several layers of plastic wrap. Refrigerate overnight.

❷ Roast the beef. About 2 hours before cooking, remove the beef from the refrigerator and let stand at room temperature. Preheat the oven to 325°F. Unwrap the beef and discard the plastic wrap. Lightly coat with about ¼ cup olive oil and season on all sides with 1 tablespoon kosher salt and 1 tablespoon pepper. Transfer the roast, rib bones down and fat side up, to a wire rack set on a sheet pan. Roast, rotating the pan every 30 minutes, for 2 hours 30 minutes to 3 hours, until an instant-read thermometer inserted into the center of the meat (not touching the bone) registers 130°F (for medium). Remove from the oven and let rest for 1½ to 2 hours.

❸ Make the jus. Transfer the roast to a cutting board. Pour the juices left in the pan into a small saucepan, scraping any browned bits (fond) into the saucepan. Skim off and discard any fat. Place the sheet pan on the stovetop and heat on medium-high. Add 1 cup of the beef stock and whisk until all of the browned bits (fond) are scraped up. Transfer to the saucepan. Add the remaining 2 cups beef stock to the saucepan and heat to boiling on high. Cook, stirring occasionally, for 14 to 16 minutes, until reduced in volume by about half. Season with salt and pepper.

❹ Slice and serve the roast. Cut off the twine and carve the beef between the bones to create 6 portions. Transfer to a serving dish and add any accumulated juices to the jus. Garnish the beef with sea salt. Serve with the jus and mushrooms on the side.

COOK'S *tip*

JUS: *If you prefer a thicker jus, make a small amount of slurry from equal parts flour and water. Stir in a little bit at a time until thickened.*

SAUTÉED MUSHROOMS
with Thyme

Serves 6 as a side

There are two secrets to perfectly sautéed mushrooms. First, allow the oil to get very hot; it should be shimmering, but not smoking, before you add the thyme sprigs. This allows the oil to quickly absorb the essence of the thyme and maintain the high temperature needed to sear the mushrooms. The second step involves patience. After you add the mushrooms, avoid the temptation to fuss with them in the pan. Instead, allow them to brown undisturbed, so that their liquid releases and evaporates to create a crispy exterior.

This recipe calls for oyster mushrooms, but feel free to use other varieties such as chanterelles, hen of the woods, beech, king trumpet, or any other that strikes your fancy; just make sure that they're cut into uniform pieces, so they'll cook evenly.

Extra virgin olive oil

4 sprigs thyme

2 pounds oyster mushrooms, heavy stems discarded, cut into bite-size pieces

1 shallot, finely chopped

1 clove garlic, finely chopped

¼ cup (½ stick) unsalted butter

Kosher salt and freshly ground black pepper

2 tablespoons coarsely chopped fresh flat-leaf parsley leaves, for garnish

❶ **Season the oil.** In a large sauté pan, heat a thin layer of olive oil on medium-high until hot. Add the thyme; it should crackle as you add it to the pan. Cook, tilting the pan to submerge the thyme in oil, for 30 seconds or until fragrant.

❷ **Cook the mushrooms.** Line a plate with paper towels. Working in batches if necessary, add the mushrooms to the sauté pan in a single, even layer. Cook, without stirring, for 12 to 14 minutes, until lightly browned. Stir in the shallot, garlic, and butter. Cook, stirring occasionally, for 1 to 2 minutes, until the shallot is softened.

❸ **Season the mushrooms.** Immediately transfer to the paper towel–lined plate. Season with salt and pepper. Remove and discard the thyme sprigs. Transfer to a serving dish. Garnish with the parsley and serve.

3

3
Slow Roasts

Slow roasts are some of our favorite things to cook because the long cooking process allows us to do most of the work ahead of time (usually just seasoning the meat) and stay hands-off for the rest of the cooking, with very little monitoring.

This means less time in the kitchen and more time with friends and family as those savory aromas float from the kitchen, making everyone hungry for the meal to come. Slow roasts are true crowd-pleasers, and an added bonus is that the leftovers, from roast beef to pork shoulder, make amazing sandwiches (pages 266, 270).

Slow roasts are exactly what they sound like—roasts cooked slowly at low temperatures (typically 325° to 350°F). Relatively inexpensive cuts (from whole chicken to lamb shoulder) transform into tender, utterly satisfying roasts. We distinguish these recipes as "slow roasts" because we're cooking tougher cuts of meat and using a dry-heat method that melts their connective tissue; this method results in a tender but sliceable texture and deeply browned crust.

The low-and-slow technique creates richly flavored pan drippings that make delicious gravy (roast beef never had it so good) and is gentle enough to allow other ingredients to cook nestled alongside the meat (think potatoes with chicken). Slow roasts pair especially well with side dishes such as polenta, root vegetable purées, or braised vegetables—especially those with a bit of acid that brightens the rich flavors, such as braised red cabbage or winter greens, melted leeks, and braised carrots and parsnips.

Tools to Have on Hand

- Heavy-duty rimmed sheet pan
- Oven-safe wire rack
- Roasting pan with elevated rack
- Instant-read thermometer
- Butcher's twine

Keys to Success

1. Start with the highest-quality meat. Even though these cuts aren't as expensive as the roasts in the previous chapter, you still want to seek out a quality butcher or meat market that sources its beef, pork, and poultry from specific farms and ranches. In general, pasture-raised meat tends to have the best flavor; the animal's diet will affect the flavor of a roast. When it comes to buying beef, pork, and lamb, look for cuts trimmed of excess connective tissue and with good marbling and firm fat caps.

2. Season generously in advance. Season the meat well in advance so the seasoning permeates throughout.

3. Roast from room temperature. Meat roasted from room temperature will cook more evenly; if the meat is too cold, the outside will dry out and burn before the inside can become fully tender.

4. Let the meat rest. A long resting time allows for maximum reabsorption of flavorful juices. With tender slow roasts, after the meat is cooked, the resting and carving options depend on how you intend to serve it (see Tip).

COOK'S tip

SERVING SLOW ROASTS: *If you're serving the roast whole and carving at the table, allow the meat to rest, and then rewarm gently in the oven before carving. If you plan to serve the meat already sliced, you'll have neater results if after it rests, you refrigerate the roast overnight, slice the cold meat, and rewarm gently in the oven. If you're shredding the meat, allow it to rest 45 minutes, and then shred and rewarm in the pan juices. As a general rule of thumb, rewarm meat in the oven at the same temperature as it was roasted (for example, if it was roasted at 325°F, warm it at that temperature too).*

Porchetta-Style Pork Shoulder

You'll be hard-pressed to find a cut that yields more succulent, flavorful results than a well-marbled pork shoulder. Here we're giving our take on classic porchetta, a popular street food in Umbria and Tuscany with a history that some say dates back to ancient Rome. Look for all the traditional flavors (think rosemary and fennel pollen and seed), but our roast is easier and much less work (you don't have to debone a whole pig). If you want something different from the classic Italian flavors, try our Cuban-inspired variation that incorporates warm spices, citrus, and chile peppers in the recipe. No matter which style you make, like all larger cuts, pork shoulder benefits from being generously seasoned in advance and refrigerated overnight so the spices and aromatics have plenty of time to permeate the meat.

12 medium or 15 small cloves garlic, coarsely chopped

2 tablespoons coarsely chopped fresh rosemary leaves, plus sprigs for serving

Grated zest and juice of 2 lemons, plus a halved lemon for serving

2 tablespoons coarsely chopped fresh sage leaves

1 teaspoon crushed red pepper flakes

1 tablespoon fennel pollen or 1 teaspoon ground coriander

1 teaspoon whole fennel seed

1 teaspoon sugar

¼ cup extra virgin olive oil, plus more for drizzling

5 tablespoons kosher salt

2½ teaspoons freshly ground black pepper

1 bone-in pork shoulder roast (also called Boston butt; about 10 pounds)

Braised Winter Greens (page 83), for serving (optional)

❶ Make the rub and prepare the pork. In a bowl, stir together the garlic, chopped rosemary, lemon zest and juice, sage, red pepper flakes, fennel pollen, fennel seed, sugar, ¼ cup olive oil, salt, and black pepper until thoroughly combined. Use a sharp knife to score the pork fat about ¼ inch deep and at ¾-inch intervals in a crosshatch pattern.

❷ Season the pork. Coat the pork all over with the seasonings, rubbing them into the meat until it is thoroughly coated. Tightly wrap the pork in several layers of plastic wrap and refrigerate overnight.

COOK'S
tip

ZESTING: *When a recipe calls for both citrus zest and juice, remember to zest your citrus before juicing.*

RECIPE CONTINUES

3 Roast the pork. About 2 hours before cooking, remove the pork from the refrigerator and let stand at room temperature. After 1 hour, unwrap the pork and discard the plastic wrap. Let stand for the remaining 1 hour. Preheat the oven to 325°F. Transfer the pork to a wire rack set on a sheet pan. Roast for 3 hours. Loosely cover the pork with aluminum foil and rotate the pan. Roast for 3 to 4 hours more, until the meat starts to separate from the bone; an instant-read thermometer inserted into the center of the meat (not touching the bone) should register 190°F. Remove from the oven. Let rest for up to 1 hour 30 minutes.

4 Slice and serve the pork. Transfer the pork to a cutting board and cut into ¼-inch-thick slices. Transfer to a serving dish. Garnish with the rosemary sprigs, drizzle with olive oil, and serve with the lemon halves and greens on the side.

Variation: Cuban Mojo-Style Pork Shoulder

For the best Cubanos (page 266) in the world, make this pork shoulder. Substitute the following ingredients for the seasonings in step 1 and proceed with the recipe.

4 medium or 6 small cloves garlic, coarsely chopped

1 tablespoon ground cumin

2 teaspoons ground coriander

1 tablespoon ground mustard

1 tablespoon whole dried oregano

2 teaspoons ground cinnamon

Grated zest and juice of 1 orange

Grated zest and juice of 2 limes

1 tablespoon smoked paprika

2 teaspoons cayenne pepper

¼ cup canola oil

5 tablespoons kosher salt

2½ teaspoons freshly ground black pepper

BRAISED WINTER GREENS

Serves 8 as a side

Braising hearty greens transforms waxy, robust leaves into a tender, comforting partner to any number of roasts and pan-seared meats. This recipe calls for kale, but you can use this basic method for any hardy, leafy green such as mustard, collards, or Swiss chard. Blanching the greens before braising helps remove excess moisture (for a more concentrated flavor), retain a vibrant color, and remove any bitterness— but this step is not necessary for young greens like spinach. Our secret to the most tender result is adding a small amount of baking soda to the water—the baking soda softens the leaves. For a richer dish, you can finish it with a generous dollop of crème fraîche, heavy cream, or Greek yogurt.

2 tablespoons unsalted butter

¼ cup extra virgin olive oil

1 large yellow onion, finely chopped (about 2 cups)

4 cloves garlic, minced

Kosher salt

½ teaspoon crushed red pepper flakes

¼ teaspoon baking soda

2 bunches green curly kale (about 1 pound total), stems removed, leaves coarsely chopped

½ cup water

⅛ teaspoon freshly grated nutmeg

Juice of ½ lemon

Freshly ground black pepper

❶ Cook the aromatics. Heat a large pot of water to boiling on high. In a large, high-sided sauté pan or a Dutch oven, heat the butter and 2 tablespoons of the olive oil on medium-low until the butter is melted. Add the onion and garlic and season with ½ teaspoon salt. Cook, stirring frequently, for 11 to 12 minutes, until the onion has softened but not browned. Stir in the red pepper flakes and remove from the heat.

❷ Blanch the kale. Generously season the boiling water with salt and stir in the baking soda. Add the kale. Use a wooden spoon or long spatula to push the kale down so it is fully submerged in the water. When the water returns to a simmer, cook for 1 to 2 minutes, until the kale is wilted and tender. Drain the kale in a colander; let stand for a few minutes to thoroughly drain.

❸ Braise the kale. Heat the sauté pan with the onion on medium. Once the onion is warmed, add the kale and stir until well combined. Stir in the remaining 2 tablespoons olive oil and cover. Cook, using the spoon to separate the kale, for 1 to 2 minutes, until combined and heated through. Add the ½ cup water. Cover and cook for 13 to 15 minutes, until the kale is very tender. Uncover and cook for 2 to 3 minutes more, until the liquid has cooked off. Remove from the heat and stir in the nutmeg and lemon juice. Season with salt and pepper. Transfer to a serving dish and serve.

Variation: Creamed Greens

To turn braised greens into creamed greens, preheat the oven to at 425°F. Heat 1 cup heavy cream in a small pot on medium-high. Cook until reduced in volume by half. Transfer the cream to a large bowl and fold in the braised greens until well combined. Transfer the mixture to an oven-safe baking dish and smooth the top. Top with ½ cup toasted breadcrumbs and 2 tablespoons unsalted butter, cut into pieces. Bake until browned and bubbling around the edges, about 10 minutes. Cool slightly before serving.

HOW TO BRAISE
Any VEGETABLE

Braising is a low-and-slow process that transforms
vegetables that are typically tough or fibrous (think turnips,
leafy winter greens, cabbage) into a dish that's
deeply flavored with a tender texture.

Once you get the basic process down (fear not: braises are very forgiving), you'll see that you're set to braise anything. A vegetable braise is simply a matter of starting with a great vegetable and then choosing the best aromatics, a cooking liquid, and a few elements to finish and elevate the dish.

For the best flavor, you'll want to finish a dish with a final layer of seasoning—anything from fresh herbs to an acid like vinegar or lemon. You can make any braise richer by finishing it with crème fraîche, heavy cream, or Greek yogurt. Braised vegetables are excellent candidates to prepare in advance because they improve with time (the flavors get the chance to meld).

Keys to Success

1. Every step matters. As with meat, a vegetable braise is built on layers of flavor, so use care when sautéing aromatics (they should soften but not brown). Choose fresh, seasonal vegetables, flavorful braising liquids (broth, wine, olive oils), and finishing flavors (fresh herbs, citrus juice, vinegar, flaky salt) that elevate the dish.

2. Cut vegetables to the same size and shape. Uniform pieces will cook more evenly and result in a nicer presentation.

3. Don't start at too high a heat. The vegetables will caramelize at a more moderate temperature—if it's too hot, they'll burn.

4. Use the right pan. The pan should be heavy and wide enough for the vegetables to cook evenly over the heat, with a tight-fitting lid so the cooking liquid doesn't evaporate too quickly.

5. Season in stages. If you wait to add all the salt at the end, right before serving, the braise will taste too salty. Instead, season the braise as you go (a pinch for the aromatics, another when you add the vegetables) to create more depth of flavor.

WINE-BRAISED FENNEL

More quicker-cooking vegetables (particularly ones with "petals") to be braised with wine: *artichokes and small heads of cabbage*

❶ Brown the fennel. Cut 2 fennel bulbs into 1½-inch-thick wedges. In a large pan or Dutch oven, heat 2 tablespoons oil on medium-high until hot. Working in batches if necessary, add the fennel cut sides down. Cook, turning occasionally, for 5 to 6 minutes, until browned. Season with salt and pepper. Add 1 tablespoon olive oil, 2 peeled and crushed garlic cloves, and 1 teaspoon fennel seed. Cook for 30 seconds to 1 minute, stirring occasionally, until fragrant. Add ¼ cup white wine. Cook, stirring occasionally, for 30 seconds to 1 minute, until reduced by half. Add 2 cups vegetable stock (page 175) or chicken stock (page 174). Increase the heat to medium-high and bring to a simmer. Once simmering, reduce the heat to medium.

❷ Braise the fennel. Cover and cook for 17 to 22 minutes, flipping the fennel halfway through, until the fennel core is tender when pierced with a knife. Use a slotted spoon to remove the fennel from the pan and place on a serving dish. Discard the garlic.

❸ Finish the fennel. Increase the heat to high and cook the braising liquid, uncovered, 6 to 8 minutes, until reduced by half and slightly thickened. Stir in 2 tablespoons chopped parsley and the juice of ½ lemon. Season with salt and pepper. Pour over the braised fennel and serve.

BRAISED POLE BEANS
with Tomato Paste

More vegetables that pair well with (and can hold up to) a tomato-based braise: *garlic scapes, zucchini, and eggplant*

❶ Brown the beans. In a large pan or Dutch oven, heat 3 tablespoons olive oil on medium-high. Add 1½ pounds trimmed green beans and cook until golden brown and slightly softened. Transfer to a paper towel–lined plate. Reduce the heat to medium-low and add 3 tablespoons olive oil. Add ½ cup tomato paste and cook for 2 to 3 minutes until the tomato paste is dark red. Stir in 2 teaspoons fennel seed, 2 teaspoons chopped fresh oregano, and ½ teaspoon crushed red pepper flakes; cook, stirring frequently, for 30 seconds, until fragrant. Add the green beans back to the pot; season generously with salt. Stir in 1 cup white wine and 1 cup water. Bring to a simmer and remove from the heat.

❷ Braise the beans. Cover and bake at 350°F for 45 minutes to 1 hour. After 30 minutes, remove from the oven and stir in 1 cup chopped green olives. Return to the oven and bake for the remaining 15 to 30 minutes, until completely softened. Remove from the oven and stir in ¼ cup red wine vinegar.

❸ Finish the beans. Let cool, uncovered, to room temperature before serving. Right before serving, top with 3 tablespoons chopped parsley, 1 tablespoon chopped mint, and 1 tablespoon chopped basil.

❶ Brown the potatoes. Wash 1½ pounds small (about 1½ inches in diameter) Yukon or red potatoes; thoroughly dry with paper towels. In a large pan or Dutch oven, heat 1 cup olive oil on medium-high until warm. Carefully add the potatoes. Season generously with salt and cook for 12 to 15 minutes, turning occasionally, until lightly browned and wrinkled. Stir in 3 small shallots halved lengthwise, 1 tablespoon whole capers (drained), ½ teaspoon crushed red pepper flakes, 4 crushed garlic cloves, 3 small rosemary sprigs, 1 small sage sprig, and 1 dried bay leaf.

❷ Braise the potatoes. Reduce the heat to low; cover and cook for 35 to 40 minutes, turning halfway through, until tender when pierced with a fork. Season with salt and pepper.

❸ Finish the potatoes. Let cool slightly. Use a slotted spoon to transfer the potatoes and aromatics to a dish (discard the herb sprigs). Top with extra oil, freshly squeezed lemon juice, 2 tablespoons chopped parsley, and flaky sea salt.

BALSAMIC-BRAISED CIPOLLINI ONIONS

More vegetables that can be braised with vinegar: *endives (balsamic vinegar), carrots (sherry vinegar), and parsnips (sherry vinegar)*

1 Brown the onions. Heat 2 tablespoons olive oil and 2 tablespoons butter on medium in a large pan or Dutch oven until hot. Add 1 pound peeled cipollini onions; season with salt. Cook, turning occasionally, for 5 to 7 minutes, until lightly browned and softened. Stir in 2 tablespoons raisins and 2 dried bay leaves. Add ½ cup balsamic vinegar and ½ cup water or chicken stock (page 174). Bring to a boil and reduce the heat to medium.

2 Braise the onions. Cook, uncovered, for 25 to 30 minutes, turning occasionally, until the liquid is reduced to a glaze and the onions have softened. Let cool to room temperature before serving.

Spiced Lamb Shoulder

Mechoui, which comes from the Arabic word for "roasted," is a North African preparation for spit-roasted or grilled lamb or goat. Found in the back alley markets of Marrakesh and family celebrations alike, *mechoui* is a famous dish known for its fall-apart texture and fragrant spices. Though the meat is traditionally roasted over a spit (if you have one for your grill at home, use it) or in an underground oven, we've adapted the dish for home ovens, cooking it low and slow.

1 tablespoon kosher salt

¾ teaspoon freshly ground black pepper

¾ teaspoon ground cumin seed

¾ teaspoon ground fennel seed

¾ teaspoon ground cardamom

1½ teaspoons sweet paprika

¾ teaspoon smoked paprika

3 cloves garlic, finely chopped

1½ teaspoons finely chopped fresh rosemary leaves

1½ teaspoons honey

2 tablespoons extra virgin olive oil

1 (3-pound) boneless lamb shoulder roast, trimmed of excess connective tissue

Coarse sea salt, for garnish

Braised Cauliflower (page 92), for serving (optional)

❶ Season the lamb. In a small bowl, stir together the kosher salt, pepper, cumin, fennel seed, cardamom, sweet and smoked paprikas, garlic, rosemary, honey, and olive oil. Coat the inner side of the lamb with half of the seasonings, rubbing them into the meat until thoroughly coated.

❷ Tie the lamb. Cut 6 to 8 long pieces (about 16 inches) of butcher's twine. Roll the lamb lengthwise into a cylinder. Place the center of the lamb on a length of twine. Tie tightly with a knot and trim off any excess twine. Continue tying at 1-inch intervals. Cut one more piece of twine to tie around the length of the lamb. The tied lamb should be a tight cylinder. Rub the outside of the lamb with the remaining half of the seasonings. Wrap in several layers of plastic wrap and refrigerate overnight.

❸ Roast the lamb. About 2 hours before cooking, remove the lamb from the refrigerator and let stand at room temperature. Preheat the oven to 350°F. Unwrap the lamb and discard the plastic wrap. Transfer to a wire rack set on a sheet pan. Roast for 3 to 4 hours, until well browned and fork-tender; an instant-read thermometer inserted into the center of the meat should register 190°F. Remove from the oven and loosely tent with aluminum foil. Let rest for 1 hour.

❹ Serve the lamb. Cut off and discard the twine. Cut the lamb into ¾-inch-thick slices and transfer to a serving dish. Sprinkle with the sea salt and serve with the cauliflower on the side.

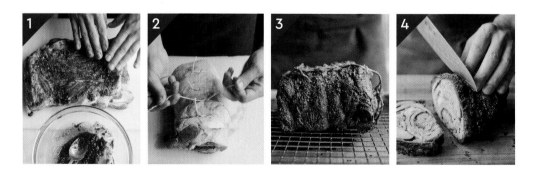

BRAISED CAULIFLOWER

Serves 4 to 6

When cauliflower is browned, then braised in a flavorful liquid enriched with butter, garlic, capers, and crushed red pepper flakes, it becomes meltingly tender and immensely flavorful—the antithesis of its alternative personality as raw, crunchy crudités. To avoid making them too soft, the florets are removed before the cooking liquid is reduced to a concentrated sauce. A final splash of white wine vinegar and plenty of fresh parsley perk up the rich flavors.

3 tablespoons extra virgin olive oil

1 head cauliflower (about 2 pounds), cut into large florets

Kosher salt and freshly ground black pepper

2 tablespoons unsalted butter

4 cloves garlic, coarsely chopped

2 teaspoons nonpareil capers in brine, drained, or salted capers

¼ teaspoon crushed red pepper flakes

2 cups vegetable stock (page 175) or chicken stock (page 174)

1 tablespoon white wine vinegar

½ cup coarsely chopped fresh flat-leaf parsley

❶ Brown the cauliflower. Preheat the oven to 375°F. In a large, high-sided, oven-safe sauté pan or Dutch oven, heat 2 tablespoons of the olive oil on medium until hot. Add the cauliflower. Cook, without stirring, for 2 to 3 minutes, until browned. Flip the cauliflower and continue cooking, stirring occasionally, for 4 to 5 minutes, until beginning to soften. Season with 2 teaspoons salt and ¼ teaspoon black pepper. Add the butter, garlic, and capers. Cook,

SALTED CAPERS

With a sharp, pungent flavor that brightens anything from tuna salad to tomato sauce, capers are an essential ingredient in Mediterranean cuisines. Capers are the unopened flower buds of a spiny shrub (the caper bush) that have been cured in salt or brined in salt and vinegar. Most Americans rely on brined nonpareil capers, which carry a vinegary pop and have a firmer texture. In Italy, many cooks prefer salted capers, which tend to be higher quality and have more nuanced flavor. To use salted capers (found in specialty stores and online), you'll need to rinse them in a fine-mesh strainer under cold water for about 30 seconds to remove the outer layer of salt. Place the rinsed capers in a shallow bowl, cover them with cold water, and soak at room temperature for a few minutes or up to a few hours, depending on how salty they are. Drain and dry on paper towels before using.

stirring occasionally, for 5 to 6 minutes, until the butter begins to brown. Add the red pepper flakes. Cook, stirring occasionally, for 30 seconds to 1 minute, until fragrant.

❷ Prepare the braise. Add the stock. Increase the heat to high and bring to a simmer. Remove from the heat, cover, and transfer to the oven. Cook for 18 to 22 minutes, until the cauliflower is very tender when pierced with a knife.

❸ Reduce the liquid. Remove from the oven and transfer to the stovetop. Use a slotted spoon to transfer the cauliflower to a serving dish. Heat the reserved braising liquid on high until boiling. Boil for 3 to 4 minutes, until reduced in volume by half. Add the white wine vinegar and the remaining 1 tablespoon olive oil. Cook for 30 seconds to 1 minute, until thoroughly combined. Remove from the heat and stir in the parsley. Pour the sauce over the cauliflower and serve.

Classic Roast Beef

Whether it's served as a Sunday roast as traditionally done in England, a festive holiday meal, or simply a warming dinner on a cold winter's night, roast beef with gravy is a classic dish that's loved by many. As with other large cuts of meat, this one benefits from being seasoned well in advance. While the meat roasts, garlic cloves and rosemary sprigs sizzle in its rendered fat, perfuming the beef and eventually the gravy.

1 (3- to 4-pound) top round or eye round beef roast

Kosher salt and freshly ground black pepper

2 tablespoons extra virgin olive oil

6 to 8 cloves garlic, unpeeled

2 large sprigs rosemary

Coarse sea salt, for garnish

GRAVY

2 tablespoons all-purpose flour

2 cups beef stock (page 176)

2 tablespoons unsalted butter at room temperature; plus 2 tablespoons chilled and cubed (optional)

2 shallots, minced

⅓ cup dry Marsala wine

1 tablespoon chopped fresh flat-leaf parsley

1 tablespoon red wine vinegar

Braised Carrots & Parsnips (page 97), for serving (optional)

❶ Season the beef. About 3 hours before cooking, generously season the beef with salt and pepper on all sides. Tightly wrap in several layers of plastic wrap. Refrigerate for 1 hour 30 minutes. Remove from the refrigerator and let stand at room temperature for 1 hour 30 minutes.

❷ Tie the beef. Position a rack in the middle of the oven and preheat the oven to 325°F. Unwrap the beef and discard the plastic wrap. Pat dry with paper towels. Cut 6 to 8 long pieces (about 16 inches) of butcher's twine. Place the center of the beef on a length of twine. Tie tightly with a knot. Continue tying the beef at 1-inch intervals. Cut one more piece of twine to tie around the length of the beef. The tied beef should be a tight cylinder. Trim off any excess twine.

❸ Roast the beef. Drizzle the beef with the olive oil; rub to thoroughly coat. Season again with salt and pepper. Transfer to a wire rack set on a sheet pan. Place the garlic and rosemary around the beef. Roast for 70 to 80 minutes, until an instant-read thermometer inserted into the center of the meat registers 130°F (for medium). Remove from the oven. Discard the rosemary and garlic. Let rest for 45 minutes on the wire rack. Transfer the beef to a cutting board, leaving any browned bits (fond) and juices in the pan.

RECIPE CONTINUES

❹ Start the gravy. Place the sheet pan on the stovetop and heat to medium. Sprinkle the flour over the drippings in the sheet pan. Whisk constantly to scrape up the fond and coat the flour in the drippings. Add 1 cup stock and continue to whisk until all of the fond is scraped up. Remove from the heat and set aside.

❺ Finish the gravy. In a small saucepan, melt the 2 tablespoons room-temperature butter on medium. Add the shallots. Cook, stirring occasionally, for 2 to 3 minutes, until the shallots are softened and fragrant. Add the wine, the remaining 1 cup stock, and the flour-stock mixture from the sheet pan. Cook, whisking occasionally, for 3 to 4 minutes, until reduced in volume by about half. If you'd like a richer gravy, add the 2 tablespoons chilled, cubed butter a little at a time, whisking constantly, for 3 to 5 minutes, until thoroughly combined and shiny. Stir in the parsley and vinegar. Season with salt and pepper. Remove from the heat and set aside in a warm place until you're ready to serve.

❻ Slice and serve the beef. Cut off and discard the twine from the beef. Cut the beef into ½-inch-thick slices and transfer to a serving dish. Spoon the gravy over the beef or serve on the side. Sprinkle the beef with sea salt just before serving with the carrots and parsnips on the side.

BRAISED CARROTS & PARSNIPS

Serves 6 to 8

Braising root vegetables like carrots and parsnips highlights their earthy flavors and concentrates their natural sugars (enhanced here by a drizzle of honey). It's always nice to balance that sweetness with sharpness and acid (such as mustard and vinegar here). You can use any color carrot, or substitute turnips or rutabagas for the parsnips; just make sure to slice them into uniform pieces for even cooking. Additional fresh herbs like rosemary or bay leaves would be right at home in the mix, as would spices like cumin or fennel seed.

4 parsnips, peeled (about 1½ pounds)

4 carrots, peeled (about 1 pound)

Extra virgin olive oil

Kosher salt

2 cloves garlic, peeled and lightly crushed

2 sprigs thyme

1 teaspoon mustard powder (such as Colman's)

2 teaspoons honey

½ cup vegetable stock (page 175) or chicken stock (page 174)

1 tablespoon white wine vinegar

½ cup chopped fresh flat-leaf parsley

Coarse sea salt, for garnish

BIAS CUTS

Cutting vegetables on the bias (at an angle) is great from a presentation point of view, but functionally, the diagonal cuts expose more surface area, which results in quicker cooking.

❶ **Prepare the vegetables.** Cut each parsnip and carrot in half lengthwise, then cut at an angle into ¾-inch pieces.

❷ **Sweat the vegetables.** In a large, high-sided sauté pan or Dutch oven, heat 6 tablespoons olive oil on medium until hot. Add the parsnips; season with salt; and cook, stirring occasionally, for 1 to 2 minutes, until they begin to release their liquid. Add the carrots and garlic and season with salt. Cook, stirring occasionally, for 1 to 2 minutes, until the carrots begin to release their liquid. Add the thyme and stir to combine. Cover; reduce the heat to low; and cook, stirring occasionally, for 6 to 7 minutes, until the vegetables start to wrinkle and soften.

❸ **Add the seasoning.** Add the mustard and honey. Cook, stirring constantly, for 30 seconds to 1 minute, until thoroughly combined. Add the stock. Increase the heat to medium and cook, stirring occasionally, for 30 seconds to 1 minute, until almost all the liquid has cooked off.

❹ **Finish the braise.** Remove and discard the thyme sprigs (any leaves that remain behind are okay) and garlic. Stir in the vinegar and parsley and season with salt and pepper. Cook, uncovered, for 30 seconds to 1 minute, until thoroughly combined. Transfer to a serving dish. Sprinkle with sea salt and serve.

Slow-Roasted Chicken

with Potatoes

This recipe showcases all of the tender, juicy qualities of a rotisserie chicken without actually requiring a rotisserie at home. It's similar to our classic roast chicken; however, this time we're cooking it low and slow. Stuffing the cavity full of aromatics like garlic, rosemary, thyme, lemon, and onion infuses the meat with flavor while creating a steaming effect that keeps the chicken moist from the inside out. Rotating the pan ensures even cooking, while roasting at a lower temperature allows you to cook the vegetables alongside the chicken without burning. This way they soak up all the flavorful juices too.

1 whole chicken (3½ to 4 pounds)

½ teaspoon sweet paprika

1 teaspoon ground fennel seed

½ teaspoon ground coriander

Kosher salt and freshly ground black pepper

2 pounds Yukon gold potatoes

1 small onion, quartered

4 sprigs thyme

2 large sprigs rosemary

Extra virgin olive oil

1 head garlic, top ½ inch cut off (you want to be able to see the tops of the cloves)

1 lemon, halved, plus 4 lemon wedges for serving

½ cup finely chopped fresh flat-leaf parsley, for garnish

Melted Leeks with White Wine (page 100), for serving (optional)

❶ Prepare the chicken. Preheat the oven to 300°F. Pat the chicken dry with paper towels inside and out. In a small bowl, combine the paprika, ground fennel, and coriander; sprinkle on the chicken inside and out. Season generously with salt and pepper inside and out. Let stand at room temperature for 1 hour.

❷ Season the potatoes. After the chicken has stood for about 50 minutes, cut the potatoes into ¾- to 1-inch-thick rounds. In a bowl, combine the potatoes, 2 of the onion quarters, 1 thyme sprig, 1 rosemary sprig, and 2 tablespoons olive oil. Season with salt and pepper. Arrange in a single, even layer in a high-sided roasting pan.

❸ Continue preparing the chicken. Stuff the garlic, the lemon halves, and the remaining

2 onion quarters, 3 thyme sprigs, and rosemary sprig inside the chicken. Truss the chicken (see page 37). Drizzle with 2 teaspoons olive oil and season lightly with salt and pepper. Place the chicken in the roasting pan, on top of the vegetables.

❹ Roast the chicken. Roast the chicken for 1 hour. Rotate the pan 180 degrees and continue to roast for 1 hour 45 minutes to 2 hours, removing the chicken from the oven every 30 minutes to drizzle with olive oil and rotate the pan. The chicken is done when it is browned and the juices run clear when the skin is pierced between the thigh and leg; an instant-read thermometer inserted into the thigh (without touching the bone) should register 170°F. Remove from the oven and let rest for 45 minutes.

❺ Serve the chicken. Transfer the chicken to a cutting board and carve (see page 37). If desired, once cool enough to handle, squeeze the garlic cloves out of the head of garlic to serve with the chicken and potatoes. Transfer the chicken to a serving dish, drizzle with olive oil, and garnish with the parsley. Serve with the potatoes, lemon wedges, and leeks on the side.

MELTED LEEKS *with White Wine*

Serves 4

A stovetop braise is the best way to transform alliums like leeks, shallots, and onions into a tender and surprisingly nuanced side dish. As the vegetables cook and soften into the thyme-infused wine, their natural sugars concentrate, creating a delicious accompaniment to rich, roasted meats.

3 large or 4 medium leeks (about 2 pounds)

½ cup (1 stick) unsalted butter, cut into 1-tablespoon pieces

Kosher salt

1 tablespoon fresh thyme leaves

¾ cup dry white wine (such as sauvignon blanc or pinot grigio)

1 teaspoon freshly squeezed lemon juice

Freshly ground black pepper

❶ Slice and clean the leeks. Slice the leeks into ½-inch-thick half-moons. Clean the leeks according to the instructions at the right.

❷ Braise the leeks. In a large saucepan or Dutch oven, melt the butter on medium-low. Add the leeks and season with 1 teaspoon salt. Increase the heat to medium. Cook, stirring frequently, for 14 to 16 minutes, until the leeks are slightly softened. Add the thyme and season with ½ teaspoon salt. Cook for 1 to 2 minutes, until fragrant. Add the white wine and bring to a simmer. Cover and reduce the heat to medium-low. Cook, stirring occasionally, for 18 to 20 minutes, until the leeks are tender. Uncover and continue cooking until the liquid is reduced to a glaze coating the leeks. Remove from the heat. Add the lemon juice and season with salt and pepper. Transfer to a serving dish and serve.

How to CLEAN LEEKS

Grit in your food, even a speck, is enough to ruin a dish. Leeks are masters at harboring grit, so it's important to soak the slices after an initial rinse. Make sure you lift the leek slices up and out of the water—if you invert the bowl you'll be pouring the dirt back over the leeks.

Cut off and discard the dark green tops and root ends of the leeks. If using the leeks in whole pieces (as in Poached Chicken with Aioli, page 212), cut the white bottoms and pale green parts in half lengthwise and rinse between the layers under running water for 30 seconds to 1 minute to clean off large pieces of dirt. If using the leeks sliced, slice according to the recipe directions. Fill a large bowl with cold water. Working in batches, place the leeks in the bowl and use your hands to agitate them, cleaning off any remaining dirt. Let the leeks float to the top and the dirt settle to the bottom of the bowl. Being careful not to disturb the dirt, scoop the leeks out of the water and transfer them to a colander. Drain thoroughly. If you have a salad spinner, use it: Place the cut leeks in the basket, fill the spinner with water, and agitate to clean the leeks. Lift out the basket to drain the leeks, leaving the dirty water behind.

BRAISED RED CABBAGE

Serves 4 to 6

When braising leafy brassicas such as cabbage or brussels sprouts, you can either do a quick braise that will leave the vegetables crunchier (like a warm coleslaw) or a longer braise, like this one, that renders them very soft. Here, the raw cabbage becomes sweet and takes on the elements it's cooked with, such as onions, apples, and red wine vinegar. Consider the following stovetop method a guideline that's open to endless variation—feel free to add other ingredients (such as bacon, pancetta, fennel, pears), use apple cider vinegar instead of red wine, or swap out the caraway seed for your favorite spice.

¼ cup (½ stick) unsalted butter

2 tablespoons extra virgin olive oil

1 yellow onion, small diced

4 cloves garlic, minced

Kosher salt

¼ teaspoon caraway seed

1 head red cabbage (about 1½ pounds), quartered, cored, and thinly sliced

2 tablespoons sugar

¼ cup full-bodied red wine (such as cabernet sauvignon, merlot, or syrah)

¼ cup veal stock, vegetable stock (page 175), or chicken stock (page 174)

1 Granny Smith apple

¼ cup sour cream (or crème fraîche)

¼ cup red wine vinegar

Freshly ground black pepper

❶ Start the braise. In a large saucepan or Dutch oven, heat the butter and olive oil on medium until the butter melts and sizzles. Add the onion and garlic and season with ¼ teaspoon salt. Cook, stirring occasionally, for 6 to 7 minutes, until the onion is softened. Add the caraway seed and cook, stirring frequently, for 30 seconds to 1 minute, until fragrant. Add the cabbage, sugar, and 1½ teaspoons salt. Cook, stirring frequently, for 11 to 12 minutes, until the cabbage begins to soften.

❷ Braise the cabbage. Add the wine and bring to a simmer. Add the stock and bring to a simmer. Reduce the heat to medium-low. Cover and cook for 28 to 30 minutes, until the cabbage is tender. Peel and grate the apple; discard the core. Increase the heat to medium and add the apple to the cabbage. Cook uncovered, stirring occasionally, for 9 to 11 minutes, until all the liquid has cooked off.

❸ Finish the cabbage. Remove from the heat and stir in the sour cream and vinegar. Season with salt and pepper. Transfer to a serving dish and serve.

Roasted Duck

Ducks have been eaten as food since the time of cavemen (it probably helped that ducks walk a bit clumsily on land, making them an easy target). Since ducks were domesticated by the Chinese centuries ago and introduced to the New World by Europeans, they developed a long and noble culinary lineage.

Despite this history, many people shy away from cooking duck at home because it seems intimidating, but that's a shame. Our method is foolproof and simple—roasting the duck slowly plus pricking the skin allows for the fat to render while the bird roasts, leaving crispy skin and flavorful duck fat that you can save for roasting potatoes and other vegetables. In this recipe, the carcass is stuffed with a shallot *piqué*, a French technique of using whole cloves to secure bay leaves to an onion or shallot—you might think of it as a secret flavor bomb.

1 (5- to 6-pound) Pekin (Long Island) duck

Kosher salt and freshly ground black pepper

1 large shallot, peeled

4 juniper berries

2 fresh bay leaves or 1 dried bay leaf

2 whole cloves

Braised Red Cabbage (page 101), for serving (optional)

❶ Prepare the duck. Use a fork to prick the skin all over the duck, being careful not to puncture the flesh. Use kitchen shears to cut away excess fat from the cavity, and cut the neck skin so that only 1 inch remains. Cut off and discard the wing tips. Season generously with salt and pepper.

❷ Make the shallot piqué. Cut the shallot into quarters without cutting through to the root; the shallot should stay intact. Open out the shallot and place the juniper berries inside. Close the shallot. Wrap the bay leaves around the shallot and stick the cloves through the leaves

and into the shallot to secure. (If the leaves don't wrap all the way around, it's okay. If using a dried bay leaf, simply secure the leaf with the cloves without wrapping.) Place the shallot piqué in the duck's cavity. Truss the duck (page 37). Let the duck stand at room temperature for 75 minutes.

❸ Roast the duck. Preheat the oven to 350°F. Transfer the duck, breast side up, to a V-shaped rack set in a deep roasting pan. Roast for 2 hours to 2 hours 30 minutes, until browned and an instant-read thermometer inserted into the thigh (not touching the bone) registers 170°F. If necessary, during roasting, carefully drain the fat that pools on the bottom of the roasting pan; you don't want the fat to burn. Remove the duck from the oven and let rest for 45 minutes to 1 hour. Transfer to a cutting board

❹ Carve and serve the duck. Remove and discard the shallot piqué. Carve as desired (see page 37). Transfer to a serving dish and serve with the cabbage on the side.

COOK'S
tip

SLOW-ROASTED DUCK FAT: *Duck fat is prized for its rich flavor, so when you have the pleasure of cooking duck, make sure to save the fat. Fry eggs in the fat, roast potatoes in it to serve alongside the duck, or even use it instead of oil for Braised Red Cabbage (page 101).*

DUCK VARIETIES

There are many breeds of duck available that offer different flavors and textures. White Pekin ducks have mild, tender meat. The breed originated in China and was brought to Long Island, New York, in 1873. The area subsequently became the center of the U.S. duck industry (hence the term "Long Island duck"). Other varieties tend to be more gamy, such as the strongly flavored Muscovy, moulard (a larger bird—a cross between Pekin and Muscovy—raised for its liver to make foie gras), and mallard (a smaller, tougher wild duck).

4
Braises

Economical and delicious, braising is a method that's been lovingly embraced in many food cultures.

Travel the world and you'll find versions of braised beef in almost every corner, whether it's an onion-and-pepper-strewn *ropa vieja* in Cuba or *carbonnade*, a Belgian stew made with dark ale.

It's easy to see why braising is one of the most satisfying cooking techniques around. With minimal effort on the cook's part, tougher cuts of meat become spoon-tender, deeply flavored one-pot meals. As the meat cooks at a low temperature, it creates its own rich sauce, a process that fills your kitchen with delightful aromas. Braising is also one of the most forgiving forms of cooking—stick to the basic formula and it's hard to mess up. And because these cuts are typically less expensive, braising is a great method for feeding a crowd without blowing your budget.

A good braise is built from the ground up, and the multiple stages of the process are key to building layers of flavor in the finished dish. The low-and-slow heat melts the collagen in the meat into gelatin, making the meat tender while enriching the braising liquid. (To us, a "stew" specifically refers to a braise that utilizes smaller pieces of meat versus a larger cut.) As the moisture in the sealed pot turns to trapped steam, the meat cooks in its own juices, concentrating flavors. We generally braise with tougher cuts of meat (such as shoulders and shanks), but you can also braise leaner, more tender meats like a whole chicken. If the tougher cuts were to be cooked in another fashion, the collagen would remain elastic, yielding chewy meat. Following the same basic principles, you can braise just about anything; lamb shanks, short ribs, pork belly, and chicken legs are all delicious options that require only a few tweaks to the basic method. As you'll discover in the following recipes, braises can easily be taken in any number of directions using various seasonings, aromatics, and cooking liquids.

Braises are best served with starches that soak up all of that rich, flavorful sauce, such as steamed rice, buttery egg noodles, mashed potatoes, or creamy polenta. For example, with our red wine–braised beef stew, we love a classic French potato purée, the silky-smooth, refined cousin of traditional mashed potatoes. Learning to make a potato purée opens the door to making a whole range of vegetable purées that can serve as comforting, nourishing bases for braises, stews, and beyond.

Tools to Have on Hand

- Dutch oven or heavy oven-safe pot
- Parchment paper

DUTCH OVENS

Braising is a moist-heat cooking method that requires a heavy, oven-safe pot with a tightly fitting lid. The weight of the pot allows the heat to conduct slowly and evenly, while a secure lid keeps the moisture inside—steam from the braise will rise, condense on the inside of the lid, and drip back into the pot. Enamel-coated cast-iron pots, such as Dutch ovens, are our go-to for braises.

Keys to Success

1. Use the right cut and the highest-quality meat.
More flavorful but tougher cuts from the hardest-working muscle groups (such as shoulder, lower leg, and neck) have more collagen and fat that break down to create exceptionally moist, tender results. Traditional cuts for braising are inexpensive and fairly easy to source. That said, you'll get the best flavor if you seek out a quality butcher or meat market that sources its beef, pork, and poultry from specific farms and ranches. In general, pasture-raised meat tends to have the best flavor; the animal's diet will affect the flavor of good meat.

For beef, choose chuck, short ribs, top blade roast, and bottom round. For veal and lamb, shoulder and shanks work well. For pork, shoulder, ribs, and belly are best; and for poultry, choose bone-in legs and thighs.

2. Start with a sear. Browning meat on all sides before braising not only creates a richer, more complex flavor, but also "sets" the exterior so that the moisture from the meat releases more slowly into the braising liquid. To get a good sear, don't rush the process, and do work in batches; overcrowding the pan creates steam that inhibits browning.

3. Enhance with aromatics. These ingredients add nuance and depth of flavor to a braise. They include classic combinations like the French *mirepoix* (carrots, onions, and celery), Spanish *sofrito* (onion, green bell pepper, garlic, sometimes tomato), and Italian *battuto* (also carrots, onions, and celery, plus garlic, parsley, and sometimes fennel). You'll come across additions like cured meats, fresh herbs, and other vegetables as well, depending on the style of braise.

4. Take it low and slow. Cooking the ingredients slowly over gentle heat is at the heart of what defines a braise. Though all braises start on the stovetop, they can finish in the oven or continue to simmer on the stove.

5. Refining the braising liquid. Depending on the style of the braise, you may want to strain and reduce the liquid after cooking to create a more refined sauce. Degreasing the braising liquid by skimming the fat off with a large spoon is also key to creating a clean finished dish.

MAKE AHEAD

Braises are perfect for making ahead and then rewarming (the easiest winter dinner party fare) because they actually taste even better the next day. The flavors in the braise soften and meld, while the meat reabsorbs some of the liquid. To make any braise ahead of time, cook the recipe through to the end of the braising step. Before finishing the braise—by skimming the fat, reducing the braising liquid, or adding any last ingredients or garnishes—let it cool to room temperature in the pot, then refrigerate, covered. (For food safety, always let food cool completely before storing in the refrigerator, and do not put hot food in plastic containers to cool.) Always leave the meat in the braising liquid when storing.

The next day, the fat in the braise will have risen to the top and congealed, making it even easier to scrape off and discard before rewarming. Rewarm gently and slowly on the stovetop on medium heat and with the lid on (resist the temptation to use additional liquid at this point), then continue with the last step of the recipe.

COOK'S tip

LEFTOVERS: *Leftover braised meats are perfect as the start to a potpie (just place in a baking dish, top with puff pastry, and bake for 30 minutes at 425°F), or even used as a filling for stuffed pastas (page 293), enchiladas, or tacos.*

Some braises are topped with a circle of parchment paper that serves as an added "lid" to seal in the steam. Cutting a hole in the center of the parchment circle will allow the liquid to reduce slightly.

❶ Cut a large piece of parchment a few inches bigger than the size of your pot or pan. Fold it in half horizontally to make a rectangle. ❷ Fold the rectangle in half again vertically to make a smaller rectangle. Line up the two closed edges to create a triangle. ❸ Fold the triangle a few more times, lining up the edges. ❹ Cut a small piece of the tip of the triangle. Hold the parchment triangle over the pan with the tip of the parchment at the center of the pan. Use your thumb to mark where the edge of the pan is and cut the paper at that point. ❺ Unfold the triangle and you should have a circle the size of the pan.

Red Wine–Braised Beef Stew

When the days shorten and temperatures sink into sweater weather, it's time to gather friends for the quintessential French braise: *boeuf bourguignon.* Described by Julia Child as "one of the most delicious beef dishes concocted by man," this famous dish comes from Burgundy, a region of France known for its excellent wines and cattle. This stew, with peasant-fare beginnings, is perfect for entertaining because it's even better if prepared in advance (see page 107). When friends arrive, all you'll need to do is slice bread to sop up every drop of sauce.

5 pounds boneless beef short ribs or stew beef, cut into 1½-inch cubes

Kosher salt and freshly ground black pepper

½ cup all-purpose flour

1 small bunch thyme

3 dried bay leaves

Extra virgin olive oil

1 head garlic, separated into cloves, peeled, and thinly sliced

2 leeks, sliced into thin half-moons and cleaned (see page 100)

3 stalks celery, cut into 1-inch slices; ¼ cup celery leaves reserved for garnish

2 cups pearl onions, peeled

1 (6-ounce) can tomato paste

1 (750-ml) bottle red wine (such as cabernet sauvignon, zinfandel, or syrah)

2 quarts beef stock (page 176), plus more if needed

1½ pounds carrots, peeled and large diced

¼ cup (½ stick) unsalted butter

1 pound cremini mushrooms, trimmed, quartered if large

1 tablespoon red wine vinegar

Classic Potato Purée (page 113), for serving (optional)

❶ Prepare the beef and herbs. Pat the beef dry with paper towels. Season on all sides with 1 tablespoon salt and ½ teaspoon pepper. Place the flour in a large bowl. Add the meat and toss to coat. Transfer the meat to a fine-mesh strainer and tap off any excess flour. Transfer to a large plate. Tie the thyme and bay leaves together with butcher's twine.

❷ Brown the beef. In a large Dutch oven, heat 1 tablespoon olive oil on medium-high until hot. Working in batches and adding more oil as needed, add the beef in a single, even layer. Cook, flipping occasionally, for 5 to 8 minutes per batch, until well browned on all sides. Transfer to a clean plate, leaving any browned bits (fond) in the pot. (If the fond is black and burned, scrape it away and discard; rinse and wipe out the pot.)

❸ Cook the aromatics. Heat the fond on medium until hot. (If the pot seems dry, add 1 tablespoon olive oil.) Add the garlic. Cook, stirring occasionally, for 1 to 2 minutes, until the garlic is lightly browned and fragrant. Add the leeks, celery, and pearl onions and season with salt and pepper. Cook, stirring occasionally, for 5 to 6 minutes, until lightly browned. Add the tomato paste and cook, stirring frequently, for 6 to 7 minutes, until the paste is dark red.

RECIPE CONTINUES

④ Reduce the wine. Add the wine and increase the heat to medium-high. Cook, stirring occasionally and scraping up any browned bits from the bottom of the pot, for 8 to 9 minutes, until the wine is reduced in volume by two-thirds.

⑤ Braise the beef. Add the stock and season with salt and pepper. Increase the heat to high and bring to a boil. Return the beef to the pot, along with any accumulated juices. Add the herb bundle. Reduce the heat to low, cover, and simmer for 2 hours 20 minutes to 2 hours 30 minutes, until the meat is close to tender. If the braise seems dry, add more stock, ½ cup at a time.

⑥ Add the carrots. If necessary, skim off any excess fat. Add the carrots and increase the heat to medium. Cook uncovered, stirring occasionally, for 40 to 45 minutes, until the carrots are tender and the braise is thickened. Season with salt and pepper.

BETTER BROWNING

The initial step of browning beef cubes is important because it creates the foundation for a richly flavored stew. For the best results, allow the oil to get nice and hot, and avoid fussing with the meat while it's sizzling in the pot. Take your time to achieve a dark crust on all sides. Since the meat is coated in flour and you're cooking over high heat, there's a chance that it can blacken. If this happens, pour out the fat and rinse the pan before continuing; otherwise the stew will have an acrid flavor.

⑦ Cook the mushrooms. While the braise simmers, in a large sauté pan on medium-high, melt the butter. Add the mushrooms. Cook, stirring only a few times, for 7 to 8 minutes, until browned. Season with salt and pepper.

⑧ Finish the braise. Stir the mushrooms into the braise. Cook for 15 to 20 minutes, until slightly thickened. Remove from the heat. Discard the herb bundle and stir in the vinegar. Season with salt and pepper. Transfer to a serving dish or individual bowls. Garnish with the celery leaves and serve with the potato purée.

COOK'S *tip*

KEEP IT CLEAN: *In making braises like this one, there's a tendency for some of the liquid (juices from the meat, the wine) from the braise to splash onto the sides of the pot. We like to periodically wipe the sides of the pot with a wet paper towel to prevent that splattered liquid from burning during the long cooking process.*

CLASSIC POTATO PURÉE

Serves 6 to 8

Buttery puréed potatoes are the ultimate creamy base for just about anything with delicious braising liquids or pan juices. The method is deceptively simple: Four basic ingredients create something far more memorable than the sum of its parts. Using a food mill to process the potatoes creates the smoothest texture; for a more rustic texture, you can use a potato masher. Don't process the potatoes in a food processor: This will release the starch and make the purée gummy. We'll confess that butter plays no small role here—yes, we're calling for a half pound of butter to two pounds of potatoes.

Yukon gold potatoes have golden flesh and a moist, waxy texture that create exceptionally creamy results; they're the best bet for this recipe. (Starchier potatoes, such as russets, are best used for other purposes, such as baking, as they won't give you that creamy texture.) After draining the potatoes, allow them to air-dry in the colander for a few minutes—this will help avoid a watery purée—but don't allow them to cool for too long. For the smoothest texture, it's essential that the butter is cold when whisked in—this helps prevent the purée from "breaking" and becoming oily.

2 pounds Yukon gold potatoes, peeled and cut into 1½-inch pieces

Kosher salt

¼ cup whole milk

1 cup (2 sticks) unsalted butter, cubed and chilled

❶ Cook the potatoes. In a large saucepan, combine the potatoes, 4 teaspoons salt, and enough cold water to cover the potatoes by 1 inch. Heat to boiling on high. Cook for 15 to 17 minutes, until tender when pierced with a fork. Drain thoroughly.

❷ Warm the milk. While the potatoes cook, heat the milk in a small pot over low until warm.

❸ Mill the potatoes. Set a food mill fitted with the finest plate over the pot used to cook the potatoes. Transfer the potatoes to the mill and process directly into the pot.

❹ Finish the potatoes. Heat the pot of potatoes on low heat. Add the milk and stir to combine. Add a few pieces of butter at a time, stirring to combine after each addition. Season with salt. Transfer to a serving dish and serve.

HOW TO MAKE
Any VEGETABLE A PURÉE OR MASH

Silky, rich, and an easy side for any number of dishes
(particularly braised meats), puréed vegetables are enticing and
endlessly versatile.

Depending on how they come together—milled, riced, or mashed by hand—the texture can be rustic or elegant. The basic process can be applied to a wide range of vegetables. Ultimately, the details depend on the vegetable's flavor and moisture content, and your desired outcome. Typically puréed or mashed vegetables are boiled, but they can also be roasted or even sautéed before processing.

Keys to Success

1. Don't overcook your vegetable. Whether you're boiling, roasting, or sautéing, cook the vegetable until it's tender but not falling apart—this will ensure that the dish has a fresh, vibrant flavor and an appealing (not mushy) texture. Also, for the best overall consistency, cut the vegetables evenly so they cook at the same rate (no overcooked pieces mixed with undercooked ones).

2. Add warm liquid. If using liquid in your purée, make sure it's warm so it will incorporate better.

3. Add fat gradually. Add the finishing fat (butter, browned butter, olive oil) slowly. If you add too much at once, the mixture will be greasy. You can always add more if you need it.

4. Don't overwork the purée. When mixing the purée together, don't stir it too vigorously for too long (particularly with starchy vegetables such as potato), or the purée will become gluey or gummy.

5. Season in stages. This will create a deeper, rounder flavor. Adding all the salt at the end will make the purée or mash overly salty.

SWEET POTATO PURÉE
with Lemon

More dense root vegetables perfect for simply smashing with a fork:
turnips, parsnips, and rutabagas

Heat a medium pot of salted water to boiling on high. Peel 2 pounds sweet potatoes; cut into 1½-inch pieces. Boil the potatoes for 14 to 16 minutes, until tender when pierced with a fork. Drain thoroughly. Return the drained potatoes to the pot. Using a potato masher or a fork, mash the potatoes until smooth. Stir in 4 tablespoons butter (cut into small pieces), 2 teaspoons lemon zest, and the juice of ½ lemon; season with salt and pepper.

SPRING PEA PURÉE

More tender, green vegetables for a vibrant quick-cooking purée:
fava, zucchini, and broccolini

In a sauté pan, heat 2 tablespoons olive oil on medium until hot. Add 1 pound shelled peas (about 3 cups), 1 chopped small onion or large shallot, and 2 cloves garlic, chopped; cook for 1 to 2 minutes, stirring occasionally, until slightly softened. Add ¼ cup chicken stock (page 174); cook for 2 to 3 minutes, until the peas are tender. Remove from the heat and stir in 1 tablespoon chopped parsley or tarragon. Transfer to a high-powered blender and add 2 tablespoons cold butter. Blend until smooth. Add 2 teaspoons freshly squeezed lemon juice and season with salt and pepper; blend briefly to combine. Top with 1 teaspoon mint leaves.

ROASTED KABOCHA PURÉE

More winter squash and root vegetables perfect for roasted, browned butter–based purées: *butternut squash, acorn squash, honeynut squash, sweet potatoes, and sunchokes*

Using a sturdy kitchen knife, cut 2 kabocha squash (about 3 pounds total) in half; scoop out and discard the seeds and pulp. Coat each squash half with olive oil. Season the cut sides of the squash generously with salt and pepper. Place the squash on a baking sheet, cut sides down; tuck 1 sprig sage under each squash half. Roast at 425°F for 45 to 50 minutes, until browned and tender when pierced with a fork. When cool enough to handle, scoop out the flesh and place in a saucepan; mash the squash until smooth. In a small pot, heat 4 tablespoons butter on medium, until the butter is browned and nutty smelling, and the foam starts to disappear. Add 2 tablespoons finely chopped sage leaves and cook, stirring constantly, for 30 seconds to 1 minute, until the sage darkens in color. Heat the pot of squash over medium until hot. Stir in the butter-sage mixture; season with salt and pepper.

CELERIAC & POTATO PURÉE

More puréed vegetables to combine with potato purée:
zucchini, kale, and spinach

In a medium pot, combine 2 pounds celeriac (peeled and cut into 1½-inch pieces), 3 cups whole milk, and 2 teaspoons salt; heat to a simmer on medium. Once simmering, cook for about 30 minutes, or until tender when pierced with a fork. Drain over a large bowl, reserving the milk. In a second medium pot, combine 1 pound Yukon gold potatoes (peeled and cut into 1½-inch pieces), 1 teaspoon salt, and enough water to cover by 1 inch. Heat to boiling on high. Once boiling, cook for 18 to 20 minutes, or until tender when pierced with a fork. Drain thoroughly.

Transfer the cooked potatoes to a food mill; process through the finest sieve directly into the pot used to cook the potatoes (or use a ricer). Transfer the cooked celeriac, 1 cup of the reserved milk, and ½ teaspoon salt to a food processor; process until smooth. Add the puréed celeriac to the pot of potatoes and stir to combine. Heat the pot on low. Add 1½ sticks butter, a few pieces at a time, stirring constantly to combine after each addition, for about 3 minutes. Season with salt and pepper.

Osso Buco

with Gremolata

Osso buco is a beloved Milanese specialty whose name translates to "pierced bone." The name refers to the star of the recipe— meaty, crosscut veal shanks that are braised with vegetables, wine, and stock until they're fall-off-the-bone tender. Tomatoes infuse the sauce with a sunny sweetness that caramelizes while the braise reduces, and the shanks' exposed marrow enriches the dish. As with most braises, this recipe is even more enjoyable the second day. Serve it with gremolata, a condiment made with minced garlic, parsley, and lemon zest that brightens the long-simmered flavors.

3 pounds crosscut veal shank (5 pieces, 2 to 3 inches thick)

Kosher salt and freshly ground black pepper

1 large bunch thyme

1 dried bay leaf

½ cup all-purpose flour

Extra virgin olive oil

¼ cup (½ stick) unsalted butter

1 medium yellow onion, small diced

2 carrots, peeled and small diced

2 stalks celery, small diced

4 cloves garlic, minced

4 tablespoons unsalted butter

Grated zest of 1 lemon

2 teaspoons tomato paste

1 cup dry white wine (such as pinot grigio)

1 (14- to 15-ounce) can diced tomatoes

2 cups beef stock (page 176)

GREMOLATA

½ cup chopped fresh flat-leaf parsley leaves

Grated zest of 1 lemon

1 clove garlic, finely grated into a paste

2 tablespoons nonpareil capers in brine or salted capers, rinsed and chopped

2 tablespoons extra virgin olive oil

❶ Prepare the veal and herb bundle. Tie each shank around its middle with butcher's twine. Pat the shanks dry with paper towels. Season on all sides with 2 tablespoons salt and ½ teaspoon pepper. Let stand at room temperature for 30 minutes. Tie the thyme and bay leaf together with butcher's twine.

❷ Brown the veal. Spread the flour on a plate. Lightly coat each shank in the flour, tapping off any excess. Heat a thin layer of oil in a large Dutch oven on medium-high until hot. When the oil is shimmering, add the shanks in batches; do not crowd the pot. Cook, flipping occasionally, for about 15 minutes per batch, until well browned on all sides. Transfer to a plate, leaving any drippings and browned bits (fond) in the pot.

RECIPE CONTINUES

❸ Cook the aromatics. Add 2 teaspoons olive oil to the pot and heat on medium until hot. Add the onion, carrots, celery, and garlic and cook, stirring occasionally and scraping up any fond from the bottom of the pot, for 3 to 4 minutes, until slightly softened. Season with salt and pepper. Add the butter and stir to combine. Add the lemon zest and stir to combine. Add the tomato paste and cook, stirring occasionally, for 1 to 2 minutes, until the paste is dark red. Season with salt and pepper. Add the wine and cook, stirring occasionally, for 2 to 3 minutes, until the liquid is reduced in volume by half.

❹ Braise the veal. Add the tomatoes with their juices, the stock, and the herb bundle. Season with salt and pepper. Bring to a simmer on high. Return the shanks to the pot along with any accumulated juices and reduce the heat to low. Top with a parchment paper circle (see page 108). Cover and cook for 3 to 4 hours, until the shanks are very tender and the meat has pulled away from the bones. Remove from the heat and let the shanks cool slightly in the braising liquid with the parchment circle on.

❺ Make the gremolata. While the braise cools, in a bowl, combine the parsley, lemon zest, garlic, and capers. Drizzle with 2 tablespoons olive oil and stir to combine.

❻ Finish the braise. Discard the parchment circle and herb bundle. Remove the osso buco from the pot and transfer to a serving dish; carefully remove and discard the butcher's twine. Top with a few generous spoonfuls of the braising liquid and vegetables. Top with the gremolata and serve.

COOK'S
tip

BRAISING LIQUID: *If the braising liquid seems thin after the braised shanks have cooled slightly, transfer the shanks to a plate and simmer the liquid on medium-high until reduced in volume by about half. Return the shanks to the pan to reheat.*

Beer-Braised Short Ribs

This recipe is a riff on *carbonnade*, a traditional stew made with beef and dark ale named for the rich color the ribs take on after browning in the pan and the deep color of the braising liquid (*carbonnade* comes from the word for charcoal). Choose dark beers like stout or porter that echo the meat's richness and lend their own nuances, such as notes of roasted malt or dark coffee. As with any meaty braise, the foundation of this dish is browning the beef to create caramelized depth. An abundance of herbs— thyme sprigs early on and a finish of fresh parsley—balances the rich flavors.

4 pounds bone-in beef short ribs

Kosher salt and freshly ground black pepper

Extra virgin olive oil

1 large bunch thyme

1 bay leaf

3 cloves garlic, quartered

1 yellow onion, large diced

3 carrots (about ½ pound), peeled and cut into ¼-inch-thick rounds

2 stalks celery, large diced

2 tablespoons tomato paste

1 (12-ounce) bottle or can dark beer (such as stout or porter)

2 cups beef stock (page 176)

½ cup chopped fresh flat-leaf parsley leaves

Polenta (page 126), for serving (optional)

1 Brown the beef. Pat the short ribs dry with paper towels. Season with 4 teaspoons salt and 1 teaspoon pepper. In a large Dutch oven, heat 2 tablespoons olive oil on medium-high until hot. Reduce the heat to medium. Working in batches, add the short ribs in a single layer; do not overcrowd the pot. Cook, flipping occasionally, for about 15 minutes per batch, until well browned on all sides. Transfer to a plate, leaving any browned bits (fond) in the pot.

2 Cook the vegetables. Tie the thyme and bay leaf together with butcher's twine. Add the garlic, onion, carrots, and celery to the fond. Season lightly with salt. Cook, stirring occasionally and scraping up any fond from the bottom of the pot, for 2 to 3 minutes, until the onion is slightly tender and fragrant. Add the tomato paste and cook, stirring occasionally, for 1 to 2 minutes, until the paste is dark red.

COOK'S tip

TOMATO PASTE: Pinçage *("pin-sahge") is a French cooking term that describes the process of sautéing tomato paste until it caramelizes and becomes dark red, which deepens its flavor.*

RECIPE CONTINUES

❸ Braise the beef. Add the beer, stock, and herb bundle and season with salt and pepper. Bring to a boil on high, occasionally scraping up any browned bits from the bottom of the pot. Return the short ribs to the pot, along with any accumulated juices, and reduce the heat to low. Top with a parchment paper circle (see page 108). Cover and cook for 5 to 6 hours, until the short ribs are tender and the liquid is reduced in volume by half. Check the braise occasionally, especially after 4 hours; if it seems dry, add water, ¼ cup at a time.

❹ Reduce the braising liquid. Discard the parchment circle. Transfer the short ribs to a serving dish, leaving the braising liquid and vegetables in the pot. Place a fine-mesh strainer over a small saucepan. Carefully strain the braising liquid, slightly pressing on the vegetables. Discard the vegetables and herbs. Skim off any excess fat. Bring the liquid to a simmer on medium-high. Simmer until reduced in volume by half.

❺ Finish the braise. Top the short ribs with a few generous spoonfuls of the reduced braising liquid. Garnish with the parsley and freshly ground black pepper and serve with the polenta.

POLENTA

Serves 4 to 6

This is our basic, go-to method for creating soft, cheesy polenta that can be served as a creamy base for braised meats, stews, and herb-roasted vegetables, and with sautéed greens like broccoli rabe. You can use any kind of cornmeal; however, stone-ground varieties will have the freshest, sweetest corn flavor. Using milk, in addition to water, to cook the polenta adds richness without making the result too heavy, but feel free to omit it and use all water if you prefer. Note that we're suggesting that you only periodically whisk the bottom of the pot—this allows a thin skin to develop on the bottom of the polenta that becomes toasted and adds a nutty flavor.

3 cups whole milk

3 cups water

Kosher salt

1 cup yellow polenta (medium-fine grind)

Grated zest of 1 lemon

¼ cup (½ stick) unsalted butter

2 tablespoons extra virgin olive oil

2 cups freshly grated Parmigiano-Reggiano cheese (about 4 ounces)

Freshly ground black pepper

❶ Start the polenta. In a large saucepan, combine the milk, water, and 2 tablespoons salt; heat to simmering on medium. Slowly add the polenta, whisking to break up any clumps. Reduce the heat to medium-low. Cook, whisking occasionally, for 25 to 30 minutes, until smooth.

❷ Finish the polenta. Reduce the heat to low. Stir in the lemon zest. Add the butter and olive oil and cook, stirring constantly, for 30 seconds to 1 minute, until melted and well combined. Remove from the heat and stir in the Parmigiano. Season with salt and pepper. Transfer to a serving dish and serve.

Polenta Variations

You can fold any number of ingredients into soft polenta, including other cheeses like cheddar or goat cheese; sautéed fresh corn, onions, peppers, or mushrooms; or chopped fresh herbs. If you don't want to serve soft polenta, transfer the polenta to an oiled baking dish, let it cool and solidify in the refrigerator, then cut into squares and grill or panfry until the edges are golden and crisp. This is also a great way to use up any leftover polenta.

Soy-Braised Pork Belly
with Steamed Buns & Marinated Cucumbers

In this recipe, we're using the Chinese technique of "red cooking," or braising with soy sauce and sugar. It gives the braising liquid (full of the warm, aromatic flavors of ginger, lemongrass, and star anise) a rich, reddish color and conjures up a caramelized sweetness that echoes the pork's natural flavor. The braised belly is sliced and pan-seared to create burnished strips of meat with a lacquered, crackly crust that are then tucked inside tender steamed buns.

If you can't find steamed buns, the pork would also partner well with steamed rice and crunchy Napa Cabbage Slaw (page 228).

3 pounds center-cut pork belly (skin removed)

Kosher salt and freshly ground black pepper

Grapeseed oil

1 (2-inch) piece ginger, peeled and cut into thin matchsticks

1 (2-inch) piece lemongrass, finely chopped (see page 131)

4 cloves garlic, thinly sliced

6 scallions, thinly sliced (keep the green tops and white bottoms separate)

¼ teaspoon ground cinnamon

½ piece whole star anise

2 whole cloves

3 tablespoons sugar

¼ cup soy sauce

1 cup Shaoxing rice wine or dry white wine (such as sauvignon blanc or pinot grigio)

1 cup water, plus more if needed

8 to 12 steamed buns, for serving

1 teaspoon fermented black bean paste (optional)

MARINATED CUCUMBERS

¼ cup rice vinegar

1 teaspoon sugar

1 teaspoon kosher salt

1½ tablespoons water

2 cups thinly sliced Persian cucumbers (about 2 cucumbers)

❶ **Season the pork.** Preheat the oven to 325°F. Score the pork belly fat by making long diagonal cuts 1 inch apart in one direction, cutting through the fat but stopping before reaching the meat. Season both sides of the pork generously with salt and pepper. Rub the seasoning into the pork with your hands.

❷ **Sear the pork.** Heat 1 tablespoon oil in a Dutch oven on medium-high until hot. Place the pork in the pot, fat side down. Cook for 7 to 9 minutes, until the fat browns and starts to blister. Flip the pork and cook the second side for 5 to 6 minutes, until browned. Transfer to a plate, leaving any browned bits (fond) in the pot.

❸ **Cook the aromatics.** Reduce the heat to medium. Add the ginger, lemongrass, garlic, and the white parts of the scallions. Cook, stirring occasionally, for about 1 minute, until fragrant and tender. Add the cinnamon, star anise, and cloves and cook for 20 to 30 seconds, until fragrant. Add the sugar and cook, stirring to coat the aromatics, for 20 to 30 seconds.

COOK'S *tip*

SPECIAL INGREDIENTS: *Shaoxing wine is a rice wine commonly used in Chinese cooking. Dry sherry, Japanese sake, or dry white wine may be used as a substitute. Fermented black bean paste will add an unmistakable, savory depth to your dish. The paste is made from a mash of fermented, salted soybeans (the fermentation process turns the beans black) and garlic. Both Shaoxing wine and black bean paste can be found at specialty Asian groceries.*

RECIPE CONTINUES

4 **Braise the pork.** Add the soy sauce and wine and bring to a simmer. Add the pork belly, fat side up, and the 1 cup water. Return to a simmer. Remove from the heat and top with a parchment paper circle (see page 108). Cover with a lid and transfer to the oven. Braise for 2 hours 45 minutes to 3 hours, until the pork is very tender. Remove from the oven and let cool in the braising liquid, uncovered but with the parchment on, for 2 hours. While the pork cools, prepare the buns according to the package directions. Set aside on a serving dish in a warm place until you're ready to serve.

5 **Marinate the cucumbers.** In a bowl, whisk together the vinegar, sugar, salt, and the 1½ tablespoons water. Add the cucumbers and toss to combine. Set aside for 10 to 15 minutes to marinate. Drain and set aside.

6 **Sear the braised pork.** Transfer the pork to a cutting board; discard the parchment circle and leave the braising liquid in the pot. Slice the pork into ½-inch-thick pieces, 2½ to 3 inches long. In a large sauté pan, heat 1 tablespoon oil on medium-high until hot. Working in batches if necessary, add the pork and season with salt and pepper. Cook, flipping once, for 3 to 4 minutes per batch, until browned and crispy on both sides. Transfer to a plate and cover loosely with aluminum foil. Set aside in a warm place.

7 **Reduce the braising liquid.** Place a fine-mesh strainer over a small saucepan. Strain the braising liquid; discard the solids. Spoon or pour off the excess fat. Bring to a simmer on medium-high. Simmer for 4 to 5 minutes, until thickened and reduced in volume by half. Whisk in the black bean paste.

8 **Serve the pork.** Divide the seared pork among the steamed buns. Drizzle the reduced braising liquid over the pork. Top the pork with the marinated cucumbers and the green tops of the scallions and serve.

Braised Chicken

with Lemongrass, Ginger & Coconut Milk

This recipe is a nod to the delicious curries of Thailand that embrace intensely flavorful curry pastes. We're using spicy red curry paste that includes aromatic ingredients such as lemongrass, galangal (a spicy Southeast Asian ginger), and red chiles. One of the keys to using curry pastes and spices is to first "bloom" them, which means gently heating them in oil to release and intensify their flavor. For this dish, we also like to use bone-in, skin-on chicken for all the depth the bones and skin impart to the broth. The fresh cilantro and lime are essential to adding the fresh, herbal, and sour notes that balance the sweet, salty, and spicy flavors of the dish—a hallmark of Thai cooking.

1 whole chicken (3½ to 4 pounds), cut into 8 pieces (breasts split, thighs and legs separated)

Kosher salt and freshly ground black pepper

3 tablespoons canola oil

½ cup finely chopped lemongrass (3 to 4 stalks)

2 cloves garlic, minced

1 (2-inch) piece ginger, peeled and finely chopped

8 scallions (about 1 bunch), thinly sliced (keep the green tops and white bottoms separate)

2 to 3 tablespoons red curry paste (depending on how spicy you'd like the dish to be)

2 (14-ounce) cans full-fat coconut milk, shaken well before opening

5 cups water

2 cups jasmine rice

½ cup whole cilantro leaves, for garnish

Coarse sea salt, for garnish

2 limes, quartered, for serving

❶ **Brown the chicken.** Pat the chicken pieces dry with paper towels. Season on all sides with 1 tablespoon kosher salt and ½ teaspoon pepper. In a large, high-sided sauté pan or Dutch oven, heat the oil on medium until hot. Working in batches if necessary, add the chicken, skin side down. Cook, flipping once halfway through, for 10 to 12 minutes per batch, until browned on all sides. Transfer to a plate, leaving any browned bits (fond) in the pan.

❷ **Cook the aromatics.** Reduce the heat to low. Add the lemongrass, garlic, ginger, and white bottoms of the scallions to the fond and season with 1 teaspoon kosher salt. Cook, stirring frequently, for 30 seconds to 1 minute, until fragrant. Add the curry paste and cook for 30 seconds to 1 minute, until darkened and fragrant.

❸ **Braise the chicken.** Return the chicken to the pan, along with any accumulated juices. Add the coconut milk and 1 cup of the water and stir to combine. Increase the heat to medium and bring to a simmer. Reduce the heat to low and cover. Cook for 45 to 50 minutes, turning the chicken halfway through, until the thighs are very tender.

❹ **Cook the rice and serve.** While the chicken cooks, combine the rice, the remaining 4 cups water, and a big pinch of kosher salt in a saucepan. Heat to boiling on high. Cover and reduce the heat to low. Simmer for 12 to 14 minutes, until the water has been absorbed and the rice is tender. Remove from the heat and fluff the cooked rice with a fork; top with the green tops of the scallions. Transfer the chicken and braising liquid to a serving dish and top with the cilantro and a sprinkle of sea salt. Serve with the rice and lime wedges on the side.

How to PREPARE LEMONGRASS

Prized for its exhilarating citrus scent, lemongrass is cultivated as a culinary and medicinal herb in Asia, Australia, and Africa, where it's used in a range of preparations including teas, soups, and curries. To use fresh lemongrass, first trim off and discard the root end of the stalk. Peel off and discard the fibrous outer layers until you reach the pliable white core, and then finely chop the core.

Moroccan Braised Lamb Shoulder

with Apricot

Tagines are sacred in Moroccan culture. "Tagine" is a word used to describe both the traditional stew recipe used for centuries and the name of the tall, conical earthenware pot in which it's traditionally prepared. Tough cuts of meat, such as lamb shoulder, are transformed into a thick, spiced stew of tender meat, vegetables, and dried fruit. In this recipe, we use a Dutch oven to achieve similar results. Subtle sweetness comes from apricots and onions, and heat and spice come from ginger and *ras el hanout*.

RAS EL HANOUT

Ras el hanout is a North African spice blend that's used in a variety of savory dishes with meat, fish, rice, and couscous, similar to the way that garam masala is used in Indian cuisine. The Arabic name translates to "head of the shop," implying a mixture of the best spices the seller has to offer. There is no definitive composition, but common ingredients include a bevy of spices such as cumin, coriander, cardamom, cloves, cinnamon, allspice, ginger, and paprika. Look for *ras el hanout* in specialty stores or make your own using one part each of cumin, coriander, and sweet paprika, and one-quarter part each of cinnamon and ground cardamom.

---

3 pounds boneless lamb shoulder, cut into 1½- to 2-inch pieces

Kosher salt and freshly ground black pepper

Extra virgin olive oil

1 yellow onion, medium diced

1 carrot, peeled and cut into ½-inch-thick rounds

4 cloves garlic, minced

1 (1-inch) piece ginger, peeled and minced

2 tablespoons *ras el hanout*

1 (14- to 15-ounce) can diced tomatoes

1 cup chicken stock (page 174)

½ cup water

½ cup dried apricots or pitted dates, chopped

Juice of ½ lemon

¼ cup blanched almonds, toasted and coarsely chopped, for garnish

¼ cup whole cilantro leaves, for garnish

❶ **Sear the lamb.** Preheat the oven to 325°F. Season the lamb with 1 tablespoon salt and 1½ teaspoons pepper. In a Dutch oven, heat 1 tablespoon olive oil on medium-high until hot. Working in batches and adding more oil as needed, add the lamb in a single layer. Cook, flipping occasionally, for 10 to 15 minutes per batch, until well browned on all sides. Transfer to a plate.

❷ **Cook the vegetables.** Discard all but 1 tablespoon fat from the pot. Add the onion, carrot, garlic, and ginger. Cook, stirring occasionally and scraping up any browned bits (fond) from the bottom of the pot, for 1 to 2 minutes, until the onion is slightly softened. Add the *ras el hanout*. Cook, stirring frequently, for about 1 minute, until fragrant. Return the lamb to the pot along with any accumulated juices and stir briefly to coat in the spices.

❸ **Braise the lamb.** Add the tomatoes and their juices, and stir to combine. Season with salt and pepper. Add the stock and water and stir to thoroughly combine. Heat to a simmer on medium-high. Remove from the heat and top with a parchment paper circle (see page 108). Cover and transfer to the oven. Braise for about 1 hour 45 minutes, until the lamb is very tender.

❹ **Finish the braise.** Remove from the oven; discard the parchment circle. Stir in the apricots and let stand for 10 to 15 minutes, until the apricots are plump. Stir in the lemon juice. Transfer the lamb to a serving dish. Garnish with the almonds and cilantro leaves and serve.

5
Pan-Seared Meats

Pan-searing is a quick and easy cooking process that creates some of our most crave-worthy meals (think steak with a caramelized crust, crispy chicken cutlets, or bone-in pork chops) and produces big flavors fast.

This chapter will teach you the basic formula to create a perfectly browned crust and juicy middle on all your favorite cuts. Pan-searing is a dry-heat cooking method that relies on moderate to high heat, and a small amount of oil. (The exception is pan-seared duck, which requires lower heat to render its fat.) The browned crust that makes these meats so flavorful is the result of the Maillard reaction, a chemical response between amino acids and reducing sugars that gives browned food a distinct and satisfying flavor. We'll also teach you how to prepare a range of flavorful pan sauces from the delicious pan drippings.

Because you're cooking over high heat, pan-searing happens quickly. To avoid burning or overcooking the meat, you'll use relatively smaller (compared with a roast), tender or tenderized cuts for these recipes. As with other meat preparations, you'll get the best flavor if you season the meat in advance and allow it to come to room temperature before cooking.

Pan-seared meats pair well with a range of side dishes, from steamed rice to boiled new potatoes, or a fresh vegetable salad to balance the rich flavors.

Tools to Have on Hand

- Heavy-bottomed sauté pan
- Cast-iron skillet
- Slotted metal spatula
- Wooden spoon

COOK'S *tip*

CHOOSE THE RIGHT SIZE PAN: *A pan that is too small will be overcrowded and cause the meat to steam, not brown; if the pan is small, pan-sear in batches.*

Keys to Success

1. Start with the right cuts of the highest-quality meat. Avoid prepackaged cuts if possible, and ask the butcher for a good ratio of fat to lean meat; too-lean cuts will dry out quickly. Seek out the freshest meats available, ideally from a market that sells pasture-raised varieties. Cuts that are tender and smaller (versus a cut from a pork shoulder or a large chicken leg, for example) will be your best bet for this quick-cooking method.

2. Pat dry before you fry. Excess moisture creates steam that inhibits browning. To avoid this, pat the cuts dry with paper towels before searing.

3. Don't flip too soon. For the best flavor and appearance, you want a nice golden-brown crust. To achieve this, avoid the temptation to fuss with the meat too soon. Your best bet is to follow our timing cues; you'll know the meat is ready to flip when the crust releases easily from the pan.

4. Allow the meat to rest. As with other meats, you'll get the best flavor and juiciest texture if you allow the meat to rest briefly before it's served. This allows the meat to reabsorb the juices. It doesn't take long; while larger, longer-cooking cuts need an extended rest, pan-seared meats need only a few minutes—typically the amount of time it will take you to prepare a pan sauce.

5. Finish with a pan sauce. To make the most of searing and to take the meat to the next level, prepare a pan sauce from the flavorful fond and drippings left in the pan. Components like acid, fresh herbs, and salt pull the flavors together.

PAN SAUCES

Pan sauces, gravies, and *jus* always start with the flavorful fond (see page 40) left in the pan by the meat you just seared or roasted. Those caramelized, browned bits will add tremendous depth to the sauce. The first step in making a pan sauce is to "deglaze" the pan with a liquid—that could mean an alcohol (wine), stock, vinegar, citrus juice, or simply water. Another way to deglaze a pan is by sautéing vegetables, such as shallots or mushrooms, in the fond to cause their moisture to release. The deglazing process allows those bits of flavor to release from the pan and into the sauce. Let the liquid bubble and cook until slightly reduced in volume. If you'd like, finish the sauce by whisking in a pat of butter or a drizzle of cream to add richness; or add finely chopped soft herbs (such as tarragon, parsley, or chives) for a burst of freshness.

Pan-Seared Pork Chops

with Apple Cider Sauce

Serves 2

The keys to the juiciest pan-seared pork chops are a hot, heavy-bottomed pan and basting. Basting is an easy step that you can add to most pan-seared meat or fish preparations. It not only keeps the meats moist but infuses them with flavor. Once you flip the pork chop (or steak or salmon fillet), simply tilt the pan and spoon the pan juices over the meat while the bottom side cooks—in this case, our pan juices are enriched with butter and herbs for even more flavor. We never let fond go to waste, so while the meat rests, incorporate the flavorful browned bits into a pan sauce spiked with apple cider.

2 (1-inch-thick) bone-in pork rib or loin chops

Kosher salt and freshly ground black pepper

2 tablespoons extra virgin olive oil, plus more for the salad greens

2 tablespoons unsalted butter

2 sprigs thyme

1 large sprig rosemary

2 cloves garlic, unpeeled, lightly crushed

¼ cup apple cider vinegar

¼ cup apple cider

¼ cup water

2 loosely packed cups mixed salad greens

2 teaspoons freshly squeezed lemon juice

❶ Prepare the pork. About 45 minutes before cooking, remove the pork chops from the refrigerator and let stand at room temperature. Pat the pork dry with paper towels. Season generously with salt and pepper on both sides.

❷ Sear the pork. Heat a large, heavy pan on medium-high until hot. Add the 2 tablespoons olive oil and swirl to coat the pan. Add the pork. Cook the first side undisturbed for 2 to 4 minutes, until browned. Flip the pork and cook for 1 minute more, until lightly browned.

❸ Baste the pork. Add the butter, thyme, rosemary, and garlic. Cook, tilting the pan and continuously spooning the butter over the pork, for 1 to 2 minutes, until thoroughly coated and cooked through. Transfer the pork to a serving dish. Remove and discard the garlic, rosemary, and thyme, leaving the fond and fat (including the butter and oil) in the pan.

❹ Make the pan sauce and serve the pork. Reduce the heat to medium. Add the vinegar, apple cider, and water. Cook, stirring and scraping up any fond from the bottom of the pan, for 2 to 4 minutes, until the liquid is slightly reduced in volume. Pour the finished sauce over the pork. In a large bowl, combine the salad greens, lemon juice, and a drizzle of olive oil; season with salt and pepper. Serve the pork with the salad on the side.

COOK'S tip

BUCKLING CHOPS: *Depending on the cut of the pork chop, sometimes it will buckle or curl up in the pan as it cooks. To prevent this, cut a slit through the connective tissue—it contracts faster than the meat cooks, causing the chop to buckle. Depending on your chop, it might mean cutting slits into the outer edge of fat around the chop or, in this case, nicking the tough tissue on the inner part of the chop.*

Hanger Steak
with Red Wine–Shallot Sauce

The humble hanger steak has come a long way over the years. Named for the way the meat hangs from the loin, hanger steak is sometimes called the "butcher's cut" because it was seen as such a lowbrow piece of meat that butchers didn't even try to sell it. Instead, they would take it home for themselves—a smart move as it is incredibly flavorful, and since it's thin, it's particularly well suited for quick cooking. While the seared steaks rest before slicing, all you need to do is stir together a rich, flavorful sauce with red wine and shallots.

2 (8-ounce) hanger steaks

Kosher salt and freshly ground black pepper

2 tablespoons extra virgin olive oil

1 large sprig rosemary

¼ cup (½ stick) unsalted butter

4 shallots, minced (about ¾ cup)

1 cup full-bodied red wine (such as cabernet sauvignon or syrah)

Coarse sea salt, for garnish

❶ **Prepare the steaks.** About 45 minutes before cooking, remove the steaks from the refrigerator and let stand at room temperature. After the steaks have tempered for 30 minutes, pat dry with paper towels. Season generously with salt and pepper on both sides.

❷ **Sear the steaks.** In a large, heavy pan, heat the olive oil on medium-high until hot. Add the steaks and cook on the first side for 2 to 4 minutes, until browned. Flip the steaks and cook for 1 to 2 minutes, until lightly browned.

❸ **Baste the steaks.** Add the rosemary and 2 tablespoons of the butter. Cook, tilting the pan and continuously spooning the butter over the steaks, for 2 to 3 minutes for medium-rare (an instant-read thermometer inserted into the thickest part of the steak should register between 130° and 135°F) or until cooked to your desired degree of doneness. Transfer the steaks to a cutting board, leaving any browned bits (fond) and fat in the pan. Remove and discard the rosemary.

❹ **Make the sauce.** While the steaks rest, add the shallots to the fond. Cook on medium, stirring occasionally, for 2 to 3 minutes, until softened and fragrant. Add the wine and cook, stirring and scraping up any fond from the bottom of the pan, for 2 to 3 minutes, until the liquid is reduced in volume by about half. Reduce the heat to low and add the remaining 2 tablespoons butter. Cook, stirring frequently, for 1 to 2 minutes, until the sauce is slightly shiny and thoroughly combined. Remove from the heat and set aside in a warm place.

❺ **Serve the steaks.** Find the grain (lines of muscle; see Cook's Tip) of the steaks; thinly slice against the grain. Transfer to a serving dish. Add any juices from the cutting board to the pan of sauce; stir to combine. Top the sliced steaks with half the sauce and serve with the remaining sauce on the side. Sprinkle with the sea salt and serve.

COOK'S tip

SLICING AGAINST THE GRAIN: *The direction in which meat muscle fibers are aligned is called the "grain." Cuts like ribeye or tenderloin have thin muscle fibers so the grain is very fine, meaning the meat will be tender no matter how you slice it. Harder-working muscles like hanger and skirt steak have thicker, more defined muscle fibers. Slicing meat against the grain shortens those fibers and makes the meat easier to chew.*

Butter-Basted Porterhouse

The first steak houses in America opened in New York City, just after the Civil War. A handful of those first steak houses are still open today, and their menus really haven't changed much, with the signature porterhouse steak for two as a mainstay. It's actually two premium steaks in one: the tenderloin and the New York strip connected by the T-bone down the center. However, the part that truly makes it special and distinct from other cuts is that it's cut from the rear end of the short loin, so it has a bigger section of tenderloin.

A thick cut like a porterhouse calls for a bit more finesse to cook than thinner steaks. First, the generously seasoned steak is pan-seared to create a flavorful, deeply browned crust. A baste of garlic-and-rosemary-infused butter coats the meat in rich flavor. Then it's finished under the broiler—just a quick hit of heat—to cook through.

1 (1½-pound) porterhouse steak

Kosher salt and freshly ground black pepper

1 tablespoon extra virgin olive oil

¼ cup (½ stick) unsalted butter

2 large sprigs rosemary

3 cloves garlic, unpeeled, lightly crushed

Coarse sea salt, for garnish

1 lemon, cut into wedges, for serving

❶ Prepare the steak. About 45 minutes before cooking, remove the steak from the refrigerator and let stand at room temperature. After the steak has tempered for 30 minutes, pat dry with paper towels. Season generously with kosher salt and pepper on both sides. After another 15 minutes, pat dry again with paper towels. Season again with kosher salt and pepper on both sides.

❷ Sear the steak. Move an oven rack to the highest position and preheat the oven broiler to high. Heat an oven-safe pan (a cast-iron skillet, if you have one) on medium-high until hot. Add the olive oil and swirl to coat the pan. Add the steak. Cook the first side for 2 to 4 minutes, until browned. Flip the steak and cook for 1 to 2 minutes, until lightly browned on the second side.

❸ Baste and broil the steak. Add the butter, rosemary, and garlic. Cook, tilting the pan and continuously spooning the butter over the steak, for 1 to 2 minutes, until thoroughly coated. Remove from the heat. Using an oven mitt or a thick kitchen towel, transfer the pan to the oven rack directly under the broiler. Broil the steak for 1 to 2 minutes, until deeply browned and cooked to your desired degree of doneness (for medium-rare, an instant-read thermometer inserted into the center of the steak should register between 130° and 135°F).

❹ Rest and serve the steak. Transfer the steak to a cutting board. Remove and discard the rosemary and garlic. Let the steak rest for at least 5 minutes. Carve the two sections of meat from the T-bone. Find the grain (lines of muscle; see page 140) of the steak; cut against the grain into ¼-inch-thick slices. Transfer to a serving dish. Add any juices from the cutting board to the butter in the pan. Stir to combine and pour over the sliced steak. Season with sea salt and serve with the lemon wedges on the side.

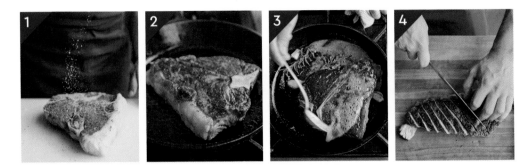

Chicken Piccata

Piccata is a wonderfully versatile technique that can be applied to any number of thinly sliced meats, such as veal, turkey, or chicken, as we use it here. "Piccata" may come from the word for "pike" or "piquant," which could refer to the lemon and briny capers commonly used in the sauce. The bright acidic elements combine with nutty browned butter to create a simple, satisfying dish using mostly staple ingredients. As with any straightforward recipe, this one is all in the details. Dredging the chicken in flour creates a flavorful crust, while the bits of the flour that remain in the pan after searing help to thicken the pan sauce you'll create. Wait until the butter begins to foam in the pan so the chicken pieces will brown quickly without overcooking.

4 (6-ounce) boneless, skinless chicken breasts (tenders removed)

½ cup all-purpose flour

Kosher salt and freshly ground black pepper

3 tablespoons extra virgin olive oil, plus more for the arugula

6 tablespoons unsalted butter

½ cup chicken stock (page 174)

5 tablespoons freshly squeezed lemon juice (about 2½ lemons)

3 tablespoons nonpareil capers in brine, drained

2 tablespoons finely chopped fresh flat-leaf parsley

3½ cups loosely packed arugula leaves (about 4 ounces)

❶ Tenderize the chicken. Pat the chicken dry with paper towels and place between two sheets of waxed paper or plastic wrap. Use a heavy pan to pound the chicken to an even ½-inch thickness.

❷ Dredge the chicken. In a shallow dish, combine the flour, 1 tablespoon salt, and ½ teaspoon pepper. Season the chicken on both sides with salt, then thoroughly coat in the seasoned flour. Tap off any excess flour and transfer the chicken to a clean plate.

❸ Sear the chicken. In a large sauté pan, heat the 3 tablespoons olive oil and 4 tablespoons of the butter on medium until the butter starts to foam. Working in batches if necessary, add the chicken and cook for 3 to 4 minutes per side, until golden brown and cooked through. Transfer the chicken to a serving dish, leaving any browned bits (fond) and fat in the pan. Loosely cover the chicken with foil and set aside in a warm place.

❹ Make the sauce. Add the stock to the fond. Heat to a simmer on medium-high, using a wooden spoon to scrape the fond from the bottom of the pan. Cook, stirring occasionally, for 30 seconds to 1 minute, until the liquid is reduced in volume by about half. Add 4 tablespoons lemon juice and the capers. Cook, stirring occasionally, for 30 seconds to 1 minute, until slightly thickened. Gradually whisk in the remaining 2 tablespoons butter, 1 tablespoon at a time. Cook, whisking constantly, for 2 to 3 minutes, until the sauce is slightly thickened. Remove from the heat. Stir in the parsley and season with salt and pepper. Top each piece of chicken with a few spoonfuls of sauce.

❺ Make the salad and serve. In a large bowl, combine the arugula, the remaining 1 tablespoon lemon juice, and a drizzle of olive oil; season with salt and pepper. Serve the chicken with the salad on the side.

Crispy Chicken Thighs

with Wild Mushrooms

Bone-in, skin-on chicken thighs are one of our favorite cuts because they offer the possibility of crispy skin and tender, flavorful dark meat. The first step is an initial sear in a hot, heavy pan. It's essential to let the fat properly render, or cook out, from the skin—it may take some patience, but it will produce crackling, thin skin and, of course, you'll be left with lots of flavorful fond to build a pan sauce. We finish the thighs in the oven to cook the meat until the connective tissue around the bone begins to break down and the meat tenderizes.

6 bone-in, skin-on chicken thighs (about 2 pounds total)

Kosher salt and freshly ground black pepper

3 tablespoons extra virgin olive oil

4 cups wild mushrooms (about 1 pound; such as yellow oyster, hen of the woods, or trumpet royale), trimmed and thinly sliced

2 shallots, minced

2 cloves garlic, coarsely chopped

2 tablespoons fresh thyme leaves

¼ cup dry white wine (such as sauvignon blanc or pinot grigio)

¼ cup heavy cream

2 tablespoons unsalted butter

3 tablespoons fresh flat-leaf parsley leaves

1 teaspoon white wine vinegar

Flaky sea salt, for garnish

❶ **Season the chicken.** Preheat the oven to 425°F. Pat the chicken dry with paper towels. Season generously with kosher salt and pepper on both sides.

❷ **Brown and roast the chicken.** In a large, oven-safe sauté pan, heat the olive oil on medium until hot. Add the chicken thighs, skin side down, and cook undisturbed for 7 to 9 minutes, until the skin is deep golden brown. Flip the chicken, skin side up, and transfer the pan to the oven. Roast for 18 to 20 minutes, until an instant-read thermometer inserted next to (but not touching) the bone registers 170°F. Remove from the oven. Transfer the chicken to a plate, leaving any browned bits (fond) in the pan. Loosely cover the chicken with foil and set aside in a warm place.

❸ **Cook the mushrooms.** Drain all but 3 tablespoons fat from the pan. Heat on medium until hot. Add the mushrooms and cook, stirring occasionally and scraping up the fond from the bottom of the pan, for 6 to 8 minutes, until the mushrooms begin to brown.

❹ **Add the aromatics.** Add the shallots, garlic, thyme, 1 teaspoon kosher salt, and ¼ teaspoon pepper. Cook, stirring occasionally, for 2 to 3 minutes, until the shallots and garlic are fragrant and slightly softened.

❺ **Finish the mushrooms.** Add the wine and cook, stirring and scraping up the fond from the bottom of the pan, for 30 to 45 seconds, until most of the liquid has been absorbed. Stir in the heavy cream and reduce the heat to low. Add the butter and stir to thoroughly combine. Stir in 2 tablespoons of the parsley. Turn off the heat and stir in the vinegar. Season with salt and pepper. Transfer the mushrooms and sauce to a serving dish; top with the chicken thighs. Sprinkle with sea salt and the remaining 1 tablespoon parsley and serve.

COOK'S
tip

DEGLAZING WITH VEGETABLES: *Deglazing a pan with mushrooms or other vegetables is a great way to pick up all the flavor of the fond (with the added benefit of making this recipe a one-pan meal). The vegetables are used instead of stock (or in addition to stock, in other cases), and the moisture released from the vegetables does the work of deglazing.*

Duck Breast

with Blood Orange Sauce

The classic French dish of *duck à l'orange* made its debut in the seventeenth century when King Louis XIV was inspired to elevate French cuisine to the best in the world. While it's fallen into and out of style since then, there's still nothing quite like crispy duck drizzled with a slightly sweet, orange-infused sauce. Our ode to the famous dish uses quick-cooking duck breasts instead of the whole bird, and rather than roasting, we pan-sear the meat over medium (not high) heat, which allows the bird's flavorful fat to fully and slowly render to create delicious, crispy skin. In our take, orange is incorporated in multiple layers: juice, zest, segments, and liqueur. The brilliant hue of blood oranges creates a strikingly beautiful sauce and presentation as well.

4 blood oranges, navel oranges, or juice oranges

2 skin-on duck breasts (Pekin or Normandy-style, about 1½ pounds total)

Kosher salt and freshly ground black pepper

Extra virgin olive oil

¼ cup apple cider vinegar

2 tablespoons Grand Marnier

⅓ cup sugar

2 tablespoons unsalted butter

❶ Prepare the oranges. Preheat the oven to 450°F. Use a peeler or paring knife to cut wide strips of zest (avoid the white pith) from half of one orange. Cut that orange and one other in half and squeeze their juice into a bowl. Peel the two remaining oranges and cut into segments (see opposite page).

❷ Blanch the orange zest. Heat a small pot of water to boiling on high. Add the zest and cook for 1 to 2 minutes, until lightened in color and slightly curled. Drain thoroughly.

❸ Prepare the duck breasts. Score the duck breasts in a cross-hatch pattern by making parallel diagonal cuts in the skin ½ inch apart, without cutting into the meat. Season with salt and pepper on both sides.

❹ Sear the duck breasts. In a heavy, oven-safe sauté pan (cast-iron skillet, if you have one), heat 1 teaspoon olive oil on medium until hot. Add the duck breasts, skin side down. Cook for 13 to 15 minutes, until deep gold and crispy; if fat begins to pool around the breasts, pour it off and continue. Flip the duck breasts and transfer the pan to the oven. Roast for 2 to 3 minutes, until an instant-read thermometer inserted into the thickest part of the breast registers 135°F (for medium-rare). Transfer the duck breasts to a cutting board, leaving any browned bits (fond) in the pan. Let the duck breasts rest while making the sauce.

❺ Make the sauce and serve the duck. Remove all but 2 tablespoons of fat from the pan. Heat the fat on medium-high. Add the orange juice, vinegar, Grand Marnier, and sugar. Cook for 6 to 7 minutes, scraping up the fond from the bottom of the pan, until reduced in volume by half. Reduce the heat to low. Add the butter ½ tablespoon at a time, whisking constantly, until thoroughly combined and slightly thickened. Remove from the heat and stir in the orange segments and blanched zest. Cut the duck into ½-inch-thick slices. Transfer to a serving dish. Spoon the sauce over the duck. Serve with any extra sauce on the side.

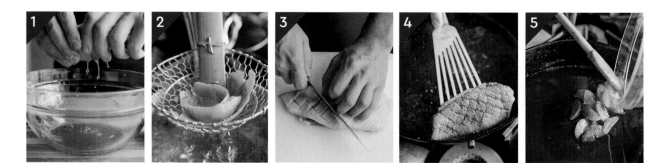

How to SUPRÊME CITRUS

❶ To suprême (meaning, cut into segments) any citrus fruit, first slice ¼ to ½ inch off the top and bottom. Place the fruit cut side down. From the top down, begin to cut away the rind peel and pith (the white part), following the curve and leaving as much fruit flesh as possible. **❷** Once all of the pith and peel are gone, cut out the segments by slicing into the fruit close to either side of the membranes, working all around the fruit.

6
Pan-Seared Fish

Cooking fish at home can seem intimidating, but when you start with the best seasonal varieties and have a few good techniques in your back pocket, it's really quite easy.

———

Remember to source the best fish or seafood that's in season, depending on where you live. We like to choose varieties that are highly rated by the Monterey Bay Aquarium, a good consumer guide that focuses on ocean conservation. For pan-searing, thicker fillets should be from fish that could be served with a range of doneness, such as wild salmon or swordfish. For thinner fillets, choose tender, flaky white fish, such as skin-on branzino and snapper, or hake, cod, sole, and flounder. We love skin-on fillets because the skin acts as a barrier that helps the flesh cook more gently while the skin itself gets crispy and delicious.

When you start with the freshest, highest-quality varieties, they often need little adornment after pan-searing: a squeeze of fresh lemon juice, a sprinkle of flaky salt, and perhaps a drizzle of olive oil. However, for a little extra excitement, we teach you how to pull together a few easy pan sauces and a lemony *beurre blanc* sauce, a classic in French kitchens. When it comes to rounding out the meal, choose sides with fresh, clean flavors (steamed asparagus, blanched vegetables, or a bright pole bean salad) that won't detract from the fish. A bottle of chilled white wine is essential.

Tools to Have on Hand

- Heavy-bottomed sauté pan
- Cast-iron skillet
- Slotted metal spatula

Keys to Success

1. Start with the freshest, highest-quality fish and seafood from a trusted source. At the store, don't hesitate to consult with the people who work at the fish counter and tell them what you'll be cooking. If the variety of fish you want isn't there, ask for alternatives that offer similar flavor and texture. Ask to smell or even touch the fish or seafood; it shouldn't have a strong, unappealing smell, and it should be firm, not slimy.

2. Pat dry before you fry. Excess moisture creates steam that inhibits browning. To avoid this, pat fish, shrimp, and scallops dry with paper towels before placing them in the pan.

3. Start skin side down in a hot pan. For the nicest presentation and the best texture, always start cooking fish in a very hot pan, skin side down. If the fish fillet has been skinned, start on the side where the skin used to be.

4. Don't flip too soon. A crispy, golden-brown crust creates the best flavor and appearance. Cook the fish most of the way through, then flip to briefly cook the other side just until finished. Avoid the temptation to fuss with the fish too soon; you'll know it's ready when the crust releases easily from the pan. If the fish sticks to the pan, allow it to cook a little longer—once the crust is caramelized, it might release. You can also add a few drops of water to the pan—the steam often helps release the skin—or lightly tap the pan against the stove.

Pan-Seared Salmon

with Thyme Butter

Serves 4

Searing salmon with its skin on protects the delicate fillets during cooking. When it's done right, it also creates a crispy exterior that will be as tasty as anything else on the plate. The secret is patience: Allow the pan to get nice and hot before you add the fish, then *do not fuss with it* for a few minutes so it has time to crisp and brown—this will also allow the skin to release from the pan and make it easier to flip. Baste the salmon with garlic-and-thyme-infused butter while it finishes cooking to create another layer of flavor and ensure moist results. However, perfectly seared salmon is delicious on its own, so feel free to skip this step and simply serve the fillets with a wedge of lemon.

4 (6-ounce) skin-on salmon fillets (preferably wild king salmon)

Kosher salt

1 tablespoon extra virgin olive oil

2 cloves garlic, peeled and lightly crushed

2 tablespoons unsalted butter

2 sprigs thyme

2 tablespoons freshly squeezed lemon juice (about ½ lemon)

2 tablespoons water

Flaky sea salt, for garnish

Pole Bean Salad with Dijon-Herb Vinaigrette (page 156), for serving (optional)

1 **Prepare the fish.** Pat the fish dry with paper towels. Season generously with salt on both sides.

2 **Start the fish.** In a large sauté pan, heat the olive oil on medium-high until hot. (The pan is hot enough when you add a drop of water and it sizzles.) Add the fish, skin side down. Cook undisturbed for 2 to 3 minutes, until cooked through (it will look opaque) halfway up the fillet. Flip each fillet and add the garlic, butter, and thyme.

3 **Baste the fish.** Tilt the pan and continuously spoon the butter over the fish, for 1 to 2 minutes, until golden brown (an instant-read thermometer inserted into the thickest part of the fish should register 125°F for medium-rare or 130°F for medium).

4 **Finish the pan sauce.** Transfer the salmon to a serving dish. Discard the garlic and thyme. Carefully add the lemon juice and water to the butter. Cook, stirring continuously, for 30 seconds to 1 minute, until thoroughly combined and slightly thickened. Pour the sauce over the fish. Sprinkle with sea salt and serve.

COOK'S *tip*

PAN SAUCE: *If your pan sauce "breaks" (separates), add a few drops of water and continue to whisk, or even add a bit of heavy cream or crème fraîche.*

POLE BEAN SALAD

with Dijon-Herb Vinaigrette

Serves 4 to 6

Consider this recipe your go-to method for any variety of pole beans (green beans, Romano beans, haricots verts, or yellow wax beans). The beans are blanched in generously salted water until they're bright green and *just* tender. They are then tossed in a sharp vinaigrette made with garlic, shallots, parsley, and tarragon. A final scattering of salt and chives creates a pretty side dish that brings the bright flavors of the garden to the table. Topped with a poached or fried egg, these beans could easily make a meal.

Kosher salt

1 pound haricots verts or other pole beans (such as yellow wax beans), trimmed

1 clove garlic, finely grated into a paste

2 shallots, minced

2 tablespoons freshly squeezed lemon juice

2 tablespoons Dijon mustard

Freshly ground black pepper

6 tablespoons extra virgin olive oil

¼ cup chopped fresh flat-leaf parsley leaves

1 tablespoon chopped fresh tarragon leaves

2 tablespoons chopped fresh chives

Flaky sea salt, for garnish

❶ Blanch the beans. Heat a large pot of salted water to boiling on high. Fill a large bowl with ice water. Add the beans to the boiling water. Cook for 3 to 5 minutes, until bright green and tender (the cooking time will vary depending on the variety of bean you're using). The beans should taste cooked but still have a snap to them.

❷ Shock the beans. Drain thoroughly and transfer to the bowl of ice water; let stand until cool. Drain thoroughly and pat dry with paper towels. Transfer to a large bowl.

❸ Make the vinaigrette. In a bowl, combine the garlic, shallots, lemon juice, and mustard and season with salt and black pepper. Slowly whisk in the olive oil until well combined.

❹ Finish the salad. Add the parsley, tarragon, and chives to the beans. Add the vinaigrette and toss to coat. Sprinkle with sea salt and serve.

COOK'S
tip

SALTING WATER: *The water you use to blanch the vegetables should taste like the sea. A good ratio is 1 tablespoon kosher salt for every quart of water.*

4

HOW TO BLANCH
Any VEGETABLE

When you want to preserve a vegetable's vibrant flavor,
color, and crisp bite, boil a pot of water.

Blanching vegetables (plunging them into boiling water, draining them, and then shocking them in an ice bath) locks in fresh flavor and snappy texture. As you'll discover, once you've blanched one variety, you're ready to take on the entire produce section to create a world of side dishes. Blanched vegetables are particularly appealing alongside pan-seared fish and meats because the clean, pure flavors don't overwhelm other elements on the plate. After they've been shocked and drained of excess moisture, the vegetables are ready for any number of enhancements, from lemon juice and flaky salt to fresh herbs, soft cheese, and toasted nuts or crumbled, crispy bacon (pages 160–161).

Keys to Success

1. Blanch one variety at a time. Various vegetables (carrots and broccoli, for instance) call for different cooking times, so to ensure the best texture, blanch each variety separately.

2. Taste the cooking water. When you're blanching multiple varieties of vegetables in batches in the same pot, be sure to taste the water before adding another vegetable. That's because the first vegetable could infuse the water during the cooking process, so if the water has a pronounced taste of the first vegetable, you'll want to dilute it with more salted water before adding the second vegetable.

3. Use the right ratios. As a general rule, when it comes to blanching, you'll want a 4:1 water-to-vegetable ratio, meaning 1 quart water to 1 cup vegetables. When it comes to salt, you'll want approximately 1 tablespoon kosher salt to 1 quart water.

4. Cook it until just tender. Be careful not to cook your vegetables beyond crisp-tender, or they will be mushy. "Crisp-tender" means the vegetable will be tender enough to bite through, but with just a slight, snappy crunch. The color should be bright and vibrant, not overly darkened. To tell when a vegetable is tender, pierce it with the tip of a sharp knife (or take a bite!). The knife should pierce the vegetable without resistance.

5. Shock in an ice bath. Shocking cooked vegetables in ice and cold water helps stop the cooking process and preserves the vegetable's bright color. Set up your ice bath before you start blanching so you're ready to go.

6. Dry before finishing. Removing excess moisture from the drained vegetables helps prevent diluted flavor. After draining, pat dry with paper towels or allow them to air-dry on a clean kitchen towel.

WARMING BLANCHED VEGETABLES: *These side dishes can be served warm or cold. For a warm dish, right after shocking, quickly reheat them in a pan with a little butter and olive oil before dressing or garnishing with the other ingredients.*

SHOCKING VEGETABLES: *If you're blanching multiple batches of vegetables, instead of fully transferring the blanched vegetables into the water bath, nestle a colander in the ice bath and place the vegetables inside to cool so you don't have to fish out the vegetables from the ice.*

For all blanched vegetables, follow the same method; the creativity comes with deciding how to finish them. Here are some of our favorite ways to finish any blanched vegetable you like:

with **LEMON & HERBS**

Toss the blanched vegetable with a drizzle of olive oil, freshly squeezed lemon juice, flaky sea salt, and 2 tablespoons chopped fresh herbs (tarragon, chervil, parsley). Works best for "early season" asparagus that is thinner and more tender.

with **HERBED BUTTERMILK DRESSING**

Serve the blanched vegetable with Herbed Buttermilk Dressing (page 236) on the side. When blanching a mix of vegetables, save green vegetables for last, since they'll leave behind a green color in the water.

with PICKLED CHILES, ALMONDS & PECORINO

Toss the blanched vegetable with a drizzle of olive oil; juice of 1 lemon; salt and pepper; ¼ cup roughly chopped, toasted, skin-on almonds; and 2 tablespoons chopped pickled chiles (such as pepperoncini). Top with coarsely grated young pecorino cheese.

with HERBS, SHALLOTS & RICOTTA

Thinly slice a large shallot crosswise and place in a small saucepan with ¼ cup red wine vinegar and 2 teaspoons sugar. Bring to a boil. Once boiling, cook, stirring occasionally, for 1 to 2 minutes, until the shallot has softened and the liquid is slightly reduced in volume. Transfer to a heatproof bowl and set aside to pickle for at least 10 minutes. Toss the blanched vegetable with a drizzle of olive oil, salt and pepper, the juice of 1 lemon, 2 tablespoons mint leaves, 2 tablespoons chopped parsley, and as much of the pickled shallot as you'd like (draining just before adding). Whisk 1 cup whole-milk ricotta with 2 tablespoons olive oil; season with salt and pepper. Spread the ricotta on a serving plate. Top with the vegetable and serve.

Sole Meunière

This dish dates back centuries to the days when villages still had a miller in town who made their flour. *Meunière* loosely translates to "in the manner of the miller's wife," referring to the flour that's used to dredge the fish in the recipe. This classic French preparation is an example of how the simplest dishes are often the most satisfying. After dredging (lightly coating) in flour, the thin sole fillets are panfried until golden brown and served with a caper-and-lemon-spiked brown butter sauce that comes together in the same pan. For the deepest flavor, allow the butter to turn a rich brown color and take on a nutty aroma before stirring in the aromatics.

1 cup all-purpose flour

4 (6-ounce) sole fillets

Kosher salt and freshly ground black pepper

2 tablespoons extra virgin olive oil

6 tablespoons (¾ stick) unsalted butter, cut into 1-tablespoon pieces

1 tablespoon nonpareil capers in brine, drained

Juice of 1 lemon

½ cup finely chopped fresh flat-leaf parsley leaves

Flaky sea salt, for garnish

❶ **Prepare the fish.** Spread the flour on a large plate or shallow dish. Pat the fish fillets dry with paper towels and season generously with kosher salt and pepper on both sides. Coat the fillets in the flour on both sides, tapping off any excess, and transfer to a plate.

❷ **Heat the oil and butter.** In a large sauté pan, heat the oil and 2 tablespoons of the butter on medium until the butter begins to foam.

❸ **Cook the fish.** Working in batches, add the fish and cook for 2 to 3 minutes, until lightly browned. Use a thin metal spatula to flip the fillets. Cook for 1 minute to 1 minute 30 seconds, until browned and cooked through. Transfer to a serving dish. Carefully discard the oil and butter, reserving the browned bits (fond) left in the pan.

❹ **Make the pan sauce.** Add the remaining 4 tablespoons butter to the fond. Cook, stirring constantly, for 30 seconds to 1 minute, until the butter begins to brown and smell nutty. Add the capers. Cook, stirring constantly, for 15 to 30 seconds, until thoroughly combined. Stir in the lemon juice. Remove from the heat. Stir in the parsley and immediately pour the sauce over the fish. Sprinkle with sea salt and serve immediately.

Shrimp

with Garlic, Cherry Tomatoes & Basil

Time to channel your inner Italian fisherman. Bursting with summery flavors, this easy-to-assemble dish is a play on *acqua pazza*, the Neapolitan dish of fish cooked in "crazy water." Traditionally, that would involve sautéing a fresh catch in the "crazy water," which consists of garlic, hot chiles, tomatoes, and wine. In our version, we add crisp green beans to our sweet pan-seared shrimp, and finish with a scattering of fresh basil. The key to perfectly cooked shrimp is simple: Don't cook it for too long—it's done when it's opaque through the center, but will retain an almost snappy texture without being tough or mealy.

1 pound large shrimp (8 to 10 shrimp per pound)

Kosher salt

½ pound green beans or Romano beans, trimmed and cut at an angle into 1-inch pieces (2 cups)

½ loosely packed cup fresh basil leaves

¼ cup extra virgin olive oil

2 cloves garlic, minced

2 cups cherry tomatoes, halved

½ teaspoon crushed red pepper flakes

¼ cup dry white wine (such as sauvignon blanc or pinot grigio)

1 tablespoon freshly squeezed lemon juice

Flaky sea salt, for garnish

❶ Clean the shrimp. Shell the shrimp. Use the tip of a knife to make a small incision down the back of the shrimp and scrape out the digestive tract or vein.

❷ Blanch and shock the beans. Heat a pot of salted water to boiling on high. Fill a bowl with ice water. Add the beans to the boiling water and cook for 1 minute 30 seconds to 2 minutes, until bright green. Drain thoroughly and transfer to the ice water; let stand until cool. Drain thoroughly and pat dry with paper towels. Thinly slice the basil leaves and set aside.

❸ Sear the shrimp. In a large sauté pan, heat 2 tablespoons of the olive oil on medium-high until hot. While the oil is heating, pat the shrimp dry with paper towels and season generously with kosher salt. When a drop of water sizzles in the pan, add the shrimp. Cook for 1 minute 30 seconds to 2 minutes on one side, until lightly browned and opaque. Transfer the shrimp to a plate.

❹ Cook the tomatoes. Reduce the heat to medium. Add the remaining 2 tablespoons olive oil, the garlic, tomatoes, and red pepper flakes and season with salt. Cook, stirring constantly, for 1 minute 30 seconds to 2 minutes, until the tomatoes start to soften and break down. Add the wine and cook, stirring frequently, for 1 minute, until mostly evaporated.

❺ Finish the shrimp. Add the shrimp, browned side up. Let the shrimp cook undisturbed for 30 seconds. Stir in the beans and cook, stirring occasionally, for 2 to 3 minutes, until the shrimp are cooked through and the sauce is slightly thickened. Remove from the heat and stir in the basil and lemon juice. Transfer to a serving dish. Sprinkle with sea salt and serve immediately.

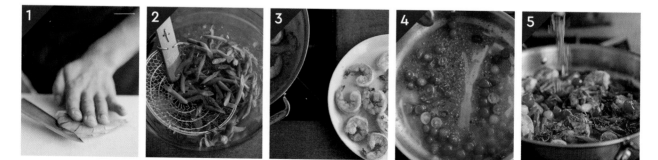

Pan-Seared Scallops

with Tarragon Butter Sauce

This elegant and impressive recipe features two important techniques: one for perfectly seared scallops (crispy, caramelized crust with a middle that's still tender, not rubbery and not overcooked) and the second for an easier take on a classic butter sauce, *beurre blanc*. Many French recipes are traditionally finished with butter, and this sauce likely evolved from that technique. At its simplest, beurre blanc is an emulsion (see page 259) of butter and a reduction of wine or vinegar, but other seasonings or elements can be added, such as lemon, herbs, and spices, as we do here. It's essential to cook the scallops in a heavy-bottomed pan, such as a cast-iron skillet—the deep, even heat will create a deeply browned exterior.

TARRAGON BUTTER SAUCE

¼ cup dry white wine (such as sauvignon blanc or pinot grigio)

¼ cup white wine vinegar

1 shallot, thinly sliced

1 teaspoon whole coriander seed

1 teaspoon whole fennel seed

1 teaspoon whole black peppercorns

1 cup (2 sticks) unsalted butter, cut into 1-tablespoon pieces, chilled

2 teaspoons finely chopped tarragon leaves

1 teaspoon finely chopped fresh flat-leaf parsley leaves

1 teaspoon kosher salt

BUYING AND CLEANING FRESH SCALLOPS

Fresh scallops are a luxury, so when you plan a meal around them, it's important to purchase the best. Start with a great fish market that has a high turnover, so you know the product is fresh—scallops should smell clean and like the ocean. Scallops are often soaked in a phosphate solution that whitens them and makes them absorb more liquid, so you'll pay significantly per pound for water. These scallops will retain too much moisture and won't brown well. Instead, seek out "chemical-free" or "dry-pack" scallops. To clean the scallops, find the small, tough side-muscle (the "foot") on each scallop. Pull it off with your fingers and discard.

12 large sea scallops (1¼ to 1½ pounds total), cleaned

Kosher salt and freshly ground black pepper

1 tablespoon canola oil

2 tablespoons unsalted butter

Flaky sea salt, for garnish

❶ Start the sauce. Set a small fine-mesh strainer over a small bowl. In a small saucepan, heat the wine, vinegar, shallot, coriander, fennel, and black peppercorns to a simmer on medium. Cook, stirring occasionally, for 5 to 7 minutes, until the liquid is reduced in volume by three-quarters (about 2 tablespoons remain). Strain into the bowl and discard any solids.

❷ Finish the sauce. Return the strained liquid to the pot. Heat to a simmer on medium. Reduce the heat to low. Gradually whisk in the 1 cup chilled butter, 1 tablespoon at a time, waiting until each tablespoon is almost completely incorporated before adding the next. When you have 1 tablespoon of butter remaining, remove from the heat and whisk it in off the heat. Whisk until the mixture is thoroughly combined and slightly thickened. Whisk in the tarragon, parsley, and salt. Transfer to a bowl and set aside in a warm place.

❸ Sear the scallops. Pat the scallops dry with paper towels. Season with salt on both sides. In a large cast-iron pan, heat the canola oil on medium-high until shimmering. Working in batches if necessary, add the scallops in a single, even layer and cook for 1 to 2 minutes, until golden brown on the bottom. Use a metal slotted spatula or spoon to flip the scallops.

❹ Baste the scallops. Add the 2 tablespoons butter and cook, tilting the pan and continuously spooning the butter over the scallops, for 20 to 30 seconds, until the scallops start to plump and are browned on the second side. Remove from the heat. Divide the scallops among four serving plates. Top with a sprinkle of sea salt and a few spoonfuls of the sauce and serve immediately.

7
Soups

Soups have long been a symbol of community
and fellowship, and learning how to make a great soup
will truly serve you for a lifetime.

There is perhaps no other dish that is so universally adaptable and equated with comfort, no matter the culture or country. The foundation of soup and countless other dishes is a flavorful stock, so we begin by teaching you how to build deeply flavored pots of chicken, beef, and vegetable stocks; you'll wind up with enough for the recipes at hand, plus more to freeze for future uses. With a bit more effort, homemade stock becomes a rich and beautiful bowl of clarified broth (consommé).

Great soup is made up of layers, a process that begins by sweating an aromatic base of vegetables (what the French call a *mirepoix*) to create depth. After that, the primary components (for example, the beef for beef and barley soup, zucchini and herbs for creamy zucchini soup) are added with stock or other cooking liquids, and the ingredients simmer together at a low and slow tempo. With these basic steps, any soup can be yours.

The word "soup" actually comes from the French *sop*, which meant the pieces of bread you would use to soak up all of the juices from the meat on your plate. Stale bread was made moist once again, while not a single drop of liquid was wasted. Given this history, it's no wonder that soup and bread make such an excellent pair.

Tools to Have on Hand

- Stockpot
- Blender
- Butcher's twine and cheesecloth

Keys to Success

1. Start with the best ingredients. Seek out the freshest seasonal produce to create soups with the most vibrant flavor. It's nice to have a selection of dried beans (cannellini, lentils), grains (barley, farro), and small shapes of pasta on hand so recipes come together quickly. As you'll discover, homemade stocks are best, but if you need to go with store-bought, look for high-quality (organic, free-range), low-sodium brands.

2. Treat every step as a building block of your soup. Take your time sweating the aromatics (gently cooking the vegetables in butter or olive oil without browning). It is an essential, flavor-building step that creates wonderful depth. After you've created an aromatic base, sauté the primary components until the flavors are combined. Depending on what you're making, add stock, cream, or milk, and simmer until the ingredients are tender (but not mushy), so they retain a vibrant flavor. If you're making a puréed soup, you'll stop and blend here.

3. Add cooked grains and pastas last. If you're including them, you'll want to add them toward the end of cooking so they won't become bloated or mushy, and won't create a cloudy stock.

4. Finish with a flavorful garnish. A drizzle of extra virgin olive oil, a sprinkling of freshly ground black pepper, a squeeze of fresh lemon juice, or a scattering of fresh herbs will brighten the flavors of the soup. A final dollop of something creamy—like yogurt or crème fraîche or a swirl of pesto—is also a quick way to add an extra layer of flavor and interest to a soup.

Rustic Bread
(page 180)

Classic Chicken Noodle Soup (page 178)

CHICKEN STOCK

Makes 4 quarts

Chicken stock is the building block of flavor in many recipes in this book. When it's made well, stock enhances the simplest of dishes with a depth of flavor—while a stock simmers, the gelatin extracted from the bones creates richness. Although most of the cooking time is unattended, there are a couple of key details to pay attention to: Briefly blanching the chicken pieces first pulls out the bitterness and impurities from the bones. Careful skimming, particularly in the early part of the process, will result in the cleanest, clearest stock and best flavor. Additionally, for the clearest stock, maintain very gentle heat; there should be only a few bubbles rising to the surface as it simmers.

HOW LONG SHOULD YOU SIMMER?

Six hours is the optimal amount of time you'll need to extract the desired amount of flavor and collagen from the bones. Feel free to simmer the stock a couple of hours longer, but no more than that—after eight hours you'll begin to extract minerals and impurities that won't improve the flavor. If you're short on time, a two- to three-hour simmer time could do in a pinch.

3 pounds chicken pieces (preferably necks, backs, and wings)

1 yellow onion, cut into wedges

2 carrots, peeled, cut into 3-inch lengths

2 stalks celery, cut into 3-inch lengths

1 head garlic, halved crosswise

1 large leek, large diced and cleaned (see page 100)

1 large sprig thyme

2 bay leaves

10 black peppercorns

6 quarts cold water

❶ Blanch the chicken pieces. Place the chicken in a large stockpot. Cover completely with tap water. Heat to simmering on high. Cook for 5 minutes, periodically skimming foam and impurities from the surface of the water. Turn off the heat and skim off any remaining impurities. Drain the chicken in a colander; rinse and wipe out the stockpot.

❷ Make the stock. Return the chicken to the stockpot and add the onion, carrots, celery, garlic, leek, thyme, bay leaves, peppercorns, and water. Heat to simmering on high. Reduce the heat to low. Cook, uncovered, occasionally skimming off foam and impurities, for 6 to 8 hours, until the liquid is reduced in volume to about 4 quarts.

❸ Strain and cool the stock. Pour the stock through a fine-mesh strainer into a second clean pot or large heatproof container. Discard the solids. Fill a large bowl or the sink with ice. Set the pot of strained stock in the ice. Cool the finished stock to room temperature. Store for up to 3 days in sealed containers in the refrigerator or freeze right away and use within 3 months.

VEGETABLE STOCK

Makes 4 quarts

Making homemade vegetable stock is very easy—this method will inspire you to start saving parsley stems, celery trimmings, fennel fronds, and all sorts of vegetable scraps. Unlike long-simmered meat stocks, vegetable stock comes together fairly quickly—80 to 90 minutes—so it retains a fresh, light, delicate flavor. Simmering too long will give too strong a flavor that will muddy your stock, so keep an eye on the pot as the stock simmers and taste it as it cooks. Choose a variety of fairly neutral vegetables like the ones we use in this recipe—stronger-flavored ones, such as crucifers (cabbage, broccoli) and green vegetables (asparagus, zucchini) should be avoided. Store-bought vegetable stocks usually have such a poor flavor that we actually recommend you use water instead if you don't have homemade vegetable stock on hand.

1 tablespoon extra virgin olive oil

1 pound white button or cremini mushrooms, quartered

2 onions, cut into wedges

2 carrots, peeled, cut into 3-inch lengths

2 stalks celery, cut into 3-inch lengths

1 large leek, large diced and cleaned (see page 100)

1 fennel bulb, large diced, fronds reserved

1 head garlic, halved crosswise

Kosher salt

Stems only from 1 bunch flat-leaf parsley

2 large sprigs thyme

2 bay leaves

10 black peppercorns

5 quarts water

❶ **Create the base.** In a large stockpot, heat the olive oil on medium-high until hot. Add the mushrooms, onions, carrots, celery, leek, fennel, fennel fronds, and garlic and season with 1 teaspoon salt. Cook, stirring frequently, for 3 to 4 minutes, until thoroughly combined. Cover and cook for about 30 minutes, stirring occasionally, until softened and fragrant.

❷ **Make the stock.** Add the parsley stems, thyme, bay leaves, peppercorns, and water. Heat to simmering on high. Reduce the heat to low. Cook for 80 to 90 minutes, uncovered and without stirring, until the liquid is light brown and reduced in volume to about 4 quarts. The stock should taste slightly sweet and vegetal, without one flavor dominating the others.

❸ **Strain and cool the stock.** Pour the stock through a fine-mesh strainer into a second clean pot or large heatproof container. Discard the solids. Fill a large bowl or the sink with ice. Set the pot of strained stock in the ice. Cool the stock to room temperature. Store for up to 3 days in sealed containers in the refrigerator or freeze right away and use within 3 months.

COOK'S tip

STOCK INGREDIENTS: *Keep in mind that anything you add to stock will concentrate in flavor as it cooks, so if you vary the ingredients, go easy on more assertive ingredients like mushrooms (fresh or dried), onions, peppercorns, and other dried herbs and spices.*

BEEF STOCK

Makes 3 quarts

When it comes to adding depth and a rich backbone of meaty flavor to everything from stews to French onion soup, nothing compares to beef stock. The key to great beef stock is roasting the bones—it imparts a deep flavor and rich color to the stock.

5 pounds beef bones (knuckle, neck, or rib bones with a thin layer of meat still attached; *not* marrow bones)

Extra virgin olive oil

Kosher salt

2 onions, cut into wedges

4 stalks celery, cut into 3-inch lengths

4 carrots, peeled, cut into 3-inch lengths

1 head garlic, halved crosswise

2 tablespoons tomato paste

5 quarts water

2 large sprigs thyme

2 bay leaves

10 black peppercorns

❶ Roast the bones. Preheat the oven to 450°F. Pat the bones dry with paper towels. Arrange the bones in a single, even layer on a large sheet pan. Lightly drizzle with olive oil and season with salt. Roast for 30 to 35 minutes, until dark brown.

❷ Caramelize the aromatics. While the bones cool, in a large stockpot, heat 1 tablespoon olive oil on medium-high until hot. Add the onions, celery, carrots, and garlic. Cook, stirring occasionally, for 5 to 7 minutes, until caramelized and fragrant.

❸ Make the pinçage. Add the tomato paste to the aromatics. Cook, stirring frequently, for 1 to 2 minutes, until the paste is dark red. Add 2 cups of the water and cook, stirring and scraping up any browned bits (fond) from the bottom of the pot, for 30 seconds to 1 minute, to deglaze the pot.

❹ Make the stock. Add the thyme, bay leaves, peppercorns, bones (scraping up and adding any browned bits from the sheet pan), and the remaining 4 quarts and 2 cups water, and season with salt. Heat to simmering on high. Reduce the heat to low. Cook, uncovered, occasionally skimming off any foam or impurities from the surface, for 6 to 8 hours, until the liquid is reduced in volume to about 3 quarts.

❺ Strain and cool the stock. Pour the stock through a fine-mesh strainer into a second clean pot or large heatproof container. Discard the solids. Fill a large bowl or the sink with ice. Set the pot of strained stock in the ice. Cool the finished stock to room temperature. Store for up to 3 days in sealed containers in the refrigerator or freeze right away and use within 3 months.

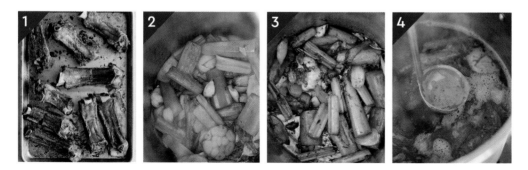

ROASTING BONES

Roasting bones imparts a deep flavor and rich color to beef stock. While the bones crisp and caramelize, the heat also extracts gelatin, which ultimately creates the rich mouthfeel that makes dishes made with this stock so satisfying. The delicious fond that remains on the sheet pan after roasting is a key flavor builder—scrape it into the stockpot!

Classic Chicken Noodle Soup

There's a reason why just about every culture has its own version of chicken soup, from Spanish *caldo de pollo* and Greek *avgolemono* to creamy Thai *tom kha gai* and Mexican *posole verde*. Few techniques will serve you and those you love best better than this one—follow it a few times and you'll come to intuitively understand how a great soup comes together. It all begins with the stock; this one has extraordinary depth because the bird is poached in a chicken stock base (think double dose of flavor).

CHICKEN AND BROTH

1 whole chicken (3½ to 4 pounds)

Kosher salt and freshly ground black pepper

5 quarts chicken stock

4 carrots, peeled and coarsely chopped

2 leeks, coarsely chopped and cleaned (see page 100)

3 stalks celery, coarsely chopped

6 cloves garlic, peeled and halved

2 bay leaves

1 small sprig rosemary

6 sprigs flat-leaf parsley

3 sprigs thyme

SOUP

3 carrots, peeled and cut into ¼-inch-thick rounds

3 stalks celery, thinly sliced

2 leeks, thinly sliced and cleaned (see page 100)

12 ounces dried egg noodles

¼ cup coarsely chopped flat-leaf parsley

2 tablespoons coarsely chopped dill

Rustic Bread (page 180), for serving (optional)

❶ Temper the chicken. Pat the chicken dry with paper towels. Truss the chicken (see page 37). Season the inside and outside with salt and pepper. Let stand at room temperature for 1 hour.

❷ Make the broth. In a large saucepan or soup pot, heat the stock to a simmer on high. Add the carrots, leeks, celery, garlic, bay leaves, rosemary, parsley, and thyme. Cook, stirring occasionally, for 6 to 7 minutes, until the vegetables are slightly softened. Add the chicken, breast side down, making sure that the chicken is mostly submerged in stock. Heat until just simmering. Reduce the heat to medium. Cook for 55 to 65 minutes, until an instant-read thermometer inserted into the thigh registers 170°F. Use tongs to carefully transfer the chicken to a large bowl to cool slightly.

❸ Strain the broth and shred the chicken. Pour the broth through a fine-mesh strainer into another large pot; discard the vegetables. Season the broth with salt. When the chicken is cool enough to handle, remove the meat from the bones. Remove and discard the skin. Use two forks or your fingers to shred the meat or use a knife to cut into bite-size pieces.

❹ Cook the soup vegetables and noodles. Add the carrots, celery, and leeks to the broth and season with salt and pepper. Cook on medium at a simmer for 25 to 30 minutes, until the carrots are tender. Add the noodles and cook according to the time on the package until tender.

❺ Finish and serve the soup. Add the shredded chicken and simmer, stirring occasionally, for 2 to 3 minutes, until heated through and well combined. Season with salt and pepper. Stir in the parsley and dill. Divide the soup among bowls and serve with the bread.

COOK'S tip

SIMMERING WITH MEAT: *To ensure perfectly moist chicken, keep an eye on the pot to ensure it simmers gently; too lively a boil will result in tough meat.*

RUSTIC BREAD

Makes 1 loaf

If you're not accustomed to working with yeast, this recipe is an ideal gateway to begin your journey to baking great loaves of bread at home. The dough comes together effortlessly with just a wooden spoon and a bowl. Adding salt early slows down the fermentation of the starter, and the slowing results in a deeper, more complex flavor. This bread will take at least 14 hours, so you'll probably want to start the night before you plan to bake. When the dough is ready, all that's required is a quick bit of folding to form the loaf.

Let the bread cool completely before slicing. This allows the starches to realign and "settle"; when they're still hot, they remain viscous, so the bread will be gummy.

1½ teaspoons active dry yeast

1¾ cups warm water (90°F)

3½ cups all-purpose flour, plus extra for dusting

2¼ teaspoons kosher salt

❶ Mix the dough. Sprinkle the yeast into the water and let stand for 5 minutes, until foamy. Place the 3½ cups flour and salt in a large bowl and stir to combine. Add the dissolved yeast and stir with a wooden spoon until a loose dough forms. It will be sticky; do not overwork. Cover the bowl with plastic wrap and let stand at room temperature for 2 hours. Transfer to the refrigerator and let ferment for 12 to 16 hours. The dough will double to triple in size and have a strong aroma from the fermentation.

❷ Fold the dough. Remove the dough from the refrigerator and let stand at room temperature for 1 hour. Lightly dust a clean, dry work surface with flour. Turn out the dough onto the work surface and dust the top with more flour. Dust your fingers with flour to prevent sticking and fold the left and right thirds of the dough over the middle, overlapping them to make a tri-fold (like a tri-fold wallet or a folded letter). Repeat with the top and bottom thirds of the dough, folding toward the middle. Fold the left and right sides of the dough together (like closing a book) and flip over, seam side down.

❸ Proof the dough. Generously dust a large, clean kitchen towel with flour. Carefully transfer the folded dough, seam side down, to the towel. Dust the top of the dough with additional flour. Loosely cover the dough with a second clean kitchen towel. Let stand at room temperature for 2 hours. The dough will double in volume.

❹ Bake the bread. When the dough has proofed for first 1 hour, place a large Dutch oven (lid on) on a rack in the center of the oven and preheat the oven to 475°F. When the dough has proofed for 2 hours, carefully remove the Dutch oven from the oven, remove the lid, and carefully turn the dough over (seam side up) into the pot. Shake gently to slightly distribute the dough, then cover with the lid. Bake for 35 minutes. Uncover and bake for 15 to 20 minutes more, until thoroughly browned and crispy; when you tap the surface of the bread, it should sound hollow. Remove the pot from the oven and let stand for 10 minutes. Transfer the bread to a wire rack to cool completely before serving.

Beef & Barley Soup

with Mixed Mushrooms

In this recipe, a time-honored classic gets new appeal from a mix of mushrooms (cremini, shiitake, white button) and a rich, meaty stock enhanced with red wine and aromatic vegetables. Making it a complete meal is the barley. Barley or farro that has been "pearled" or "semi-pearled" means that the grain's hull and outer bran layers have been entirely or partially removed ("pearled" refers to the grain being polished). These grains have shorter cook times than their whole counterparts and a softer texture. When you incorporate cooked grains like barley into soup, it's important to add them toward the end of cooking so they retain an appealing texture and don't overcook and bloat, which in turn would add too much starch to the soup.

1 pound London broil or beef top round

Kosher salt and freshly ground black pepper

Extra virgin olive oil

½ pound mixed mushrooms (such as cremini, shiitake, and/or white button), trimmed and coarsely chopped

2 tablespoons unsalted butter

4 carrots, peeled and small diced

1 parsnip, peeled and small diced

1 onion, small diced

2 leeks, small diced and cleaned (see page 100)

4 cloves garlic, minced

¼ cup tomato paste

1 cup full-bodied red wine (such as cabernet sauvignon, merlot, or syrah)

3 quarts beef stock (page 176)

1 cup pearled barley

2 teaspoons red wine vinegar

½ cup finely chopped fresh flat-leaf parsley leaves

1 (1-inch) piece horseradish root, grated (optional)

❶ **Brown the beef.** Pat the beef dry with paper towels. Cut the beef into 1-inch cubes. Transfer to a large bowl, season with ½ teaspoon salt and ¼ teaspoon pepper, and toss to coat. In a large saucepan or soup pot, heat 2 tablespoons olive oil on medium-high until hot. Working in batches and adding more oil as needed, add the beef in a single layer. Cook, turning occasionally, for 6 to 8 minutes, until browned on all sides. Transfer to a plate, leaving any browned bits (fond) in the pan.

❷ **Cook the vegetables.** Add the mushrooms to the fond. Cook on medium, stirring and scraping up the fond, for 2 to 4 minutes, until the mushrooms have softened. Add the butter, carrots, parsnip, onion, leeks, and garlic and season with 2 teaspoons salt and ½ teaspoon pepper. Cook for 8 to 10 minutes, stirring occasionally, until the onion is softened and the vegetables are sticking to the bottom of the pan.

RECIPE CONTINUES

❸ Add the tomato paste. Add the tomato paste and cook, stirring frequently, for 3 to 5 minutes, until the paste is dark red.

❹ Deglaze the pan. Add the wine and cook, stirring frequently and scraping up any fond from the bottom of the pan, for 2 to 3 minutes, until the wine is reduced in volume by three-quarters.

❺ Simmer the beef. Add the beef, along with any accumulated juices, and 2 quarts of the stock. Heat to simmering on medium-high. Reduce the heat to medium-low and cover. Cook for 70 to 80 minutes, until the beef is tender enough to pull apart with a spoon.

❻ Cook the barley. While the soup is simmering, in a separate saucepan, heat the remaining 1 quart stock to simmering on medium. Add the barley and 1 teaspoon salt. Reduce the heat to medium-low. Cover and cook for about 30 minutes, until the barley is al dente (slightly firm to the bite). The barley will not absorb all the liquid; do not drain. Remove from the heat and set aside.

❼ Finish and serve the soup. Add the barley with the stock. Cover and cook for 11 to 13 minutes, until the barley is tender. Remove from the heat and stir in the vinegar. Season with salt and pepper. Divide the soup among bowls. Top with the parsley and horseradish and serve.

White Bean Soup

with Escarole & Pancetta

Minestre, or hearty soups, have humble roots in *cucina povera*, the Italian tradition of peasant cooking. The word *minestra* comes from "to administer," which referred to the way that soup was often served from one main bowl by the matriarch or patriarch of the household. Soups incorporated simple staple ingredients or, to avoid waste, items that were leftovers— some greens, a little meat (in this case, pancetta), beans, good homemade broth, and a Parmigiano rind. To extend the soup even further, add leftover rustic bread to the broth to make a *ribollita*.

½ pound dried cannellini beans

1 (4-ounce) block Parmigiano-Reggiano cheese, with rind

2 bay leaves

6 sprigs thyme

3 quarts chicken stock (page 174)

Extra virgin olive oil

Kosher salt

¼ pound pancetta, small diced

5 cloves garlic, thinly sliced

BOUQUET GARNI

A bouquet garni, or bundle of herbs such as thyme, parsley, and bay leaves used to flavor soups, stocks, and stews, is typically wrapped in cheesecloth and tied with butcher's twine. Sometimes other flavorings are included, such as Parmigiano-Reggiano rind. You can also secure the ingredients with a 4- or 5-inch section of cleaned leek green, sturdy kale, or collard leaf, or even tuck them into a loose-leaf tea sachet.

½ teaspoon crushed red pepper flakes

2 onions, small diced

2 carrots, peeled and small diced

2 stalks celery, small diced

2 teaspoons chopped fresh rosemary leaves

1 large head escarole, thinly sliced crosswise and thoroughly washed

Freshly ground black pepper

High-quality extra virgin olive oil, for serving

❶ Prepare the beans. At least 12 hours or up to 2 days ahead, place the beans in a fine-mesh strainer; rinse under cold water to clean thoroughly and remove any debris. Transfer the beans to a large bowl or a plastic container with a securable lid; add at least 3 times their volume of water. Cover and place in the refrigerator. When ready to cook, drain the soaked beans and rinse under cold water.

❷ Make the bouquet garni. Shave or grate the cheese and set aside, for garnish. Cut a 6-inch square of cheesecloth. Place the cheese rind, bay leaves, and thyme in the center of the cheesecloth; wrap together to create a small sachet. Tie it closed securely with butcher's twine.

RECIPE CONTINUES

3 Cook the beans. In a large saucepan, combine the beans, bouquet garni, and 2 quarts of the chicken stock. Heat to simmering on medium. Reduce the heat to low and skim off any foam that has risen to the top. Stir in 2 tablespoons olive oil. Cover and cook for about 1 hour, until the beans are completely cooked through (they will have a creamy texture; taste a few at a time). Remove from the heat and season generously with salt.

4 Cook the pancetta. In a large saucepan or soup pot, heat 2 teaspoons olive oil on medium-high until hot. Add the pancetta and cook, stirring occasionally, for 7 to 9 minutes, until browned and slightly crispy. Set a small fine-mesh strainer over a bowl. Drain the pancetta in the strainer, leaving any browned bits (fond) in the pot. Let the pancetta stand for 30 seconds to 1 minute, until most of the fat has drained off; set the pancetta aside.

5 Sauté the vegetables. Return the pancetta fat to the pot and heat on medium-low until hot. Add the garlic and red pepper flakes. Cook, stirring frequently, for 1 to 2 minutes, until the garlic is fragrant and the red pepper flakes are lightly toasted. Add the onions, carrots, celery, and rosemary and season with ½ teaspoon salt. Cook, stirring occasionally, for 5 to 7 minutes, until the onions are slightly softened and fragrant. Add the escarole and season with ½ teaspoon salt. Increase the heat to medium and cook, stirring occasionally, for 3 to 5 minutes, until the escarole is wilted.

6 Simmer and serve the soup. Remove the bouquet garni from the beans and discard. To the vegetables, add the beans and their cooking liquid, the pancetta, and the remaining 1 quart chicken stock. Cook on medium-high, stirring occasionally, for 12 to 14 minutes, until simmering. Reduce the heat to medium-low and cook, stirring occasionally, for 9 to 11 minutes, until the escarole is dark green and the vegetables are tender. Divide the soup among bowls. Top with shaved or grated Parmigiano and season with black pepper. Drizzle each bowl with 2 teaspoons olive oil and serve.

New England Clam Chowder

It may come as no surprise that chowders in America originated with the fishermen along the shores of New England in the eighteenth century. It's believed that French fishermen came across the Atlantic with their *chaudières* (or cauldrons) and those pots soon were filled with hearty stews made from the region's fish and seafood. The dish made its way down from Nova Scotia to New England, where "chowdah" became king.

This style of chowder is thickened with a roux (though some traditionalists may balk) that binds the ingredients and results in a velvety texture. Unlike gumbo, which relies on a dark, deeply flavored roux, this chowder has a roux that is cooked quickly—just long enough for the flour to lose its raw taste—so it thickens without overpowering the other flavors.

3 dozen littleneck clams

Extra virgin olive oil

3 cloves garlic, peeled and smashed

2 bay leaves

1 cup dry white wine (such as sauvignon blanc or pinot grigio)

½ pound bacon, small diced

2 stalks celery, small diced

1 large onion, small diced

Kosher salt and freshly ground black pepper

1 pound Yukon gold potatoes, peeled and small diced

2 tablespoons unsalted butter

¼ cup all-purpose flour

1½ cups whole milk

1 bunch thyme, tied in a bundle with butcher's twine

½ cup heavy cream

1 bunch chives, finely chopped, for garnish

Classic Dinner Rolls (page 191), for serving (optional)

❶ **Clean the clams.** Place the clams in a large bowl. Cover with cold water and soak for 1 to 2 minutes. Drain and repeat, rinsing and soaking, three or four more times, until the soaking water is clear and free of grit.

❷ **Steam the clams.** In a large saucepan or soup pot, heat 2 teaspoons olive oil on medium until hot. Add the garlic and 1 of the bay leaves. Cook, stirring occasionally, for 1 to 2 minutes, until fragrant. Add the clams and wine. Cover and steam for 5 to 7 minutes, until the clams begin to open.

Carefully remove any opened clams from the pot and transfer to a large bowl. Replace the lid and continue to steam, checking periodically and removing other opened clams, for 6 to 8 minutes, until every clam is opened. (If any clams have not opened by now, remove and discard them.)

Line a fine-mesh strainer with cheesecloth and set over a bowl. Pour the steaming liquid through the strainer to remove any grit or sand; set the liquid aside. When cool enough to handle, remove the clams from their shells. Strain and reserve any accumulated liquid from the bowl of clams; add to the reserved bowl of steaming liquid. Rinse and wipe out the pot.

RECIPE CONTINUES

❸ Render the bacon. Line a plate with paper towels. Heat 1 tablespoon olive oil in the clam pot on medium-high until hot. Add the bacon. Cook, stirring occasionally, for 6 to 8 minutes, until the bacon is browned and crispy. Use a slotted spoon to transfer to the plate to drain, leaving the bacon fat in the pot.

❹ Start the soup. Heat the fat on medium until hot. Add the celery and onion and season with 1 teaspoon salt and ¼ teaspoon black pepper. Cook, stirring occasionally, for 7 to 9 minutes, until softened. Add the potatoes and season with ½ teaspoon salt. Cook, stirring occasionally, for 2 to 4 minutes, until the potatoes are translucent. Add the butter and let it melt. Sprinkle with the flour. Cook, stirring frequently, for 1 to 2 minutes, until thoroughly combined and golden.

FRESH CLAMS

Clams open on their own terms, which is to say not all of them will open at once. That's why it's important to keep an eye on the pot and remove them in stages, as soon as they've opened. That way, when you add the steamed clams to the chowder at the end of simmering time, they'll be *just cooked* and tender, not tough. Feel free to use other varieties of clam, such as cherrystone or surf clams (chop into ½-inch pieces once steamed). Since they're larger, they also tend to be harbor more grit, so straining the steaming liquid through a cheesecloth- or kitchen towel–lined strainer is even more important.

❺ Add the liquids. Add the milk, the reserved steaming liquid, thyme bundle, and the remaining bay leaf. Heat to boiling on medium-high, stirring frequently. Reduce the heat to low. Cook, stirring occasionally, for 3 to 5 minutes, until the potatoes are tender. Add the cream and cook, stirring frequently, for 2 to 3 minutes, until thoroughly combined.

❻ Finish the soup and serve. Add the clams and season with salt and pepper. Cook, stirring frequently, for 1 to 2 minutes, until heated through. Discard the thyme bundle and bay leaf. Divide the chowder among serving bowls. Top with the bacon and chives and serve with the rolls.

CLASSIC DINNER ROLLS

Makes 24 rolls

These dinner rolls are inspired by Parker House rolls, first made famous by the Parker House in Boston in the nineteenth century. Traditional Parker House rolls call for flattening and folding the dough, but we're opting for a round shape.

Enriching the dough with butter creates the rolls' characteristic flavor and light texture. Feel free to make the dough the day before baking and proof it in the refrigerator; this will slow down the process and create more flavor. Unlike other breads that need to cool, rolls are best served warm from the oven, after they've been brushed with melted butter and sprinkled with sea salt. Expect them to disappear from the bread basket quickly.

1½ cups whole milk, warm (90°F)

1½ teaspoons active dry yeast

4 cups all-purpose flour, plus more for dusting

1 tablespoon kosher salt

1½ teaspoons sugar

12 tablespoons (¾ cup; 1½ sticks) unsalted butter:
    6 tablespoons at room temperature, and
    6 tablespoons melted for serving

2 teaspoons canola oil

2 teaspoons coarse sea salt, for finishing

❶ Mix the dough. In the bowl of a stand mixer fitted with the dough hook attachment, combine the milk and yeast. Let stand for 5 minutes, until foamy. Add the flour, salt, and sugar and mix on low speed for about 3 minutes, until evenly blended. Add 5 tablespoons of the room-temperature butter and increase the speed to medium. Mix for 6 to 8 minutes, until a springy dough has formed; when you press a finger gently into the dough, it will spring back.

❷ Proof the dough. Use a paper towel to grease the inside of a glass or stainless steel mixing bowl with the canola oil. Transfer the dough to the bowl and cover with a clean, barely damp kitchen towel. Let stand at room temperature for 2 hours, until the dough has doubled in size. (If shaping and baking the next day, cover with plastic wrap and place in the refrigerator overnight. Remove from the refrigerator 2 hours before baking.)

❸ Form the rolls. Grease a large sheet pan with the remaining 1 tablespoon room-temperature butter. Transfer the dough to a clean, dry work surface and cut into 24 equal pieces. Moisten a small area of a wooden cutting board with water. Keep the pieces loosely covered with the damp towel as you work. Working with one piece of dough at a time, fold and pinch the bottom together to create a beggar's purse shape, dabbing with a small amount of water if needed. Gently roll the pinched side of the dough on the moistened cutting board with a cupped hand until smooth.

❹ Proof the rolls. Place the rolls on the sheet pan ½ inch apart. Cover again with the damp towel and let stand at room temperature for 1 hour 30 minutes, until the rolls begin to expand and touch.

❺ Bake the rolls. While the rolls are proofing, preheat the oven to 350°F. When the rolls have proofed, brush the tops with 3 tablespoons of the melted butter. Bake for 25 to 30 minutes, until golden and puffed. Remove from the oven and brush with the remaining 3 tablespoons melted butter. Sprinkle with sea salt and serve warm.

Creamy Kabocha Soup

with Crispy Sage Leaves

Turning hard winter squash (butternut, acorn, shokichi, kabocha) into soup is one of the easiest and most satisfying techniques when the season arrives. With a hard green rind and pale orange flesh, kabocha squash has a slightly sweet flavor and a silky texture. When the squash is roasted in the oven, the flavor concentrates and the squash doesn't need more than a quick simmer with a base of aromatics and a flavorful liquid like vegetable stock.

Keep in mind that puréed soups vary in consistency (depending on the variety and size of squash; you can also use butternut or even pumpkin in this recipe), and they can thicken upon standing. Feel free to add more or less liquid to create your desired texture.

3½ pounds kabocha squash (about 2 medium or 1 large squash)

1 bunch sage, leaves picked, stems reserved

⅔ cup extra virgin olive oil, plus more for drizzling the squash and for serving

FRYING FRESH HERBS Flash-frying fresh herbs in hot olive oil crisps them to create a crackly texture and a slightly toasted flavor that make them a beautiful and delicious garnish for a range of dishes. Velvety sage leaves work particularly well, but you can also use fresh oregano, marjoram, parsley, or basil. It's a fast process: As soon as the herbs sizzle and turn a darker shade, transfer them to a paper towel–lined plate. Save the oil; the process infuses it with the herbs' essence. You can use herb oil for sautéing aromatics in the same dish (a nice way to echo flavors), drizzled over toasted bread, or tossed with tomatoes and avocados for a quick salad.

Kosher salt and freshly ground black pepper

2 cups thinly sliced leeks (about 2 large leeks), cleaned (page 100)

2 stalks celery, thinly sliced

3 quarts vegetable stock (page 175)

2 teaspoons white wine vinegar

Nutmeg, for grating

Cornbread (page 195), for serving (optional)

❶ **Prepare the squash.** Preheat the oven to 400°F. Wash any visible dirt off the squash. Use a sturdy kitchen knife to quarter the squash; scoop out and discard the seeds and strings. Cut off and reserve the stems.

❷ **Roast the squash.** Place the squash, cut side up, on a sheet pan with the sage stems among them. Drizzle the squash with the olive oil; use your hands to rub the olive oil on the squash. Season with 1 tablespoon salt and 1½ teaspoons pepper. Turn the squash pieces cut side down. Roast for 30 to 35 minutes, flip the squash, then continue to roast for 5 to 10 minutes, until the squash is tender when pierced with a knife and lightly browned. Remove from the oven and set aside to cool. Discard the sage stems. When the squash is cool enough to handle, cut off and discard the skin; medium-dice the flesh.

RECIPE CONTINUES

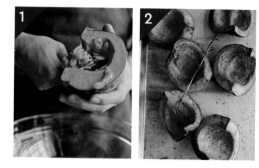

3 **Fry the sage leaves.** Line a plate with paper towels. In a large saucepan or soup pot, heat a ½-inch layer (⅔ cup) of olive oil on medium until hot. Add the sage leaves and cook for 2 to 4 minutes, until dark green and crispy. Remove from the heat. Use a slotted spoon to transfer to the plate, leaving the infused oil in the pot. Immediately season the leaves with ¼ teaspoon salt. Set aside.

4 **Start the soup.** Heat the sage-infused oil on medium-high until hot. Add the leeks and celery and season with salt and pepper. Cook, stirring occasionally, for 7 to 9 minutes, until the celery is slightly softened. Add the squash and stock. Heat to simmering on high, then reduce the heat to medium. Season with 1 teaspoon salt. Cook, stirring occasionally, for 20 to 25 minutes, until the squash is completely tender and broken down, and the soup has slightly thickened. Set aside to cool slightly.

5 **Purée and finish the soup.** Working in batches, transfer the soup to a high-powered blender. Purée each batch on high for 2 to 3 minutes, until thoroughly smooth. Pour the batches of soup into a clean pot. (Alternatively, use an immersion blender and purée in the pot.) If the soup is too thick, add ¼ cup stock or water at a time until the desired consistency is reached. Heat the soup over low until warmed through. Slowly add in the white wine vinegar, to taste. Season with salt and pepper. Divide the soup among bowls. Top with a drizzle of olive oil, freshly grated nutmeg, and a few leaves of crispy sage, and serve with the cornbread.

BLENDING HOT LIQUIDS

Be very careful when blending hot liquids. The steam from the liquid can accumulate in the blender as you purée, causing the lid to explode and splattering hot soup everywhere. To prevent this, always purée in batches, never filling the blender more than halfway. Remove the center cap from the blender lid. Replace the lid and hold it down very firmly with a folded kitchen towel (over the hole where the cap was) as you purée.

CORNBREAD

Makes 2 (8-inch) round or square pans

There are many schools of thought on cornbread—
some versions are more savory and breadlike; others
are sweeter with a denser crumb. Our version uses a
touch of sugar in the pan for sweetness and sour cream
for a rich texture. The recipe makes two pans, so you'll
have plenty to share or delicious leftovers to enjoy,
reheated in the oven or toasted in a cast-iron skillet.

¼ cup (½ stick) unsalted butter, melted, plus more
   for greasing the pans

⅔ cup sugar, plus more for dusting

1½ cups yellow cornmeal (medium-grind, *not* coarse)

2 cups all-purpose flour

2 teaspoons baking soda

4 teaspoons cream of tartar

1½ teaspoons kosher salt

2 large eggs

2 cups sour cream

½ cup whole milk

❶ **Prepare the pans.** Preheat the oven to 425°F.
Lightly grease two 8-inch round or square baking pans
with butter. Line the bottoms of the pans with parchment
and grease with additional butter. Lightly dust each
with 1½ teaspoons sugar.

❷ **Mix the ingredients separately.** In a medium bowl,
whisk together the cornmeal, flour, ⅔ cup sugar, baking
soda, cream of tartar, and salt. In a large bowl, whisk
together the eggs, sour cream, milk, and ¼ cup butter to
combine.

❸ **Finish and bake the cornbread.** Use a spatula to
fold the dry ingredients into the wet until well combined.
Divide the batter evenly between the two pans; use a
spatula to smooth the tops. Bake for 18 to 20 minutes,
rotating the pans halfway through, until golden brown
and a toothpick inserted in the center comes out clean.
Remove the pans from the oven and cool on a wire rack.
When cool enough to handle, unmold, cut into pieces, and
serve.

Creamy Zucchini Soup

Historically, *potage* is a French term that meant "what is in the pot," and first referred to just about anything cooked in that vessel, but particularly hearty one-pot meals. Eventually, the term came to refer to soups in general, but with the legendary French chef Escoffier came a further classification—a refined first-course soup, usually made of vegetables, then puréed. The technique works particularly well for flavorful, seasonal vegetables like the zucchini in this recipe. A swirl of cream gives ours an extra creamy texture without any need for a traditional velouté (which involves a roux). Take this technique and use it for any number of vegetables, such as broccoli, asparagus, carrots, cauliflower, or anything else that strikes your fancy.

Extra virgin olive oil

3 pounds zucchini, trimmed and medium diced

6 cloves garlic, coarsely chopped

1 onion, thinly sliced

Kosher salt and freshly ground black pepper

1 cup coarsely chopped fresh flat-leaf parsley

1 quart water or vegetable stock (page 175)

¾ cup finely chopped fresh basil leaves, plus whole small leaves for garnish

½ cup heavy cream

¼ cup freshly grated Parmigiano-Reggiano cheese

Juice of ½ lemon

❶ Brown the zucchini. In a large saucepan or soup pot, heat 1½ tablespoons olive oil on medium-high until hot. Working in batches if necessary, add the zucchini in a single, even layer. (If the pan seems dry, add more olive oil between batches.) Cook, stirring occasionally, for 4 to 5 minutes, until the zucchini is browned. Transfer to a plate or bowl.

❷ Cook the aromatics. In the same pot, add 2 tablespoons olive oil and heat on medium until hot. Add the garlic and onion. Season with salt and pepper. Cook, stirring occasionally and scraping up any browned bits (fond) from the bottom of the pan, for 6 to 7 minutes, until softened and fragrant.

❸ Cook the zucchini. Return the zucchini to the pot along with any accumulated juices. Add half the parsley, ½ teaspoon salt, and a pinch of pepper. Cover and cook, stirring a few times, for 14 to 16 minutes, until the vegetables have softened.

❹ Simmer the soup. Add the water and heat on high to a simmer. Reduce the heat to medium. Cook uncovered, stirring occasionally, for 20 to 25 minutes, until the liquid is reduced to below the level of the vegetables and they are completely tender. Remove from the heat. Add the remaining parsley and half the chopped basil, and stir to combine.

❺ Purée and finish the soup. Transfer two-thirds of the soup to a high-powered blender and blend until completely smooth. Return to the pot. If necessary, heat on medium until warm again. Remove from the heat. Stir in the heavy cream, Parmigiano, and the remaining chopped basil. Stir in the lemon juice and season with salt and pepper. Divide among bowls, garnish with the whole basil leaves, and serve.

Chicken Consommé

Making consommé (clarified stock) is an old-school, time-honored French technique that's been around for centuries ("consommé" comes from a French word meaning to consummate or finish). According to culinary legend, King Louis XIV demanded his chef make a soup so crystal clear that he could see himself in it. To create the broth's pristine appearance, lightly beaten egg whites are combined with chicken stock and brought to a gentle simmer. As the egg whites poach, they create a "raft" that collects impurities from the liquid. The egg white raft is carefully skimmed from the liquid and the broth gets a final strain through a damp, clean kitchen towel. The result is a delicate soup that tastes like the essence of the meat or fish used for the stock.

2 large egg whites

3 quarts chicken stock (page 174), at room temperature

Vegetable or herb garnishes (optional; see "Consommé Garnishes" following step 5)

❶ **Whip the egg whites.** In a small bowl, whisk the egg whites until light and frothy. Be careful not to beat until they hold a peak; you want to get a lot of air into them, but you are not making meringue.

❷ **Heat the stock.** In a large saucepan or soup pot, combine the stock and egg whites and briefly stir. Bring to a simmer on medium and cook for 16 to 18 minutes, until the egg whites float to the top of the pot and form a "raft" and bubbles form at the edges of the pot. Occasionally skim off any grayish impurities that rise to the surface; do not skim off the raft at this point.

❸ **Prepare to strain.** While the stock heats, rinse a clean kitchen towel under cold water several times and wring dry. Place the towel over a large pot. Allow the towel to slightly sag in the center. Use butcher's twine to tightly tie the towel to the pot.

❹ **Skim for impurities.** Reduce the heat to medium-low and pull the pot halfway off the heat. Cook for 1 to 2 minutes, until consistent bubbles show up around the edges of the pot. Use a spoon, skimmer, or ladle to skim off as much of the raft as you can. (It's okay if there's still a little in the pot.) Turn off the heat.

❺ **Strain the broth and serve.** Carefully ladle the stock through the towel-lined strainer into the pot. (It may take a few minutes for the stock to strain through; do not force or push it through.) Serve the consommé garnished as desired. If using garnishes such as vegetables, place them in the bottom of the bowls and pour the consommé on top.

Consommé Garnishes (page 171) Fresh shelled peas and seasonal baby vegetables are some of our favorite garnishes for consommé. To incorporate, simply blanch vegetables briefly in boiling water. Drain them and set them at the bottom of the bowl. Add the consommé broth and top with fresh herbs such as feathery leaves of chervil, thinly sliced chives, or tarragon. No matter what you choose, always keep it fresh and simple to let the clean flavor of the consommé shine through.

COOK'S *tip*

PASTA SAUCE: *If you have leftover consommé, heat it in a saucepan on medium-high until reduced in volume by three-quarters. Toss with hot pasta, a little pasta cooking water, butter, and Parmigiano-Reggiano cheese.*

8
Steaming & Poaching

Steaming and poaching foods are two of the
oldest culinary techniques and perhaps two of the easiest—
in most cases, all they take is boiling water.

The recipes in this chapter show the versatility of these techniques, from steaming an entire fish served with a gingery Asian dipping sauce to shallow poaching (think a fresh fillet gently cooked in a pan) and deep poaching (chicken in a pot). Because they require less fat and preserve more nutrients than other cooking methods, steaming and poaching are indisputably healthful ways to prepare foods. But dismiss any notion that the results are bland. Although steamed or poached foods may not have the in-your-face impact of roasted or pan-seared foods, they have simple, clean flavors that allow you to savor the essence of each ingredient. The results are more delicate but no less delicious than their browned or caramelized counterparts. When steamed or poached foods are cooked with care and finished thoughtfully— say, with a sprinkle of flaky salt, a drizzle of fruity olive oil, or a dollop of homemade aioli—the refreshingly pure, discernible flavors can make for some of the most satisfying meals around.

Whether you're steaming in a packet (en papillote or even in a banana leaf) or simply poaching a chicken breast, the aromatics are a key part of suffusing flavor into your dish. After you learn the basic methods, the fun is in switching up the aromatics or ingredients to suit your whim or the season. As you'll see from the following recipes, this is an accessible and straightforward process, but it shouldn't be rushed. You'll want to start at a lower heat and increase it gradually so you don't set the exterior of the meat or fish too quickly and intensely before the interior has time to cook through. If you're steaming, remember that whatever you're preparing shouldn't touch the cooking vessel—pots and pans retain heat, so they'll disrupt the gentle, even cooking (exception: steamed mussels, because of their shells).

When you're planning your menu, keep in mind that poached and steamed foods don't reheat well—warming them a second time alters the tender, delicate texture—so plan to enjoy the results immediately. Another major bonus of these methods: There's typically a broth or sauce created in the process. You get to eat the delicately cooked meat or fish with the flavorful liquid in which it was prepared.

Keys to Success

1. Make every ingredient count. When it comes to poaching, the more flavorful the cooking liquid, the better the dish, so use the best-quality stock available. Choose tender or thinly sliced vegetables so they cook evenly, and all the way through. For this technique, it's important to seek out the freshest meat and seafood available, because the flavors are subtle—there's nothing to hide behind.

2. Infuse with aromatics. Whether you're steaming or poaching, infuse the cooking liquid with aromatics (such as leeks, garlic, carrots) to create depth of flavor.

3. Maintain a steady heat. Poaching and steaming are gentle processes that rely on relatively low, even heat or indirect heat (from the steam). Cooking too quickly or aggressively will yield tough or uneven results.

4. Cool in the broth. Allow poached fish or chicken to cool slightly in the broth for the best texture and fullest flavor.

STEAMING VESSELS

Collapsible metal steamer baskets elevate food above the simmering liquid. Designs with extendable, pop-up handles provide for easier removal; the handles can often be detached for steaming larger items like whole fish. Large pots with steamer basket inserts make it easy to steam vegetables, dim sum, or fish, and you can use the pot on its own for canning or preparing larger batches of soups, stocks, and stews.

Bamboo steamer baskets are designed to nestle into a wok or large pot, 2 to 3 inches above the water; bamboo steamers make it easy to steam tender vegetables, rice, seafood, and dumplings. Steamers with stackable layers allow you to cook a variety of foods at once.

If the item you're steaming (such as a whole fish) is too large for the steamer insert or basket, you can get creative: Place a sheet pan on a heatproof plate or shallow bowl set in the middle of a roasting pan. Fill the roasting pan with a few inches of water; make sure the sheet pan does not touch the water. Cover the roasting pan with aluminum foil and another large sheet pan.

Steamed Mussels

with White Wine & Garlic

Steamed mussels can take on many flavor profiles, but we start with the classic. In this recipe, based on the French dish *moules marinière* found in Normandy, the mussels are steamed simply in white wine and garlic. *Marinière* means mariner-style, referring to the coastal towns and sailors who originated the dish. For the easiest prep and cleanest flavor, you'll want to use aqua-farmed, rope-cultured mussels. These mollusks were grown on ropes strung from wooden poles in the sea, so they'll mostly be grit- and barnacle-free and have a particularly sweet flavor.

2 pounds fresh mussels
(preferably rope-grown)

Kosher salt

¼ cup extra virgin olive oil

10 cloves garlic, thinly sliced

2 loosely packed cups fresh flat-leaf parsley leaves, coarsely chopped

2 cups dry white wine (such as sauvignon blanc or pinot grigio)

2 tablespoons unsalted butter, cut into pieces

Freshly ground black pepper

❶ Clean the mussels. Place the mussels in a large bowl. Fill the bowl with cold water and add 1 teaspoon salt; stir to combine. Let the mussels stand for 2 minutes. (Small air bubbles will rise to the surface, which means the mussels are spitting out their dirt.) Working with one mussel at a time, use your thumb and forefinger to pull down on the small fibrous tuft (beard) sticking out of the shell. Discard the beards and place the mussels in a separate large bowl. Discard any mussels that have broken shells or that don't close when you try to press them closed.

❷ Cook the aromatics. In a large saucepan or soup pot, heat the olive oil on medium until hot. Add the garlic and ¼ teaspoon salt. Cook, stirring occasionally, for 30 seconds to 1 minute, until fragrant and softened. Add half the parsley and cook, stirring occasionally, for 30 seconds to 1 minute, until bright green and wilted.

❸ Cook the mussels. Add the wine and cook, stirring occasionally, for 5 to 7 minutes, until reduced in volume by one-third. Add the mussels, leaving any residual liquid in the bowl behind. Cover and cook for 5 to 6 minutes, until all the mussels have opened. Discard any that remain closed.

❹ Finish and serve the mussels. Uncover the pot and stir in the butter and remaining parsley. Remove from the heat. Use a slotted spoon to transfer the mussels to a wide serving bowl. Season the remaining broth with salt and pepper. Ladle the broth over the mussels and serve immediately.

Variations

This is a classic French-style recipe for steamed mussels, but you can take it in any number of directions by changing up the basic elements. Try adding to the aromatics seasonal vegetables like chopped fresh tomatoes or thinly sliced fennel, or spices like fennel seed, crushed red pepper, and saffron. For a Thai twist, use ginger, lemongrass, chiles, and curry paste as the aromatics; coconut milk instead of wine; and lime and cilantro to finish.

> **BUYING MUSSELS**
>
> If you've had an unfortunate encounter with a less-than-fresh mussel, you're not alone—it happens, now and then. But there's no reason to be daunted by preparing mussels at home, especially when you start with a great product from a trusted source. The quality test is simple: A fresh mussel should smell like the sea. If a mussel is bad, it won't smell like anything you want to eat. Before cleaning, discard any mussels with broken or open shells.

Fish en Papillote
(Fish in Parchment)

Although *en papillote* (in parchment paper) is a French term, cultures all over the world steam in packets, whether they're made from banana leaves in Southeast Asia or dried corn husks in Latin America. In this recipe, we use cherry tomatoes, fennel, garlic, and thyme, but feel free to adjust the vegetables and aromatics to your preference. The fish and vegetables steam over a bed of cooked grain (in this case, farro) that soaks up all their delicious flavors and makes this recipe a complete meal. Use care when cutting open the packets after cooking—they will release a waft of very hot steam.

4 (6-ounce) hake or haddock fillets (1½ to 2 inches thick)

Kosher salt and freshly ground black pepper

¼ cup extra virgin olive oil, plus more for drizzling

1⅓ cups cooked farro or other grain

½ fennel bulb, halved, cored, and thinly sliced, fronds reserved

¼ cup (½ stick) unsalted butter, cut into tablespoons

4 sprigs thyme

2 cloves garlic, thinly sliced

2 cups cherry tomatoes, halved

¼ cup dry white wine (such as sauvignon blanc or pinot grigio)

Flaky sea salt, for garnish

1 lemon, cut into wedges, for serving

COOK'S tip

PAPILLOTE POINTERS: *Feel free to switch up the vegetables, but always slice them very thinly or dice them small so that they cook through completely in the packet. If your fish is thinner or thicker than what's called for, adjust the cook time accordingly—longer cook time for thicker fish, shorter for thinner. And no matter the shape of your folded packet, the most important thing is that it's tightly sealed so that the steam does not escape.*

❶ Prepare the parchment paper. Preheat the oven to 500°F. Cut four 24-inch-long rectangles of parchment paper. Stack the sheets and fold in half the short way (like a book). Starting near the edge of the fold, draw a U-shape that fills the half-sheet. Secure the edges of the paper with a few paper clips. Use scissors to cut out the shapes, tightly holding the sheets together with your other hand.

❷ Assemble the packets. Generously season the fish fillets with kosher salt and pepper on both sides. Working one at a time, unfold a parchment shape and lay it flat on the cutting board. Drizzle 1 tablespoon olive oil in the center of one of the parchment halves. Place one-quarter of the farro on the oil, followed by one-quarter of the fennel slices and 1 fish fillet. Top the fish with 1 tablespoon butter, 1 thyme sprig, a few fennel fronds, a few slivers of garlic, ½ cup tomatoes (some may fall around the fish), and 1 tablespoon wine.

❸ Fold the packets. Fold the other half of the parchment over the fish, lining up the edges. Starting at one end, make 2-inch pleats, each slightly overlapping the previous fold, following the shape of the paper to create a tight seal. Use a butter knife or the edge of your fingernail to crease each fold very well. Repeat with the remaining parchment pieces and ingredients.

❹ Bake the packets. Divide the assembled packets between 2 large sheet pans. Bake for 12 minutes or until the packets are puffed and dark around the edges.

❺ Serve the fish. Use scissors or a sharp knife to cut along the top of the packet just inside the fold (you can do this at the dining table as well). Being careful of the hot steam, roll back the top of the parchment. Drizzle the fish with olive oil and sprinkle with sea salt. Serve with lemon wedges on the side.

Steamed Whole Red Snapper
with Ginger & Scallions

Serves 4 to 6

There's no better way to showcase a fresh catch like red snapper or branzino than by steaming the whole fish, a popular (and auspicious) method in Asian cooking that produces nearly foolproof, moist results. The gentle cooking preserves moisture, and stuffing the cavity with aromatics such as scallions, ginger, lemongrass, garlic, and fresh herbs infuses the delicate fish with remarkable flavor.

1 (2-pound) or 2 (1-pound) whole fish (such as red snapper or branzino, or other white, flaky fish), rinsed, scaled, and gutted

Canola oil

Kosher salt

1 (4-inch) piece lemongrass (see page 131), beaten with the back of the knife blade

2 sprigs cilantro, plus additional leaves for garnish

2 sprigs Thai basil, plus additional leaves for garnish

1 clove garlic, thinly sliced

4 scallions, thinly sliced at a sharp angle (keep the green tops and white bottoms separate)

1 (2-inch) piece ginger, peeled and cut into thin matchsticks

1 Thai bird chile, stemmed and thinly sliced

1 tablespoon rice vinegar

2 tablespoons soy sauce

1 tablespoon mirin

2 teaspoons toasted sesame oil

2 lemons, quartered, for garnish

❶ Prepare the fish. Pat the fish dry with paper towels. Place on a heatproof platter or small sheet pan. Use a sharp paring knife to score the skin and meat about ¼ inch deep in three parallel lines at an angle on both sides of the fish. Brush the fish lightly with canola oil. Season the fish inside and outside with salt. Place the lemongrass, cilantro sprigs, Thai basil sprigs, garlic, half of the white bottoms of the scallions, and one-quarter of the ginger in the cavity of the fish.

❷ Prepare the steamer. Place a small plate or shallow bowl upside down in a high-sided roasting pan. Transfer to the stovetop. Fill a kettle with water and heat to boiling. (Alternatively, use a steamer basket insert large enough to hold the fish.) Place the platter of fish on top of the plate in the roasting pan. Carefully add the boiling water to the roasting pan to a depth of 1½ inches.

❸ Cook the fish. Tightly cover the pan with foil. Heat the pan on high. Steam for 18 to 20 minutes, until the fish is cooked through and flakes easily. To check the fish for doneness, very carefully peel the foil back from the far side of the pan, so the steam releases away from you. When the fish is cooked through, turn off the heat and carefully remove the foil.

❹ Make the sauce. In a small pot, heat 1 tablespoon canola oil on medium-low until hot. Add the remaining ginger, the remaining white bottoms of the scallions, Thai chile, and ½ teaspoon salt. Cook, stirring frequently, for 45 seconds to 1 minute, until softened. Transfer to a small bowl and stir in the vinegar, soy sauce, mirin, and sesame oil.

❺ Serve the fish. With folded kitchen towels or pot holders, carefully remove the platter from the roasting pan. Remove the herbs from the cavity and discard. Garnish the fish with the green tops of the scallions, cilantro, and Thai basil leaves. Serve with the sauce and lemon wedges.

208   The Blue Apron Cookbook

Shallow-Poached Fish

with Aromatic Vegetables

Shallow-poached fish gets the benefit of both poaching and steaming, since the fillet isn't fully submerged in the liquid. It's also why the French call this preparation *à la nage*, which means swimming. The original technique called for cooking the fish in a lightly acidic broth with white wine or citrus juice, but now it has expanded to include more elements, like the aromatic vegetables used here—fennel, garlic, and bay leaf. Sealing the pan with a parchment paper circle just large enough to fit in the pan directly over the fish traps all the moisture while the fish cooks, to steam it and keep it from drying out. (See page 108 for how to cut a parchment circle.)

¼ cup extra virgin olive oil, plus more for finishing

1 teaspoon whole fennel seed

¼ teaspoon crushed red pepper flakes

2 cloves garlic, chopped

1 cup medium-diced fennel bulb (½ bulb)

1 cup medium-diced white onion (1 small onion)

1 cup medium-diced celery (about 2 stalks)

Kosher salt

2 cups medium-diced zucchini (1 to 2 large zucchini)

1 tablespoon tomato paste

1 cup dry white wine (such as sauvignon blanc or pinot grigio)

1 dried bay leaf

½ cup water

4 (6-ounce) skinless fillets firm-fleshed white fish (1½ to 2 inches thick; such as tilefish, pollock, hake, grouper, or snapper)

2 tablespoons thinly sliced fresh basil leaves

Flaky sea salt, for finishing

2 tablespoons fresh parsley leaves, coarsely chopped

1 lemon, cut into wedges, for serving

❶ Make the broth. In a large, high-sided sauté pan, heat the olive oil on medium until hot. Add the fennel seed and red pepper flakes and cook, stirring frequently, for 30 seconds or until fragrant. Add the garlic, fennel, onion, and celery and season with salt. Cook, stirring occasionally, for 5 to 7 minutes, until the vegetables are slightly softened. Add the zucchini, tomato paste, and ¼ teaspoon kosher salt and cook, stirring occasionally, for 2 to 4 minutes, until the vegetables are thoroughly coated and the tomato paste is beginning to darken. Add the white wine and bay leaf and heat to a simmer. Cook, stirring occasionally, for 4 to 6 minutes, until the liquid is reduced in volume by half. Add the water and return to a simmer. Reduce the heat to low.

❷ Add the fish. Pat the fish dry with paper towels and generously season with salt on both sides. Gently nestle the fish, skinned side down, in the vegetables.

❸ Cook the fish. Top with a parchment paper circle (see page 108). Cover and cook, without disturbing, for 10 to 12 minutes, until an instant-read thermometer inserted into the thickest part of the fish registers 130°F. Discard the parchment circle, carefully flip the fish, and turn off the heat. Let stand for 30 seconds to 1 minute, uncovered, to finish cooking the fish.

❹ Serve the fish. Carefully transfer the cooked fish to a serving dish, leaving the vegetables and broth in the pan. Stir the basil into the broth. Spoon the vegetables and broth over the fish. Finish with a sprinkle of sea salt and a drizzle of olive oil. Garnish with the parsley. Serve with the lemon wedges on the side.

210 The Blue Apron Cookbook

Poached Chicken

with Aioli

Poached chicken and aioli are a very classic French pairing. In the traditional Provençal dish, *bourride de volaille*, the aioli is used to thicken the broth that the chicken and vegetables are cooked in. While we're not stirring it into the broth, all the components are here. A final drizzle of the homemade aioli over the whole dish creates a flavorful punch of garlic in every bite.

The simple flavors of this meal have nothing to hide, so it's important to pay close attention to the details. Start with the best pasture-raised chicken and local vegetables you can find. Simmering the broth with a bouquet garni adds a subtle layer of flavor to both the chicken and the vegetables. Finally, using an instant-read thermometer to maintain steady, gentle heat and to check for doneness is key—cooking over too high a heat will result in tough, dry chicken meat.

1 whole chicken (3½ to 4 pounds)

Kosher salt and freshly ground black pepper

2 large leeks, trimmed

3 sprigs thyme

6 sprigs parsley

1 small sprig rosemary

2 dried bay leaves

5 quarts chicken stock

4 carrots, peeled and cut into 4-inch pieces

3 stalks celery, cut into 4-inch pieces

6 cloves garlic, peeled and halved

Flaky sea salt, for finishing

Aioli (page 272), for serving

❶ Prepare the chicken. Pat the chicken dry with paper towels. Season the inside and outside with kosher salt and pepper. Let stand at room temperature for 30 minutes. Truss the chicken (see page 37).

❷ Make the bouquet garni. Cut off the root ends and dark green tops from the leeks. Rinse 4 of the leek greens thoroughly; discard the rest. Wrap the thyme, parsley, rosemary, and bay leaves in the leek greens and secure with butcher's twine. Halve the leeks lengthwise, stopping 1 inch before the bottom; the leeks should remain intact. Rinse thoroughly, then tie each leek closed with twine.

❸ Poach the chicken. In a large pot on medium, heat the stock to 180°F. Add the carrots, leeks, celery, garlic, and bouquet garni and cook, without stirring, for 3 to 5 minutes, until the temperature returns to 180°F. Add the trussed chicken, breast side down. Heat until just below a simmer. The broth will occasionally bubble, but should not have a steady stream of bubbles. Do not let the broth heat above 180°F; if necessary, reduce the heat. Cook the chicken, uncovered, for 80 to 90 minutes, until an instant-read thermometer inserted into the thigh (not touching the bone) registers 170°F. Remove from the heat. Carefully transfer the chicken to a large bowl, leaving the poaching liquid and vegetables in the pot.

❹ Cut the chicken and vegetables. When cool enough to handle, cut the cooked chicken into 8 pieces; remove and discard the skin. Transfer the carrots and celery to a serving dish. Transfer the leeks to a cutting board and cut crosswise at an angle into 2-inch pieces; transfer to the serving dish. Arrange the chicken pieces on top of the vegetables. Ladle ½ cup of the broth over the chicken and vegetables. Top the chicken with a sprinkle of sea salt and a drizzle of aioli.

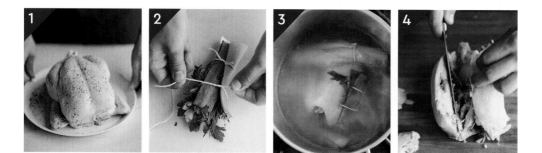

COOK'S *tip*

SAVE THE BROTH: *The beauty of this recipe lies in the flavorful, enriched chicken broth you create in the process. Save any leftover broth and use it as the start of a soup— just add chopped vegetables and cooked grains or beans of your choice. Better yet, use it as the start of Classic Chicken Noodle Soup (page 178).*

9
Frying

Crispy, crunchy, and deeply satisfying, fried foods are pretty irresistible. Dating back to as early as 1600 BC, frying is one of the oldest techniques for preparing food.

From the creation of tempura in Japan to the start of fried chicken in the American South, each region has had its own spin, but the basic principles of frying are essentially the same. With perfectly fried foods, the hot oil immediately cooks the exterior of the item you're frying when it hits the oil. The heat from the oil then causes the food to steam and cook on the inside without getting greasy. When frying is done right, the result is a crisp exterior and a moist, perfectly cooked interior, whether it's a schnitzel, a tempura, or a fried drumstick.

We often save our indulgence in fried foods for restaurants, but frying at home is easier than you think, especially with a few tools and tips that provide consistent results. Not all foods are fried at the same heat. Relying on a deep-fry thermometer is the best way to ensure that you're frying at the right temperature. Thicker cuts like pieces of bone-in chicken need to cook at a slightly lower heat to stay perfectly golden and not darken too much before they're cooked through.

Technically speaking, frying is a moist cooking method that relies on more than just a thin layer of oil (that's sautéing or pan-searing). For frying, you'll typically need enough oil to come one-third of the way up the sides of the vessel you're cooking in (but no more than halfway up). Prepping foods for their hot oil immersion is a pretty straightforward process. For the best flavor, it's important to season both the meat or fish or vegetable and the flour dredge. A batter is simple to stir together, but aim for the right consistency: thick enough that it will evenly coat whatever you're frying and not so thin that it runs

right off before the meat or vegetable hits the oil. Avoid overworking the batter, as this will develop the gluten in the flour and create tough, chewy results. Finally, keep in mind that every batch you fry will lower the temperature of the oil, so you'll need to give the oil a bit of recovery time to return to the proper temperature before adding the next round.

When it comes to rounding out the meal, go for super-fresh vegetable-based sides, such as crunchy napa cabbage slaw; a French-inspired potato salad; or a tomato, cucumber, and onion salad to balance the rich flavors.

Tools to Have on Hand

- Deep-fry thermometer
- Instant-read thermometer
- Dutch oven or other deep, heavy pot
- Cast-iron skillet
- Spider strainer

Keys to Success

1. Pay attention to prep. Use high-quality all-purpose flour for dredging, and fresh breadcrumbs (regular or panko) or cornmeal to create a crisp crust. Make friends with your local butchers and ask them to pound chicken or pork cutlets for you. For the most consistent results, aim to fry foods (chicken pieces, vegetables) of the same size and thickness—thicker or bigger pieces will take longer, while thinner or smaller pieces will need shorter cook times.

2. Use the right oil with a deep-fry thermometer. When it comes to frying, you'll need to use relatively neutral oils with a high smoking point, such as canola, grapeseed, or peanut oil. A thermometer is the best way to ensure that you're cooking at the right temperature. If you don't have a thermometer, drop a few breadcrumbs or a few globules of batter into the oil—they should bubble and start to brown. If they just sit in the oil without bubbling, the oil isn't hot enough, and conversely, if they start to smoke or immediately turn from brown to burned, the oil may be too hot.

3. Add the food carefully. Though the hot oil may seem intimidating, resist the urge to quickly drop food into the oil from high above because it seems that the distance will keep your hand safe. Adding food to the oil in this way is actually more dangerous, as it causes the hot oil to splash. Instead, use tongs, a spider strainer, or a stainless steel slotted spoon to carefully and slowly slide the food into the oil.

4. Pause between batches and don't overcrowd the oil. Adding too many items to the oil at once will quickly reduce the temperature of the oil. Also, allow a few minutes of recovery time after you fry each batch so the oil can reheat to the right temperature. Even within a single batch, as you add each piece of meat or vegetable to the oil, wait a few beats between additions so the oil can reheat (your pieces may finish frying at slightly different times).

5. Drain excess oil. After frying, use tongs to transfer foods to a plate lined with paper towels (or a wire rack placed over a sheet pan).

6. Immediately season hot foods. A final sprinkle of salt will adhere to the hot, moist surface and intensify the flavor of every bite.

LEFTOVER FRYING OIL

Once you're done deep-frying with a large amount of oil, let it cool completely in the pot. (Do not try to deal with the oil even when it's slightly warm; this is dangerous.) Strain it through a fine-mesh strainer lined with cheesecloth into a sealable container to reuse. (If using the original container it came in, use a funnel when pouring.)

Keep in mind that oil takes on the flavor of the ingredient that's been fried in it—for strongly flavored foods such as fish, you may not want to reuse it more than one or two times (and not again for, say, doughnuts). The more oil is heated, the more it breaks down—once it starts to have a rancid smell or is dark or cloudy, stop using it. When you're ready to dispose of it, do not pour the oil down the drain as it will damage the pipes. Pour the cooled oil into a container (coffee can, empty milk carton), make sure it's sealed completely, and throw it into the garbage. Alternatively, your community may have recycling centers for used oil you can bring it to.

Chicken Schnitzel

Although the most famous versions hail from Germany and Austria, many cultures serve some version of schnitzel. From Japanese katsu to Italian milanese, meat cutlets pounded thin, breaded, then quickly fried are hard not to love. Schnitzel loosely translates to "slice," which refers to the thin cut of the meat. Traditional schnitzel is made with veal, but variations made with pork, turkey, or chicken, as in this instance, are increasingly popular. Pounding the meat to a uniform thinness means it cooks in a flash, so be prepared to serve the chicken immediately or keep it warm in an oven heated to 250°F, uncovered (to preserve its crust).

4 boneless, skinless chicken breasts (about 1½ pounds total)

6 tablespoons all-purpose flour

Kosher salt and freshly ground black pepper

2 large eggs

1 cup plain dried breadcrumbs

Canola oil, for frying

1 lemon, cut into wedges, for serving

New Potato Salad (page 220), for serving (optional)

BETTER BREADING

Whether you're breading meat or vegetables, it's important to avoid breading your hands as well—or you'll end up with a mess. To avoid this, use the "dry hand, wet hand" method. Use one hand (your "dry hand") to coat the food in flour, then transfer to the eggs (without touching the eggs). Use your other hand (your "wet hand") to coat with the eggs and transfer to the breadcrumbs. Finally, use your "dry hand" to coat the food in the breadcrumbs. This way, one hand touches only the flour and breadcrumbs, while the other touches only the egg, keeping your hands neat.

❶ Pound the chicken. Pat the chicken dry with paper towels and place between two large pieces of plastic wrap. Use the bottom of a heavy pan to lightly pound the chicken until uniformly ¼ inch thick.

❷ Prepare the breading. Spread the flour on a shallow dish and season with salt and pepper. Crack the eggs into a shallow bowl and beat just until combined. Spread the breadcrumbs on another shallow dish and season with salt and pepper.

❸ Bread the chicken. Pat the chicken dry with paper towels again. Season with salt and pepper on both sides. Working with one piece at a time, coat both sides of the chicken in the flour; shake off any excess. Dip both sides in the eggs, letting the excess drip off, then in the breadcrumbs; shake off any excess. Transfer to a plate. Repeat with the remaining chicken. Discard any leftover flour, eggs, and breadcrumbs. Let stand for 10 to 15 minutes for the breading to set up.

❹ Fry the chicken. Set a wire rack on top of a sheet pan. In a large cast-iron skillet, heat ¼ inch oil on medium until hot. (The oil is hot enough when a few breadcrumbs sizzle immediately when dropped in.) Add two of the chicken pieces. Cook, occasionally spooning the oil over the chicken, for 3 to 5 minutes per side, until golden brown and cooked through. Transfer to the wire rack; immediately season with salt and pepper. Repeat with the remaining chicken pieces, adding oil if necessary. Serve with the lemon wedges and potato salad on the side.

Variation: Tonkatsu
Instead of chicken, use boneless pork chops, pounded to ½ inch thick. Substitute panko (Japanese breadcrumbs) for the plain breadcrumbs and add 1 tablespoon mustard powder (preferably Colman's) to the flour.

NEW POTATO SALAD

Serves 4 to 6

Potato salads are loved all over the world in a variety of forms: creamy and mayo-based in America, warm with bacon in Germany, with kewpie and cucumber in Japan, and more. In this French-inspired recipe, we marinate the potatoes in a vinaigrette flavored with shallots, Dijon mustard, and red wine vinegar, allowing them to absorb the tart, savory flavors.

2 pounds new potatoes or other small round potatoes (such as Yukon or red)

1 dried bay leaf

Kosher salt

2 small shallots, minced

1 tablespoon Dijon mustard

¼ cup red wine vinegar

Freshly ground black pepper

¾ cup high-quality extra virgin olive oil

½ cup finely chopped parsley leaves

1 tablespoon finely chopped tarragon leaves

❶ Cook the potatoes. Put into a large saucepan the potatoes, bay leaf, and enough cold water to cover the potatoes by 2 inches. Heat to simmering on medium-high. Reduce the heat to medium-low. Cook for 20 to 25 minutes, until tender when pierced with a knife. Remove from the heat and add 4 teaspoons salt. Let stand for 10 minutes in the cooking water. Drain thoroughly and let stand for 10 to 12 minutes at room temperature to cool slightly. Remove and discard the bay leaf.

❷ Make the vinaigrette. While the potatoes cool, in a small bowl, combine the shallots, mustard, and vinegar. Season with 1 teaspoon salt and ¼ teaspoon pepper. Slowly whisk in the olive oil until thoroughly combined.

❸ Dress the salad. Quarter the potatoes and transfer to a large bowl. Add the parsley, tarragon, and ¾ cup of the vinaigrette (you will have extra). Toss to combine and let stand for 1 hour before serving. Season with salt and pepper. Transfer to a serving dish and serve.

NOTE: *The new potatoes are cooked more gently—on a lower heat and for a longer period of time—than regular potatoes because of their thin skin and waxy interior. This way, the delicate potato skin won't be broken down by the boiling water before the inside is cooked through. The gentler heat also helps keep the waxy interior tender—not crumbly and not falling apart.*

MARINATED TOMATO, CUCUMBER & ONION

Serves 4 to 6

The bright flavors and acidic punch of marinated vegetables balance the richness of fried foods. This combination showcases summer's best bounty. First, the cucumber-and-onion mixture and tomatoes marinate separately with salt; this brings each ingredient to its fullest flavor without watering it down. Then they're combined—carefully, so the juicy tomatoes hold their shape—with a vinaigrette that brightens all the components further. We're partial to heirloom varieties, but by all means mix and match any seasonal selection you can get your hands on, such as a mix of yellow, green, and red streaky tomatoes; lemon cucumbers; or sweet onions such as Vidalia, Walla Walla, or Kelsae.

1 cup thinly sliced red or sweet onion

½ pound cucumbers, halved lengthwise and cut crosswise into ¼-inch slices (about 2 cups)

1 teaspoon sugar

Kosher salt

2 to 3 large heirloom tomatoes (about 2 pounds total), cored and cut into thick wedges

Flaky sea salt (such as Maldon)

2 tablespoons red wine vinegar

1 clove garlic, peeled and crushed

¼ cup plus 2 tablespoons extra virgin olive oil

Freshly ground black pepper

❶ Prepare the vegetables. In a large bowl, combine the onion, cucumbers, sugar, and 1 teaspoon kosher salt. Set aside to marinate, stirring occasionally, for 10 minutes. At the same time, in a separate bowl, season the tomatoes with 2 teaspoons sea salt.

❷ Make the vinaigrette. In a small bowl, combine the vinegar and garlic. Season with ½ teaspoon kosher salt. Slowly whisk in ¼ cup olive oil until thoroughly combined. Let stand for 10 minutes. Discard the garlic.

❸ Dress the salad. Add the vinaigrette to the cucumber and onion and toss to combine. Gently fold in the tomatoes and their juices until just combined. Season with salt and pepper. Transfer to a serving dish. Top with the remaining 2 tablespoons olive oil and a sprinkle of the sea salt and serve.

Buttermilk Fried Chicken

Fried chicken is an institution in the American South that evolved from being a fancy dish for aristocrats to becoming the centerpiece of Sunday family suppers (and finally, fast food in that familiar red-and-white-striped bucket). It's a dish with a lot of history and heart. The keys to ours lie in the batter. First, the lactic acid in the buttermilk marinade tenderizes the meat, while the seasonings infuse it with flavor. Second, double-dipping the chicken creates a thicker, flakier crust. To ensure a crisp coating, it's essential to dredge the chicken just before you place it in the hot oil.

Serve this chicken warm or at room temperature—or even cold—with whatever condiments suit your mood and menu, including maple syrup, ranch dressing, or sriracha stirred into honey for a quick hot honey.

1 tablespoon sweet paprika

1 tablespoon garlic powder

1 tablespoon onion powder

1 teaspoon cayenne pepper

3 cups buttermilk

Kosher salt and freshly ground black pepper

1 whole chicken (3½ to 4 pounds), cut into 10 pieces (2 wings, 2 breasts split horizontally, 2 drumsticks, 2 thighs)

Canola oil

5 cups all-purpose flour

Marinated Tomato, Cucumber & Onion (page 221), for serving (optional)

❶ Marinate the chicken. In a large bowl or shallow baking dish, combine the paprika, garlic powder, onion powder, cayenne, buttermilk, 2 tablespoons salt, and ½ teaspoon black pepper. Stir to combine. Add the chicken and toss to coat. Cover with plastic wrap and refrigerate for 6 to 12 hours to marinate.

❷ Double-coat the chicken. Set a wire rack on a large sheet pan. One hour before cooking, remove the chicken from the refrigerator. In a large, heavy pot on medium, heat 2 inches of oil to 350°F. While the oil is heating, in a large bowl, combine the flour, 1½ teaspoons salt, and ¼ teaspoon black pepper. Working with one piece at a time, lift a chicken piece from the buttermilk, letting the excess drip off. Transfer to the seasoned flour and toss to thoroughly coat. Return the piece to the buttermilk, then back to the flour (double battering). Shake off any excess flour and immediately transfer to the hot oil. Working in batches, repeat the process with the remaining chicken pieces, being careful not to overcrowd the pan.

❸ Fry the chicken. Cook the chicken, flipping once halfway through, for 13 to 17 minutes, until golden brown and cooked through (an instant-read thermometer inserted into the thickest part of the chicken piece should register 175°F). The smaller pieces like the wings and split breasts will cook slightly more quickly than the drumsticks and thighs. Transfer to the wire rack; immediately season with salt and pepper. Serve warm or at room temperature with the salad.

Beer-Battered Fish Tacos

with Red Cabbage Slaw & Chipotle Mayo

Fish tacos are a staple in Baja, a region in Mexico known for its abundance of seafood. Fresh fish markets are flush with fish taco stands that highlight the best of the day's catch. Here we draw inspiration from those taco stands with light and crispy beer-battered fish paired with crisp cabbage slaw and smoky chipotle mayo. With its light hoppy character and fizzy fermentation, beer creates the ultimate batter. A wet, thick batter that fries into a crackly, golden-brown crust enhances fish, helping to hold the delicate fillets together. Using a slotted spoon or wire-mesh strainer to remove the fish from the pot allows excess oil to drain off, which helps maintain a crispy coating.

½ head red cabbage, thinly sliced (about 3 cups)

Juice of ½ lime

Kosher salt

½ cup mayonnaise

1 chipotle pepper in adobo sauce, finely chopped

Canola oil or other vegetable oil, for frying

4 cups all-purpose flour

1 teaspoon paprika

½ teaspoon cayenne pepper

4½ cups pilsner beer or other light lager

2 pounds mild, flaky white fish fillets (such as hake, cod, or grouper), cut into 4 by 1-inch strips

Freshly ground black pepper

8 to 12 corn tortillas, warmed

2 avocados, pitted, peeled, and thinly sliced

Leaves from ½ bunch cilantro

3 limes, cut into wedges

❶ Prepare the slaw and mayonnaise. In a large bowl, combine the cabbage, lime juice, and a big pinch of salt. Toss to combine and set aside to marinate, stirring occasionally, for 15 minutes. In a small bowl, combine the mayonnaise and as much of the chipotle as you like (depending on how spicy you'd like it).

❷ Heat the oil and make the batter. In a large, heavy pot on medium, heat 1½ inches of oil to 375°F. While the oil heats, in a large bowl, whisk together the flour, paprika, cayenne, and 2 tablespoons salt. Whisk in the beer just until smooth.

❸ Fry the fish. Line a sheet pan with paper towels. Pat the fish fillets dry with paper towels; place in the batter. When a drop of batter sizzles immediately when added to the pot, the oil is hot enough. Using your hand or a pair of rubber-tipped tongs (so as not to break the flesh of the fish) and working with one piece at a time, lift a fish fillet out of the batter, letting any excess drip off, and carefully add to the hot oil. Continue adding more fish to the pot, being careful not to overcrowd. Cook for 3 to 4 minutes, flipping occasionally, until the fish is golden brown and cooked through. Use a slotted spoon or wire-mesh strainer to carefully transfer the fish to the sheet pan. Season immediately with salt and pepper. Repeat with the remaining fish fillets, making sure the oil returns to 365° to 375°F before frying each batch.

❹ Assemble and serve the tacos. Divide the fried fish among the tortillas; top as desired with the slaw, chipotle mayonnaise, avocado, and cilantro. Serve with the lime wedges on the side.

Vegetable Tempura

Tempura, a traditional dish of Japan, is one of the earliest known forms of deep frying, inspired by a method from Portuguese missionaries. Vegetables and fish are coated in batter and then deep fried. Frying in oil or fat was rare in Japanese cooking up until this point, but unsurprisingly, it quickly became very popular. When it's done correctly, the process creates a "lighter" version of each of the ingredients, including fresh seasonal vegetables. The trick is an exceptionally light, relatively thin batter—the secret ingredient is club soda—that creates a bubbly crust that won't mask the vegetables' flavor.

2 to 3 pounds vegetables (such as summer squash, broccoli, green beans, or sweet potato), trimmed

Kosher salt and freshly ground black pepper

Canola oil or other vegetable oil, for frying

1½ cups all-purpose flour

½ cup cornstarch

2 cups club soda, chilled

Napa Cabbage Slaw (page 228), for serving (optional)

❶ **Prepare the vegetables.** Depending on the type of vegetable, cut them into bite-sized pieces, ¼- to ½-inch-thick rounds, or small florets. Transfer them to a large bowl. Season with 1 teaspoon salt. Toss to combine. Transfer to a colander and let drain for 30 minutes. Rinse the vegetables under cold water. Drain thoroughly and pat dry with paper towels.

❷ **Heat the oil and make the batter.** In a large, heavy-bottomed pot on medium-high, heat 1 inch of oil to between 330° and 350°F. Line a plate with several layers of paper towels. While the oil heats, in a bowl, whisk together the flour and cornstarch. Gently whisk in the club soda until just combined; do not overmix. It should resemble very thin pancake batter.

❸ **Fry the vegetables.** The oil is hot enough when a drop of batter sizzles immediately when added to the pot. Working in batches, dip the vegetables in the batter and turn them to fully coat. With one piece at a time, lift the vegetables out of the batter, letting any excess drip off, and carefully add to the hot oil. Continue adding vegetables, being careful not to overcrowd the pot. Cook for 3 to 4 minutes, until golden, crispy, and tender. Use a wire-mesh strainer or slotted spoon to transfer to the plate; immediately season with salt and pepper. Repeat with the remaining vegetables. Transfer to a serving dish and serve immediately with the slaw.

COOK'S *tip*

PREPARING THE VEGETABLES:
For uniform frying (and the easiest eating), you'll want to cut larger vegetables, such as summer squash and eggplant, into bite-size pieces (no bigger than 2 inches) or into ¼- to ½-inch-thick rounds; cruciferous vegetables like cauliflower and broccoli into florets; and long, thin vegetables, such as asparagus or scallions, into manageable 2- to 3-inch lengths. Salting the vegetables, then patting them dry before they're cooked, removes excess moisture and helps create crispy results.

TEMPURA DIPPING SAUCE

Tempura is traditionally served with a light dipping sauce made with dashi, a Japanese stock made from kombu (dried seaweed) and dried bonito flakes. To make the sauce, combine ½ cup dashi with ¼ cup soy sauce, 2 tablespoons mirin, and 2 tablespoons finely grated daikon radish. If you can't find dashi and/or daikon, we also like serving tempura with a bright, soy-based sauce using ½ cup soy sauce, ¼ cup rice vinegar, and 2 tablespoons mirin.

NAPA CABBAGE SLAW

Serves 6 to 8

Whether they're creamy or vinegar-based, slaws are classic sidekicks to fried and grilled foods because their fresh crunch and brightness balance the foods' rich flavors. We love the endless possibilities of vinegar-based slaws when you utilize a range of vinegars, oils, and spices—ours uses rice vinegar, sesame oil, and a kick of cayenne. Salting the ingredients before they're tossed with the dressing concentrates their flavor and results in a more toothsome, less rubbery texture.

1 (2-pound) head napa cabbage, quartered, cored, and thinly sliced crosswise

1 red onion, halved and thinly sliced

4 stalks celery, cut into thin matchsticks

2 carrots, peeled and cut into thin matchsticks

2½ teaspoons sugar

Kosher salt

3 tablespoons rice vinegar

⅛ teaspoon cayenne pepper

¼ cup high-quality extra virgin olive oil

1 teaspoon toasted sesame oil

Freshly ground black pepper

❶ Prepare the vegetables. In a large bowl, combine the cabbage, onion, celery, carrots, 2 teaspoons of the sugar, and 2 tablespoons salt; toss to thoroughly combine. Set aside to marinate, stirring occasionally, for 30 minutes or until slightly softened.

❷ Make the vinaigrette. In a small bowl, combine the vinegar, the remaining ½ teaspoon sugar, and the cayenne. Slowly whisk in the olive oil until thoroughly combined. Slowly whisk in the sesame oil. Season with salt and black pepper.

❸ Dress the slaw. Add the vinaigrette to the vegetables and toss to combine. Transfer to a serving dish and serve.

10
Salads

Salads are about more than just lettuces and leafy greens; they're about celebrating and savoring the season's best fresh vegetables and fruits.

Mastering a great salad is one of the easiest things you'll learn in the kitchen, and it's also one of the most creatively satisfying. Peruse a market, gather ingredients that pique your interest, add a handful of adornments (toasted nuts or croutons, high-quality cheese, picked herbs), then whisk together a flavorful dressing. Taste your ingredients as you go— heirloom tomatoes in season, peppery greens, chicories with a bitter bite—and think about how you want to highlight or balance those flavors.

Although we think of a green salad tossed with vinegar and olive oil as a staple on our tables today, it was once an indulgence of only the upper class because of how expensive olive oil was. High-quality olive oils and vinegars are more accessible today, and we encourage you to seek out the best—you'll be using only a small amount at a time, and they'll really make your salads shine.

Of course, a salad isn't limited to green leaves, so we've included a mix of seasonal vegetable, noodle, and hearty grain compositions that make a complete meal. The primary characteristic of most salads is freshness, but dishes like a roasted root vegetable salad with farro or a snap pea salad made with sautéed morels remind us that salads don't have to be 100 percent raw, either.

Tools to Have on Hand

- Salad spinner
- Large mixing bowls
- Whisk

Keys to Success

1. Start with the best ingredients. As in any dish made of few ingredients—particularly fresh ingredients with nothing to hide behind—quality is key. For the best salads, seek out the freshest locally grown produce. For dressings, use your best extra virgin olive oil (unless we indicate otherwise), preferably from a single origin so it carries the distinct flavor of a place. Good olive oils typically have a one-year shelf life; look for a production date on the back label. Store oils and vinegars in a cool, dark place away from sunlight. Just as with olive oil, you typically get what you pay for with vinegars. Seek out trusted brands of wine vinegars for everyday use. Aged, syrupy vinegars like balsamic vinegar from Modena are very strong and should be used in moderation.

2. Layer textures and flavors. A great salad consists of diverse colors, flavors, and textures. When you're planning yours, consider the details. Add a blend of crunchy textures (croutons, toasted nuts or seeds) and creamy textures (avocado, fresh cheeses), and balance bitter, sweet, salty, and acidic ingredients.

3. Avoid soggy salads. Always use a salad spinner to dry your greens very well. The dressings will cling to the leaves better and your salad won't be too wet. Also, start by dressing lightly, and then add more to taste.

4. Choose the right dressing. Pair greens and other components with a complementary dressing. As a general rule, the more aggressive the green, the more assertive the dressing: For example, pair chicories or dandelion greens with a pungent anchovy dressing. Young, tender lettuces should be paired with milder dressings, such as herbed buttermilk, that don't mask their delicate flavor. When you're preparing the dressing, remember that you can always add but you can't take away, so season judiciously— you can always finish with additional salt, pepper, or lemon juice as desired.

Carrot-Miso Dressing
(page 237)

Caesar Dressing
(page 235)

Red Wine Vinaigrette
(page 234)

Herbed Buttermilk Dressing
(page 236)

RED WINE VINAIGRETTE

Makes 2 cups

This is our standard vinaigrette—to our taste, the perfect ratio of oil and vinegar—that you can toss with an endless variety of leafy green, grain, and shaved vegetable salads. Allowing the shallots to briefly macerate with the Dijon mustard, vinegar, and sugar softens their sharp, raw flavor; coaxes out their sweetness; and results in a more balanced dressing.

Feel free to vary the acid according to your whim and the other components in the salad. For instance, lemon juice, white wine vinegar, or champagne vinegar is a great choice for more delicate salads (think butter lettuce and avocado), while the deep flavor of sherry vinegar is a better choice for heartier mixtures including beans, aged cheeses, olives, or cured meats. However, you don't want to use balsamic vinegar as a substitute—it will overpower the other ingredients and disrupt the balance of flavors.

Stored in a sealed container in the refrigerator, leftover vinaigrette will last 4 to 5 days, so you'll be armed for improvisational salads throughout the week.

2 shallots, minced (about ½ cup)
¼ cup Dijon mustard
½ cup red wine vinegar
Kosher salt and freshly ground black pepper
1¼ cups extra virgin olive oil

In a medium bowl, whisk together the shallots, mustard, vinegar, 1½ teaspoons salt, and ½ teaspoon pepper. Let stand for 1 minute. In a slow, steady stream, whisk in the olive oil. Season with salt and pepper. Store in a sealed container in the refrigerator for up to 5 days.

CAESAR DRESSING

Makes 1 cup

The biggest surprise about Caesar dressing and salad is that they were created in Mexico, not Italy. An Italian named Caesar Cardini owned restaurants in Tijuana that became a popular destination for Hollywood types during Prohibition. The salad came together by accident. With few things in the pantry one night, he threw together some ingredients he had on hand. Customers loved it, and the salad became a regular on the menu and eventually was seen in restaurants in Southern California. Like ours, the first version of this dressing did not include anchovies. They were added to the dressing a few years later. Our dressing relies on savory ingredients like garlic, Dijon mustard, Worcestershire sauce, and Parmigiano-Reggiano cheese to provide that characteristic salty edge and depth.

For a classic Caesar salad, toss a generous amount of dressing with cold, crisp, young leaves of romaine lettuce and croutons and serve it with shaved Parmigiano on top. But don't limit yourself to that combination—this creamy, luscious dressing is also delicious with bitter greens such as escarole, chicory, and frisée, and with peppery watercress.

2 cloves garlic, finely grated into a paste

2 tablespoons freshly squeezed lemon juice

4 teaspoons Dijon mustard

2 teaspoons Worcestershire sauce

Kosher salt and freshly ground black pepper

2 large egg yolks

½ cup canola oil or other vegetable oil, chilled

¼ cup extra virgin olive oil, chilled

6 tablespoons freshly grated Parmigiano-Reggiano cheese

In a bowl, whisk together the garlic, lemon juice, mustard, Worcestershire sauce, ½ teaspoon salt, and ¼ teaspoon pepper until thoroughly combined. Whisk in the egg yolks until thoroughly combined. In a slow, steady stream, whisk in the canola oil, then the olive oil, until the dressing is emulsified and creamy. Whisk in the Parmigiano. Season with salt and pepper. Store in a sealed container in the refrigerator for up to 2 days.

COOK'S
tips

TAME THE BITE: *We love incorporating garlic and shallot into dressings, but some may find the raw taste of these ingredients to be too strong. To take the bite out of garlic and shallot, combine them with the acid (the vinegar or lemon) in the recipe first and let stand for 5 to 10 minutes to soften the flavors. For even less of a garlic taste, use a whole clove of garlic crushed instead of grated or minced; remove the garlic before using the dressing.*

EASY EMULSIONS: *Whisking the oil into the dressing in a slow, steady stream is key; this helps it emulsify into a smooth, creamy texture—like mayonnaise, the most famous emulsion. Chilling the oil beforehand helps keep the mixture from separating. Since you're working with raw eggs,* seek out the safest, best, pasture-raised variety.*

*Consuming raw eggs may increase your risk of food-borne illness.

HERBED BUTTERMILK DRESSING

Makes 2 cups

With a mix of fresh herbs, such as chives, parsley, and dill, this recipe delivers the satisfying flavors of a classic ranch-style dressing. It's no surprise that ranch dressing is often cited as Americans' most preferred dressing. Making it yourself is easy and the result beats any bottled version. A blend of buttermilk and sour cream provides creaminess and a subtle tang. You can substitute mayonnaise (homemade or store-bought) for the sour cream with similar results. In addition to salad dressing, this recipe also makes a great dip for blanched vegetables.

1 clove garlic, finely grated into a paste, or 1½ teaspoons garlic powder

1 small shallot, minced, or 2 teaspoons onion powder

¾ teaspoon Dijon mustard

1½ tablespoons white wine vinegar

1½ teaspoons sugar

Kosher salt

1 cup sour cream

½ cup buttermilk

3 tablespoons thinly sliced fresh chives

3 tablespoons finely chopped fresh flat-leaf parsley

2 tablespoons finely chopped fresh dill

1½ teaspoons freshly ground black pepper

In a bowl, whisk together the garlic, shallot, mustard, vinegar, sugar, and 1½ teaspoons salt. Whisk in the sour cream, then the buttermilk. Add the chives, parsley, and dill; whisk until thoroughly combined. Whisk in the pepper and season with salt. Store in a sealed container in the refrigerator for up to 2 days.

CARROT-MISO DRESSING

Makes 1½ cups

A favorite in Japanese American restaurants, this vibrant dressing is based on the traditional *sumiso* sauce, which is usually made with miso, rice vinegar (*su* means vinegar in Japanese), sugar, and mirin (a sweet rice wine similar to sake). The addition of carrots gives the sauce its vibrant color and slightly sweet flavor, while ginger gives it a kick.

½ pound carrots, peeled and thinly sliced (about 4 medium)

1 (1-inch) piece ginger, peeled and minced

¼ cup white miso paste

5 tablespoons rice vinegar

1 tablespoon mirin

1 tablespoon honey

2 tablespoons water

2 tablespoons toasted sesame oil

5 tablespoons extra virgin olive oil

Kosher salt and freshly ground black pepper

In a high-powered blender, combine the carrots, ginger, miso, vinegar, mirin, honey, and water. Blend until almost smooth; use a spatula to scrape down the sides and stir together. Add the sesame oil and olive oil. Blend until completely smooth. Season with salt and pepper. Store in a sealed container in the refrigerator for up to 5 days.

MISO PASTE: *Miso paste is a traditional Japanese ingredient made from fermented soybeans and salt and is used to make soup, broth, sauces, and dressings. There are several varieties, but we most commonly use white (shiro miso), which is sweet and mellow.*

Chicory & Citrus Salad

with Shaved Fennel

Winter salads provide an opportunity to use more assertive seasonal ingredients that are no less vibrant than their warm-weather counterparts. In cool weather, chicories and endives abound—radicchio, Castelfranco, Belgian endive, escarole, puntarelle, and more. These beautiful leaves have plenty of personality, so you need to balance their bitter and peppery bite with a generous amount of fruity, rich olive oil and other ingredients that add richness (like nuts, cheese, croutons, or eggs) or sweetness, such as the citrus we use here, another seasonal favorite. Look for chicories and endives from farmers' markets, where you'll find interesting varieties beyond the regular grocery store offerings.

2 tablespoons red wine vinegar

Kosher salt and freshly ground black pepper

3 tablespoons extra virgin olive oil, plus more for drizzling

1 small red onion, halved and thinly sliced

2 navel oranges

Flaky sea salt

1 cup thinly sliced fennel bulb (about ½ bulb)

½ pound mixed chicories (such as red or Castelfranco radicchio, or frisée), trimmed, leaves separated and torn into large pieces

½ loosely packed cup fresh flat-leaf parsley leaves

¼ cup roasted unsalted pistachios, chopped

❶ Marinate the onion. Place the vinegar in a large bowl. Whisk in 1 teaspoon kosher salt and ¼ teaspoon pepper. Slowly whisk in the tablespoons olive oil. Add the onion and toss to combine. Set aside for 10 minutes to marinate.

❷ Prepare the oranges. Cut a small section off the top and bottom of the oranges so they can stand flat. Use a sharp knife to cut away the peel (including the pith) and then cut the oranges crosswise into ¼-inch-thick rounds. Arrange the orange slices on a large serving plate. Season with flaky salt.

❸ Finish and serve the salad. Add the fennel, chicories, parsley, and pistachios to the bowl of onion. Lightly drizzle with olive oil and season with salt and pepper. Toss to combine. Arrange the salad on top of the orange slices and serve.

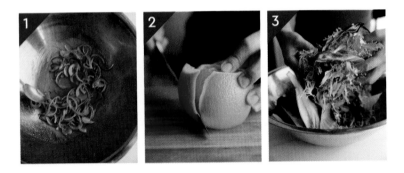

Morel & Snap Pea Salad

with Fresh Herbs & Parmigiano-Reggiano

Serves 4

Morels are an ingredient treasured by many chefs, not only for their flavor but for their limited availability, even in spring. They are especially hard to cultivate, which means the majority of them are foraged. Morels look like small sponges with a hollow body, and this porosity makes them lose their integrity very quickly. Here we're letting them shine with another spring favorite, sweet snap peas, and mixing in fresh herbs and thin shavings of Parmigiano-Reggiano cheese. The most important step (other than seasoning) is ensuring that the morels are well washed and completely dry before you sauté them—this will help you avoid a gritty or soggy salad.

½ pound fresh morel mushrooms, stemmed; large mushrooms halved lengthwise

Kosher salt

¾ pound sugar snap peas (4 cups), stems ends and strings removed

2 tablespoons unsalted butter

1 clove garlic, peeled

1 sprig thyme

Freshly ground black pepper

¼ cup dry white wine (such as sauvignon blanc or pinot grigio)

¼ cup freshly squeezed lemon juice (about 2 lemons)

1 teaspoon Dijon mustard

½ teaspoon sugar

1 small shallot, minced

⅔ cup extra virgin olive oil

1 tablespoon finely chopped fresh mint leaves

2 teaspoons coarsely chopped fresh tarragon

½ loosely packed cup fresh flat-leaf parsley leaves

2 tablespoons finely chopped fresh chives

1 (2-ounce) block Parmigiano-Reggiano cheese, shaved into strips with a vegetable peeler

❶ **Wash the mushrooms.** Line a sheet pan with paper towels. Fill a large bowl with cold water and add the mushrooms. Use your hands to gently submerge and stir to remove any excess dirt. Lift the mushrooms from the bowl and refill the bowl with cold water. Repeat washing and draining two more times, or until no dirt appears at the bottom of the bowl. Drain thoroughly and transfer to the sheet pan. (If you have a salad spinner, you can use it for the entire cleaning process. Place the mushrooms in the basket, fill the spinner with water, and agitate to clean the mushrooms. Lift out the basket to drain the mushrooms, leaving the dirty water behind. Repeat until the water is clean.)

❷ **Prepare the peas.** Heat a pot of heavily salted water to boiling on high. Fill a large bowl with ice water. Add the peas to the boiling water. Cook for 2 to 3 minutes, until bright green and just tender. Drain thoroughly and transfer to the ice water; let stand until cool. Drain again thoroughly and pat dry with paper towels. Transfer to a cutting board and cut in half at an angle.

❸ **Sauté the mushrooms.** In a sauté pan on medium-high, melt the butter. Add the mushrooms and cook, stirring occasionally, for 2 to 4 minutes, until slightly softened. Add the garlic and thyme and season with 1 teaspoon salt and ¼ teaspoon pepper. Cook, stirring occasionally, for 3 to 4 minutes, until fragrant. Add the wine and ½ teaspoon salt and cook until the wine is almost completely absorbed. Remove and discard the garlic and thyme. Set the mushrooms aside to cool.

❹ **Make the vinaigrette.** In a small bowl, combine the lemon juice, mustard, sugar, and shallot. Season with 1 teaspoon salt and ¼ teaspoon pepper. Slowly whisk in the olive oil until thoroughly combined.

❺ **Finish and serve the salad.** In a large bowl, combine the snap peas and mushrooms, mint, tarragon, parsley, chives, and enough vinaigrette to coat the salad (you may have extra). Toss to coat. Gently mix in the Parmigiano, until just combined. Season with salt and pepper. Divide among serving dishes. Lightly season with black pepper. Serve immediately.

Asparagus & Herb Salad

with Soft-Boiled Eggs & Lemon Dressing

Asparagus, one of the harbingers of spring, takes a lot of patience to grow—two to three years to harvest from planting. Look for local asparagus with tight tips; if the tips are broken, bruised, or flowering, take a pass. Domestic, local asparagus will taste much better than imported varieties at the grocery store. Don't worry if you can find asparagus only in a variety of sizes; just separate the larger and smaller tips and blanch them in batches, adjusting cooking times as necessary.

Learning how to perfectly soft-boil an egg is an essential technique that will serve you very well in many future meals, from brunches to bowls of ramen at home.

2 pounds asparagus (not pencil-thin)

Kosher salt

4 large eggs

1 loosely packed cup fresh flat-leaf parsley leaves

½ loosely packed cup fresh basil leaves

2 tablespoons fresh tarragon leaves

1 tablespoon fresh mint leaves

¼ cup freshly squeezed lemon juice (about 2 lemons)

3 tablespoons extra virgin olive oil, plus more for drizzling

Flaky sea salt, for garnish

3 tablespoons thinly sliced chives, for garnish

❶ Prepare the asparagus. Snap off and discard the tough, woody ends of the asparagus. Cut off the tips (about 2 inches from the top) and set aside. Slice the remaining stalks at an angle into 2-inch pieces.

❷ Blanch the asparagus tips. Fill a bowl with ice water. Heat a large pot of salted water to boiling on high. Add the asparagus tips to the boiling water. Cook for 1 to 2 minutes for fatter tips or 30 seconds to 1 minute for thinner tips, until bright green and slightly tender.

❸ Shock the asparagus tips. Use a slotted spoon or strainer to transfer the asparagus tips to the ice water; keep the pot of water boiling. Let the tips stand until cool. Use a slotted spoon to transfer them to a colander. Drain thoroughly and pat dry with paper towels. Transfer to a large bowl.

❹ Cook the eggs. Carefully add the eggs to the boiling water. Cook for exactly 6 minutes. Drain thoroughly and transfer to the ice water. When cool enough to handle, lightly crack the shell of each egg and return to the ice water for 1 minute. Working carefully, gently peel the eggs and set aside.

❺ Finish and serve the salad. Just before serving, coarsely chop the parsley, basil, tarragon, and mint leaves and add to the asparagus tips. Add the raw asparagus stalks, lemon juice, 3 tablespoons olive oil, and 2 teaspoons kosher salt. Toss to thoroughly combine. Divide the salad among serving dishes. Top each with an egg; drizzle with olive oil and sprinkle with the sea salt. Top with the chives and serve.

COOK'S tip

EASY PEELING: *Gently cracking the shells of the soft-boiled eggs and returning them to the cold water will allow the water to seep between the membrane and the shell, making them easier to peel.*

Roasted Beet Salad

with Crispy Goat Cheese & Walnuts

This salad makes the most of the entire beet, from the beautiful, nutrient-packed leaves to the root. Roasting the beets in a sealed baking dish with a little bit of water creates a steam-roasting effect that produces the most flavorful, tender beets. They are easy to peel too—the skins slip right off, which (along with being fork-tender) is how you'll know they're ready. Although simply crumbling the goat cheese is an easy and delicious way to finish the salad, the crispy goat cheese is worth the time to make as the crunchiness of the panko along with the walnuts gives the salad great texture.

2 pounds baby beets (red, yellow, and/or Chioggia), trimmed, stems and leaves reserved

Extra virgin olive oil

Kosher salt

½ cup minced shallots (about 2 medium shallots)

7 tablespoons red wine vinegar

Freshly ground black pepper

8 ounces fresh soft goat cheese

3 tablespoons thinly sliced fresh chives

½ cup all-purpose flour

2 large eggs

1 cup panko breadcrumbs

Grapeseed oil or other vegetable oil

1 cup fresh flat-leaf parsley, coarsely chopped

½ cup toasted walnuts, coarsely chopped

① **Roast the beets.** Preheat the oven to 450°F. Arrange the beets in a single layer in a 9 by 13-inch baking dish. Add enough water to come halfway up the sides of the beets. Drizzle with olive oil and season generously with salt. Cover the baking dish with aluminum foil and tightly seal. Roast the beets for 1 hour to 1 hour 15 minutes, or until tender when pierced with a fork.

② **Make the marinade.** While the beets roast, in a medium bowl, combine ¼ cup shallots, 6 tablespoons of the red wine vinegar, and ½ teaspoon salt.

③ **Peel and marinate the beets.** When the beets are cool enough to handle, but still warm, use a paper towel to gently rub their skin off. Halve or quarter the beets and transfer them to a large bowl. Season with salt and pepper to taste. Pour the marinade over the beets; toss to coat. Let stand for 30 minutes to marinate.

COOK'S
tip

ROASTING BEETS: *Beets are naturally alkaline, which is why they have such an earthy (some would say "muddy") flavor. That's why we marinate the roasted beets in an acidic mixture of vinegar and shallot to bring balance and accentuate their sweetness. Baby beets come in various shapes and sizes, so be sure to check doneness after an hour to prevent overcooking. You can also follow this method for larger beets; they'll just need to cook for additional time. If you roast more than one variety, use separate pans so the colors don't bleed together.*

RECIPE CONTINUES

4 **Cook the beet stems and leaves.** Cut the beet stems into 2-inch pieces. Roll the leaves into a tight log and cut at an angle into long, 1-inch-wide strips. In a sauté pan, heat 1 tablespoon olive oil on medium until hot. Add the stems and season with salt. Cook, stirring occasionally, for 3 to 5 minutes, until slightly tender. Add the beet leaves and season with salt and pepper. Cook, stirring occasionally, for 2 to 4 minutes, until wilted. Stir in the remaining 1 tablespoon red wine vinegar. Remove from the heat.

5 **Form the goat cheese rounds.** Remove the goat cheese from the refrigerator and let stand at room temperature for about 10 minutes, until slightly softened. In a bowl, combine the chives, the remaining ¼ cup shallots, and the goat cheese. Season with 1 teaspoon salt and ½ teaspoon pepper. Mix until thoroughly combined. Use your hands to form into four equal balls, then carefully flatten each into a ¼-inch-thick round. Transfer the rounds to a plate.

6 **Bread the goat cheese.** Spread the flour on a shallow dish and season with salt and pepper. Crack the eggs into a shallow bowl and beat until just combined. Spread the breadcrumbs on another shallow dish. Working with one at a time, thoroughly coat the goat cheese rounds in the flour; tap off

COOKING ROOT TO STEM TO LEAF

When you're making the effort to seek out local produce and the freshest seasonal ingredients, it only makes sense to incorporate all of the edible components into your recipes. It's a healthful and complete approach to cooking, and it also adds delicious complexity of tastes and textures to your dishes. In addition to beets, you can apply more or less the same method (roasting or boiling the meaty root and sautéing the leafy greens) to turnips, radishes, and other root vegetables with flavorful tops. Don't forget about feathery carrot tops and fennel fronds—they can be tossed into herb salads, puréed into green sauces, or used as a flavorful garnish for soups and pasta.

any excess. Dip both sides in the eggs, letting the excess drip off, then in the breadcrumbs; press to make sure the breadcrumbs adhere. Transfer the rounds to a plate and cover with plastic wrap; chill in the refrigerator until just before frying.

7 **Crisp the goat cheese.** Just before serving, remove the goat cheese rounds from the refrigerator. Line a plate with paper towels. In a cast-iron skillet or sauté pan, heat a thin layer of grapeseed oil on medium-high until hot. The oil is hot enough when a few breadcrumbs sizzle immediately when added to the pan. Add the goat cheese rounds. Cook for 2 to 4 minutes per side, until golden brown and crispy. Transfer to the plate and season with salt and pepper.

8 **Finish and serve the salad.** Add the parsley and walnuts to the roasted beets; stir to thoroughly combine. Divide the beet greens (leaves), stems, and roasted beets among serving dishes. Top each with a goat cheese round and serve.

Summer Soba Noodle Salad

Traditionally, soba noodles can be served in hot broth or chilled and served alongside a dipping sauce, but we're tossing ours with a ginger-spiked dressing made with toasted sesame oil. Most soba noodles are made from buckwheat flour combined with a little wheat flour, which helps bind the noodle dough together. Feel free to vary the mix of vegetables based on what's in season or what you have on hand. Blanched snap or snow peas, thinly shaved carrots, radishes (any variety), and red cabbage would also be delicious additions.

1 tablespoon unsweetened creamy peanut butter

1 tablespoon honey

½ cup rice vinegar

2 tablespoons mirin

2 tablespoons soy sauce

1 (1-inch) piece ginger, peeled and finely grated into a paste

2 scallions, thinly sliced (keep the green tops and white bottoms separate)

1 clove garlic, minced

¼ cup plus 1 tablespoon grapeseed or canola oil

2 tablespoons toasted sesame oil

Kosher salt

1 pound dried soba noodles

¾ pound pole beans (such as green, wax, or Romano), trimmed and cut into 2-inch pieces at an angle (2 cups)

1 large green zucchini, halved crosswise and cut into thin matchsticks

1 large red bell pepper, stemmed, seeded, and cut into thin matchsticks

2 thin-skinned cucumbers (such as kirby or Persian), halved lengthwise and cut into ¼-inch half-moons

2 tablespoons toasted sesame seeds

❶ Make the vinaigrette. In a bowl, whisk together the peanut butter, honey, vinegar, mirin, soy sauce, ginger, the white bottoms of the scallions, and the garlic. Slowly whisk in the ¼ cup grapeseed oil until thoroughly combined. Slowly whisk in the sesame oil.

❷ Cook the noodles. Heat a large pot of heavily salted water to boiling on high. Add the noodles and cook for 1 to 2 minutes less than the package directions, until al dente (slightly firm to the bite). Drain thoroughly and rinse under cold water for 30 seconds to 1 minute to stop the cooking process and prevent sticking. Set aside to drain and cool.

❸ Sauté the pole beans. In a small sauté pan, heat the remaining 1 tablespoon grapeseed oil on medium-high until hot. Add the beans and season with salt. Cook, stirring occasionally, for 4 to 6 minutes, until just softened and lightly browned. Remove from the heat. Season with salt. Transfer to a plate and set aside to cool.

❹ Finish and serve the salad. In a large bowl, combine the noodles, beans, zucchini, bell pepper, cucumbers, and vinaigrette to taste; mix gently. Season with more vinaigrette and salt, if needed. Transfer to a serving dish. Garnish with the green tops of the scallions and the sesame seeds and serve.

Roasted Root Vegetable & Farro Salad

Robust grains like barley or farro (an heirloom wheat that was a staple in ancient Rome) make stellar, satisfying salads. Here we pair farro's nutty flavor with a colorful mix of herb-roasted root vegetables and crunchy hazelnuts. Grain salads like this one are actually better the next day, so it's an ideal recipe to make in advance. If you do make the salad in advance, reserve some of the dressing or make a little extra. The grains will soak it up, so you may want a little extra dressing to toss in just before serving.

2 cups raw, skin-on hazelnuts or almonds

5½ cups peeled and medium-diced root vegetables (such as celery root, carrots, parsnips, rutabagas, and/or sweet potatoes; about 3 pounds total)

2 sprigs sage

2 sprigs thyme

Extra virgin olive oil

Kosher salt and freshly ground black pepper

2 cups semi-pearled farro

¼ cup plus 1 tablespoon apple cider vinegar

2 shallots, minced

½ cup coarsely chopped fresh flat-leaf parsley leaves

❶ Toast the nuts. Preheat the oven to 350°F. Spread the nuts on a sheet pan in a single, even layer. Toast hazelnuts in the oven for 12 to 15 minutes, or almonds for 15 to 17 minutes, until lightly browned and fragrant. Transfer to a bowl and set aside to cool slightly, tossing the nuts occasionally. If using hazelnuts, when the nuts are cool enough to handle, transfer to a clean kitchen towel. Cover with the sides of the towel and rub back and forth to loosen the skins. Discard the skins. (If using almonds, no need to remove the skins.) Transfer the nuts to a cutting board and coarsely chop.

❷ Roast the vegetables. Increase the oven temperature to 450°F. In a large bowl, combine the root vegetables, sage, and thyme. Drizzle with 2 tablespoons olive oil, season with 2 teaspoons salt and ¼ teaspoon pepper, and toss to thoroughly coat. Spread on a sheet pan in a single, even layer. Roast for 20 to 25 minutes, until browned and tender when pierced with a fork. Remove from the oven and set aside to cool to room temperature for 15 to 20 minutes. Remove and discard the sage and thyme.

❸ Cook the farro. While the vegetables roast, heat a pot of water to boiling on high. Add the farro and 1½ teaspoons salt. Cook for 20 to 22 minutes, until tender. Drain thoroughly and transfer to a large bowl; stir in ¼ cup of the vinegar and season generously with salt and pepper. Gently toss to combine. Set aside to cool to room temperature, gently stirring occasionally, for 15 to 20 minutes.

❹ Compose the salad. In a small bowl, combine the shallots and remaining 1 tablespoon vinegar. Season with 1 teaspoon salt. Marinate for 2 minutes. Add the root vegetables, marinated shallots (including the vinegar), nuts, and parsley to the farro. Drizzle with ⅓ cup olive oil and toss gently to combine. Season with salt and pepper. Transfer to a serving dish and serve.

COOK'S
tip

COOLING: *Transferring the toasted nuts to a bowl to cool allows you to toss them periodically to speed up cooling. It prevents "carryover cooking" from the hot pan, which can cause the nuts to overcook.*

11
Sandwiches

When the Earl of Sandwich, an eighteenth-century
English nobleman, decided to put cheese
and meat between two slices of bread rather than stop
his card game to eat, a legend was born.

It wasn't that no one had ever eaten meat between bread slices before (in fact, European peasants had been doing it long before, and some say the Passover "hillel" sandwich made with matzo may be the oldest of them all), but the name stuck and its popularity grew. Today, sandwiches are well loved all over the world, whether it's ham and butter on a baguette in France, *cemitas* and *tortas* in Latin America, a *banh mi* in Vietnam, or a falafel sandwich in the Middle East. They're the ultimate fast food, eaten on the go, packed in school lunches, or devoured in a rush at your desk. Though sandwiches are ubiquitous, we believe they deserve to be elevated, in the sense that they should be made with care and the best ingredients.

The art of sandwich making teaches us to transform ordinary products into something greater. Building an amazing sandwich comes down to a few basic principles, but begins with great bread. The next step is high-quality condiments, homemade if you can make them: As you'll discover in the following recipes, mayonnaise, aioli, or red onion marmalade made from scratch will dramatically transform a sandwich from good to stellar. Crisp, tart pickles are a sandwich's best ally. Extend the season for your favorite vegetables by preserving them. That way, you'll be stocked with homemade pickles to use as a condiment or sidekick for big-flavored sandwiches like muffalettas and Cubanos. Of course, sandwiches are the perfect vehicle for elevating leftovers, particularly when it comes to roasted meats. That's why we've included combinations that rely on roasted meats from other chapters (cold roast beef with onion marmalade or thinly sliced roasted lamb with aioli and arugula on ciabatta).

Tools to Have on Hand

- Salad spinner
- Serrated knife
- Mason jars with sealable lids

Keys to Success

1. Choose the right bread, of the highest quality.
Every great sandwich starts with great bread. Choose
bread that's the right texture—sturdier breads for heartier
sandwich fillings, lighter breads for softer fillings—but
make sure the bread is still easy to bite through. Toasting
bread with a drizzle of olive oil, or directly in the pan after
cooking your bacon or meat, does more than add flavor
and a crisp texture. The fat creates a barrier to moist
ingredients, such as juicy tomatoes or cucumbers, that
keeps the bread from getting soggy. Spreading mayonnaise
or butter on the bread serves the same purpose.

**2. Choose components with care and season
them.** Every ingredient in your sandwich serves a
purpose and should be chosen with care and with
freshness and flavor in mind. Choose in-season
vegetables—say no to mealy, out-of-season tomatoes.
Fresh lettuce leaves—ruffled leaves of green, red, or
butter lettuce—will have more flavor than prepacked
baby lettuce. To make lots of pickles, buy produce at peak
season, and buy in bulk. Lightly seasoning your vegetables
(such as dressing your arugula with olive oil, salt, and
pepper or sprinkling your tomatoes with a little flaky
salt) before adding them to your sandwich is a small but
important step that will lead to more flavor throughout.

3. Balance flavors and textures. Building the perfect
sandwich means a mix of flavors and textures—think
toasted bread, creamy spread, tender meat, crisp lettuce,
juicy tomato, and the crunchy bite of pickles.

4. Condiments are key—be generous. Condiments
can make or break a sandwich, which is why we encourage
you to make your own. Mayonnaise and mustards are
classics, of course, but don't be afraid to branch out to
all kinds of sauces and spreads like pestos, chutneys,
and dressings. Don't be afraid to be generous with your
condiments as they add the key element of moisture—no
one wants a dry sandwich.

5. Build it better. A sandwich that falls apart is a very
sad thing indeed. Layer denser items like meat on the
bottom of the sandwich and lighter items like vegetables
on top. If a filling isn't easy to bite through (say, broccoli
rabe for a classic roast pork sandwich), cut it into a smaller,
uniform size so it doesn't pull out when you take a bite.

All-American Burgers

The recipe for this remarkable burger has been perfected by our chefs over many years. There are a few elements that make it really special when it all comes together. First, onions that are gently dehydrated in the oven create that familiar, savory bite throughout. Second, use a light hand when combining the ground meat with the seasonings (overmixing will result in a tough burger) and make the patties very thin as they will shrink once cooked. The best part, however, has to be our tangy "special sauce"—don't be afraid to slather it on.

These thin patties will cook in a flash, so have the other components ready—lettuce sliced, condiments good to go— so you can show your stuff as a short-order cook.

BURGERS

1 small onion, small diced

Kosher salt and freshly ground black pepper

¾ pound ground beef (80% lean)

2 potato burger buns, halved horizontally

1 tablespoon unsalted butter

4 slices American cheese

¼ cup drained Pour-Over Pickles (page 260)

½ cup loosely packed, finely shredded iceberg or romaine lettuce

SPECIAL SAUCE

½ cup mayonnaise (page 259)

¼ cup ketchup

2 tablespoons sweet pickle relish, drained

½ teaspoon mustard powder (such as Colman's)

½ teaspoon garlic powder

½ teaspoon onion powder

¼ teaspoon sugar

❶ Dehydrate the onion. Preheat the oven to 325°F. Spread the onion on a small sheet pan in a single, even layer. Season with salt and pepper. Bake for 25 to 27 minutes, until shriveled and just beginning to brown around the edges. Remove from the oven and set aside to cool.

❷ Form the burgers. Place the ground beef in a large bowl and season with ½ teaspoon salt and ¼ teaspoon pepper. Use your hands to gently mix until just combined. Divide the beef into 4 equal-sized balls. Place the balls a few inches apart, between two layers of waxed paper. Press the balls into thin patties, ⅛ to ¼ inch thick, 4½ inches in diameter. Chill the patties in the refrigerator for at least 5 minutes.

❸ Make the sauce. In a small bowl, combine the mayonnaise, ketchup, relish, mustard powder, garlic powder, onion powder, and sugar. Season with salt and pepper.

RECIPE CONTINUES

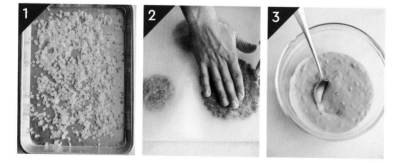

4 **Toast the buns.** Heat a large cast-iron skillet on medium-high. Working in batches, toast the buns in the dry pan, cut side down, for 1 to 2 minutes, until lightly browned. Transfer to a clean, dry work surface. Spread a thin layer of sauce on the bun bottoms and tops.

5 **Cook the burgers.** Remove the patties from the refrigerator. In the same pan used to toast the buns, melt the butter on medium-high. Right before cooking, season the top side of the patties with salt. Place two of the patties in the pan, salted side down. Season the top with salt. Cook for 2 minutes on the first side, or until browned. Flip the burgers and cook for 1 minute more, or until browned. Transfer to the bun bottoms and immediately top each burger with a slice of cheese. Place the remaining two patties in the pan, salted side down. Season the top with salt. Cook for 2 minutes on the first side, or until browned. Flip the burgers and top each with a slice of cheese. Cook 1 minute more, or until browned and the cheese is melted. Immediately transfer the cooked patties to the cheese-topped burgers. Let stand for 1 minute to allow the top patty to melt the cheese on the bottom patty.

6 **Assemble the burgers.** Top each burger with 1 tablespoon onion, a few pickle slices, a small handful of lettuce, and the bun tops. Transfer to serving plates and serve.

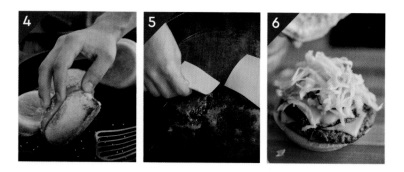

HOMEMADE MAYONNAISE

Makes 3 cups

Preparing homemade mayo can be daunting for some cooks, but that shouldn't be the case. Paying attention to a few key details makes the process easy, and the luscious, creamy results are more satisfying—and less sweet—than store-bought varieties. Chilling the ingredients and mixing bowl before whisking helps the ingredients emulsify. Since you're working with raw eggs,* use the safest, best pasture-raised variety you can find.

2 large egg yolks

4 teaspoons freshly squeezed lemon juice

2½ cups canola oil

2 tablespoons ice water

Kosher salt

❶ Make the mayonnaise base. Place the egg yolks in a large bowl, the lemon juice in a small bowl, and the canola oil in a large measuring cup. Chill them all in the refrigerator for 30 minutes. Remove from the refrigerator. Wrap the bottom of the chilled egg yolk bowl in a damp kitchen towel to prevent it from moving around. Add the lemon juice and ice water to the egg yolks and whisk to thoroughly combine.

❷ Drizzle in the oil. Slowly drizzle in the oil, whisking constantly and vigorously, until thoroughly combined and emulsified. Generously season with salt and whisk again to combine. Store in a sealed container in the refrigerator for up to 2 days.

EMULSIONS

Emulsification occurs when two liquids that for chemical reasons do not normally mix (oil and vinegar, for example) combine into one cohesive mixture, an emulsion. (Technically, one liquid is suspended in the other.) To make a longer-lasting emulsion, an "emulsifier" or "emulsifying agent" is needed—that means mustard for a vinaigrette and egg yolks for mayonnaise, aioli, or Caesar dressing. The emulsifier stabilizes the mixture by surrounding the oil droplets, preventing them from recombining—in other words, it acts as a bridge that connects the two opposing liquids. Another essential process in making an emulsion is breaking up the particles in the liquids so that the emulsifier can do its work. This requires sheer force, whether from vigorous whisking, shaking in a jar, or the rotating blades of a blender.

Most emulsions begin by combining the water-based liquid (vinegar, lemon juice) with the emulsifier (mustard, egg yolk). The fat-based ingredient (oil for a vinaigrette or butter for a *beurre blanc*) should be incorporated slowly and gradually. You'll know that your mixture is emulsified when it is thickened and completely combined.

For emulsions such as mayonnaise or aioli, if the mixture "breaks" (as in separating into its components), use more emulsifier to fix it: Whisk together an additional egg yolk, 1 teaspoon water, and ¼ teaspoon vinegar in a separate bowl. Slowly whisk the broken emulsion into the egg yolk until combined. When emulsions like vinaigrettes separate, simply whisk again until recombined.

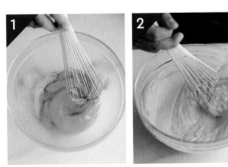

Consuming raw eggs may increase your risk of food-borne illness.

POUR-OVER PICKLES

Makes 1 quart

Making pour-over or refrigerator pickles is a quick way to capture seasonal vegetables for future enjoyment—and much easier than the boiling-water-bath and jar-sealing process required for canning. Thin-skinned kirby cucumbers make the snappiest pickles, but the following method also works for other watery or thin-skinned vegetables, including Persian cucumbers, peeled daikon, and watermelon radishes. This recipe creates subtly sweet pickles that would honor any cheeseburger, but feel free to follow your whim and add other aromatics like fresh bay leaves, sliced onion, coriander seeds, fennel fronds, or sliced fresh chile peppers such as jalapeño, serrano, or red Fresno. These are ready to go the day after they're made, but they taste even better after they've pickled for a week. They can be stored in the refrigerator for up to 6 months.

1½ pounds kirby cucumbers, thinly sliced into rounds

2 sprigs dill

Kosher salt

2 cups white wine vinegar

1 cup water

⅓ cup sugar

2 dried chiles de arbol (optional)

3 cloves garlic, peeled

❶ Prepare the cucumbers. In a nonreactive, heatproof bowl, toss the cucumbers with the dill and 1½ teaspoons salt.

❷ Make the pickling liquid. In a small saucepan, combine the vinegar, water, 2 tablespoons salt, the sugar, chiles (if using), and garlic. Bring to a simmer on high, stirring occasionally to make sure nothing has settled to the bottom. Simmer until the salt and sugar have dissolved. Remove from the heat and pour the liquid over the cucumbers.

❸ Let the cucumbers pickle. Let stand for 9 to 11 minutes, until most of the skin on the cucumbers has turned pale green. Partially fill a larger bowl with ice. Place the entire bowl of cucumbers in the bowl of ice to cool completely.

❹ Store the pickles. Use a slotted spoon to transfer the pickles to an airtight container. Pour the pickling liquid (including the dill, chiles, and garlic) over the pickles to cover. (You may have extra pickling liquid.) Tightly cover the container and refrigerate for at least 24 hours before using.

COOK'S tip

SAVE THE PICKLING LIQUID: *If you have extra pickling liquid, don't waste it—use it as a salad dressing base (instead of vinegar or lemon), stir it into mayonnaise, or use it as a marinade for roasted or grilled vegetables.*

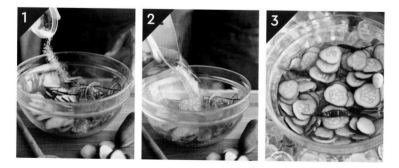

4

Muffaletta

The quintessential New Orleans lunch and the pride of its Italian community is a savory, multilayered force to be reckoned with. Layers of cured meats, cheese, and a tangy salad of briny olives and pickled vegetables are combined on a sturdy Italian loaf that can hold the ingredients without getting soggy. After it's assembled, the sandwich is wrapped and "pressed" or weighted down so the piquant flavors meld and the bread absorbs the seasoned oil (the primary condiment here). This sandwich can be made on individual rolls or on one large round loaf that's then quartered, as it's done at Central Grocery in New Orleans, where the first muffaletta sandwich is said to have been made in 1906.

In the spirit of Crescent City, serve this two-handed sandwich with plenty of napkins (the best versions are a little bit messy and that's part of the fun), a cold Abita beer, and Zapp's potato chips.

½ cup chopped green olives

1½ cups Giardiniera (page 264)

Extra virgin olive oil

1 large round bread loaf (preferably seeded Italian)

Kosher salt and freshly ground black pepper

¼ pound sliced salami

½ pound sliced ham

½ pound sliced mortadella

¼ pound sliced swiss or provolone cheese

❶ Prepare the ingredients.
In a bowl, combine the olives, giardiniera, and ¼ cup olive oil. Cut the bread in half horizontally. Place the bread on a clean, dry work surface, cut side up. Drizzle with olive oil and season with salt and pepper.

❷ Assemble the sandwich.
Layer the bread bottom with the salami, ham, mortadella, and cheese. Mound the olive-giardiniera mixture in the center of the sandwich, leaving a 1-inch border around the edge. Drizzle with olive oil. Cover with the bread top. Wrap tightly in several layers of plastic wrap.

❸ Weight the sandwich.
Place heavy pans on top of the sandwich. Let stand, weighted, at room temperature for 1 hour, or refrigerate overnight. Unwrap, cut into quarters, and serve.

GIARDINIERA

Makes about 10 cups

Giardiniera is an Italian American mix of seasonal vegetables pickled in white vinegar. The pickles are an adaptation of a traditional dish served around Christmas in Naples, where it was a dish you ate on its own, rather than as a condiment, as we do with our Muffaletta (page 262). This recipe uses a pretty classic mix of vegetables (cauliflower, onion, and celery), but feel free to follow the method for a single vegetable (such as green tomatoes, diced zucchini, sunchokes, or baby turnips) that you want to preserve.

2 teaspoons whole fennel seed

6 dried chiles de arbol

2 bay leaves

1 tablespoon whole coriander seed

2 teaspoons whole mustard seed

6 cloves garlic, peeled and lightly crushed

1 quart water

2 quarts white wine vinegar

7 tablespoons kosher salt

1½ cups sugar

1 small head cauliflower (about ¾ to 1 pound), cut into florets

2 stalks celery, sliced ¼ inch thick

3 carrots, peeled and thinly sliced

2 fennel bulbs, trimmed, halved, cored, and thinly sliced

1 large white onion, medium diced

1 tablespoon dried oregano

❶ **Prepare the sachet.** Cut a 6-inch square of cheesecloth. Place the fennel seed, dried chiles, bay leaves, coriander seed, mustard seed, and garlic in the center of the cheesecloth; wrap together to create a small sachet. (If the cheesecloth for the sachet isn't as tightly woven as you'd like, cut out another square and double-layer them so the seeds won't fall through.) Use butcher's twine to tie it securely closed.

❷ **Make the pickling liquid.** In a large, nonreactive (such as stainless steel) stockpot, combine the sachet, water, vinegar, salt, and sugar. Bring to a simmer on medium-high and cook, stirring occasionally, for 10 minutes or until the sugar and salt are completely dissolved.

❸ **Cook the vegetables.** Reduce the heat to medium. Add the cauliflower and cook, stirring occasionally, for 6 to 8 minutes, until it begins to soften. Add the celery and carrots and cook, stirring occasionally, for 6 to 7 minutes more, until they begin to soften. Add the fennel and onion and cook, stirring occasionally, for 4 to 5 minutes, until the fennel is crisp-tender. While the giardiniera is cooking, fill a very large bowl with ice and water.

❹ **Finish the giardiniera.** Remove from the heat and stir in the oregano. Transfer the vegetables and liquid to a large heatproof bowl. Place that bowl in the ice water to cool. Discard the sachet.

❺ **Store the giardiniera.** When the giardiniera is cool, use a slotted spoon to transfer the vegetables to airtight containers. Pour the pickling liquid over the vegetables to cover. (You may have extra pickling liquid.) Cover tightly and refrigerate for at least 24 hours before using. Store in the refrigerator for up to 6 months.

Cubanos

Pressing a cold sandwich to make it a warm and crispy one transforms its components from good to extraordinary. There's no better example of this technique's possibilities than a Cubano, which was a favorite of cigar factory and sugar mill workers who traveled between Cuba and Florida, where it became the sandwich as we know it today. The classic Cuban sandwich combines sliced pork shoulder and ham with pickles, cheese, and the bright pop of spicy mustard on a buttered roll. (The keys to our Cubano are all the homemade ingredients.) After assembly, the sandwich is pressed and flattened on a hot skillet or griddle, where the butter browns the bread and the sandwich fillings meld together. If you don't have a heavy enough pot to press down the sandwiches, fill a regular pot with large cans from your pantry.

4 (6-inch) hero rolls

¼ cup (½ stick) unsalted butter, at room temperature

4 teaspoons Dijon mustard

¼ cup mayonnaise (store-bought or homemade, page 259)

½ pound thinly sliced swiss cheese

1 cup drained Pour-Over Pickles (page 260) or thinly sliced dill pickles

½ pound thinly sliced leftover roast pork shoulder (page 80; about 6 slices)

½ pound thinly sliced ham (such as prosciutto cotto, boiled ham, or smoked ham)

❶ **Butter the bread.** Slice the rolls in half horizontally. Spread the outside of each half with butter. Place on a sheet pan, cut side up.

❷ **Build the sandwich.** Spread each roll bottom with 1 teaspoon mustard and each roll top with 1 tablespoon mayonnaise. Cut the cheese slices in half and divide among the roll bottoms. Top with a layer of pickles, roast pork, and ham. Cover with the roll tops.

❸ **Griddle the sandwiches.** Heat a large cast-iron skillet over medium-low until hot. Working in batches if necessary, carefully transfer the sandwiches to the skillet. Cover with aluminum foil and place a large heavy pot on top. Cook, occasionally pressing down on the pot, for 4 to 5 minutes, until the bottoms are golden brown and crispy. Flip the sandwiches and replace the aluminum foil and heavy pot. Cook for 4 to 5 minutes, until the second side is golden brown and the cheese is fully melted. Transfer to a cutting board and cut the sandwiches in half at an angle. Transfer to serving dishes and serve.

Roasted Lamb Sandwiches

Serves 4

This recipe is another lesson in turning last night's dinner into today's lunch. This sandwich harks back to the restaurant days of one of our chefs, when he and his fellow line cooks would use the restaurant's leftover roasted lamb to make these amazing sandwiches. Sometimes leftovers have a stigma attached to them, but these sandwiches will have you hoping for leftovers every time you make roasted lamb. Simply dressed arugula and a spread of homemade aioli round out these hearty sandwiches.

4 small ciabatta rolls, halved horizontally

Extra virgin olive oil

2 cups arugula leaves or mixed greens

Juice of ½ lemon

Kosher salt and freshly ground black pepper

½ cup Aioli (page 272)

½ pound thinly sliced leftover leg of lamb (page 70), at room temperature (8 to 10 slices)

1 **Toast the rolls.** Preheat the broiler on high. Place the rolls on a sheet pan, cut side up. Generously brush each half with olive oil. Toast under the broiler for 2 to 4 minutes, until golden brown. Remove from the broiler.

2 **Dress the arugula.** Place the arugula in a large bowl. Drizzle with the lemon juice and 1 tablespoon olive oil. Season with salt and pepper. Toss to combine.

3 **Make the sandwiches.** Spread the cut sides of the bread with the aioli. Divide the lamb among the bread bottoms. Top with with arugula and cover with the bread tops. Transfer to serving dishes and serve.

Roast Beef Sandwiches

Serves 4

Whether it's as a dipped "Italian beef" in Chicago, served on a soft seeded roll on the North Shore outside Boston, "on weck" in Western New York, pit beef in Baltimore, or a po' boy topped with "debris" (pan drippings) in New Orleans—in America, there are a lot of ways to love a roast beef sandwich. Our version here is another lesson in transforming delicious leftover roasted meats with a few choice condiments. We keep it pretty simple (and neater than some of our other favorites) with an easy herbed mayo and homemade red onion marmalade.

8 (½-inch-thick) slices whole grain bread

Extra virgin olive oil

Kosher salt

¼ cup mayonnaise (page 259)

2 tablespoons nonpareil capers in brine, drained and finely chopped

¼ cup finely chopped fresh flat-leaf parsley

1 tablespoon thinly sliced fresh chives

¾ pound thinly sliced medium-rare roast beef (page 94), at room temperature (about 8 slices)

Freshly ground black pepper

1 teaspoon red wine vinegar

¼ cup Red Onion Marmalade (page 273)

¼ pound thinly sliced Comté cheese

8 butter lettuce leaves

❶ **Toast the bread.** Preheat the broiler on high. Place the bread on a sheet pan and generously brush each side with olive oil. Season lightly with salt and toast under the broiler for 2 to 4 minutes, until golden brown. Remove from the oven and set aside to cool slightly for 2 to 3 minutes.

❷ **Make the herbed mayonnaise.** In a small bowl, combine the mayonnaise, capers, parsley, and chives.

❸ **Build the sandwich.** Season the sliced roast beef with salt and freshly ground black pepper. In a large bowl, combine the lettuce, vinegar, and 2 teaspoons olive oil. Toss to coat. Place the bread on a clean, dry work surface. Spread the herb mayonnaise on four of the slices. Spread the onion marmalade on the other four slices. Top the marmalade with the cheese, roast beef, and lettuce. Cover with the mayonnaise-topped bread slices. Transfer to serving dishes and serve.

AIOLI

Makes about 2 cups

Literally translating to "oil and garlic," aioli (or *aïoli*) is garlicky mayonnaise, the quintessential Provençal condiment. This pungent sauce enhances everything from crispy *frites* to fish stew, crudités, and roasted meat sandwiches. While mayonnaise relies on canola oil for its neutral flavor, aioli is traditionally made with olive oil. As with mayonnaise (page 259), since you're using raw eggs,* seek out the safest, best pasture-raised variety.

2 cloves garlic, finely grated into a paste

2 large egg yolks

2 tablespoons freshly squeezed lemon juice

1½ cups extra virgin olive oil

1 tablespoon ice water

Kosher salt

❶ **Make the aioli base.** Place the garlic and egg yolks in a large bowl, the lemon juice in a small cup, and the olive oil in a large measuring cup. Chill them all in the refrigerator for 30 minutes. Remove from the refrigerator. Wrap the bottom of the chilled egg yolk bowl in a damp kitchen towel to prevent it from moving around. Add the lemon juice and ice water to the egg yolks and whisk until pale yellow.

❷ **Drizzle in the oil.** Slowly drizzle in the olive oil, whisking constantly and vigorously, until thoroughly combined and emulsified. Generously season with salt and whisk again to combine. Store in a sealed container in the refrigerator for up to 2 days.

Consuming raw eggs may increase your risk of food-borne illness.

RED ONION MARMALADE

Makes 1 cup

With a pop of sharpness from whole mustard seed, this sweet-and-tart condiment is made by gently cooking onion, sugar, and vinegar down to a jam-like consistency. This recipe calls for a red onion but feel free to use a sweet yellow variety. Stored in an airtight container in the refrigerator, the marmalade will keep for up to 2 weeks.

¼ cup extra virgin olive oil

2 tablespoons whole yellow mustard seed

1 large red onion, small diced (about 2 cups)

Kosher salt

½ cup plus 2 tablespoons sugar

2 cups apple cider vinegar

❶ **Toast the mustard seed.** In a nonreactive saucepan, heat the olive oil on medium until hot. Add the mustard seed. Cook, stirring occasionally, for 1 to 2 minutes, until toasted and beginning to pop.

❷ **Add the onion and sugar.** Add the onion and season with 1½ teaspoons salt. Cook, stirring occasionally, for 4 to 5 minutes, until softened. Add the sugar and cook, stirring constantly, for 30 seconds to 1 minute, until thoroughly combined.

❸ **Finish the marmalade.** Add the vinegar and heat to simmering on medium-high. Cook, stirring occasionally, for 18 to 20 minutes, until the mixture is thickened and has a jam-like consistency. Transfer to a large plate and spread into a thin, even layer to cool. Store in a sealed container in the refrigerator for up to 2 weeks.

12
Risotto

Risotto with Parmigiano-Reggiano Cheese 278 •
Pea & Pancetta Risotto with Mint 280 • Wild Mushroom Risotto 282 •
Beet & Barley Risotto 285 • Farrotto with Roasted Squash 288 •
Risotto-Style Tubetti with Saffron 290

In Italian cuisine, risotto is an iconic dish that dates back to the eighteenth century.

The earliest forms of risotto simply meant boiling rice in a large pot with broth and other ingredients, particularly in northern Italy. The shorter risotto-style grain became more popular and developed because of this culinary preference (versus the more Arabic-influenced pilaf-style dishes in the south).

There are only a few ingredients in a basic Parmigiano-Reggiano risotto, but the technique creates surprising depth of flavor and risotto's famous creamy texture. Risotto is made from a short- to medium-grain rice with a high starch content. As the grains are stirred, the starches break down into a milky consistency and begin to bind the other ingredients in the pot. There are about a dozen common risotto varieties (with more always being developed). Arborio rice is most commonly used in the United States (where these days it's also cultivated). Italians use several different types of rice to make their country's beloved dish. Known as the "king of Italian rice," carnaroli rice is considered the best. The variety is grown in the northern region of Italy and has an even higher starch content than Arborio, resulting in a lush, velvety consistency.

The recipes in this chapter run the gamut from a basic and endlessly versatile Parmigiano-Reggiano risotto to seasonal varieties with a more distinct character, like pea and pancetta risotto with mint or wild mushroom risotto. We'll also explore applying risotto's technique to other grains, like farro and barley, and even small pasta shapes. You'll be amazed at how the process transforms grains and noodles into a distinctive, richly flavored dish with an entirely different personality.

Tools to Have on Hand

- Heavy, high-sided saucepan
- Wooden spoon

Keys to Success

1. Start with the best ingredients. We use Arborio rice in our recipes because it's a great option and most widely available. If you can find it, carnaroli rice is often considered the best risotto rice. It comes from the Piedmont and Lombardy regions and is available online. You can use the two varieties interchangeably. To maintain the best flavor, store rice away from light in a cool area, and after the rice package has been opened, store it in the freezer. If you need to use store-bought stock, buy a high-quality, low-sodium brand, preferably organic. The wine you add to risotto should be good enough to drink. For the best results, use freshly grated Parmigiano-Reggiano cheese.

2. Do sweat the small stuff. Risotto is built on layers of flavor, a process that begins by sweating aromatics (such as onions, shallots, scallions, garlic) and herbs in butter or olive oil, until mostly tender but not browned. Don't rush this step.

3. Toast the rice. Before adding the liquid, make sure you sauté the rice with the aromatics until the grains of rice turn opaque and take on a toasted, nutty aroma. This small step will create a risotto with a much deeper flavor.

4. Add the cooking liquid gradually. So you won't lower the heat in the pan and disrupt the cooking, you'll add warm cooking liquid at intervals, allowing the rice to slowly absorb the liquid before you pour in another ladleful. Having a small pot of warmed stock on the stove keeps the risotto process moving.

5. Finish with fat. When the rice is cooked al dente, swirl in a touch of butter, cheese, or crème fraîche to elevate the flavors and create the creamiest texture.

COOK'S tip

PARM RINDS: *Whenever you grate Parmigiano-Reggiano cheese, save the rinds. Wrap them in foil and freeze for up to several weeks, until needed. Simmering the rinds in stock for risotto, soup, white beans, and other recipes infuses the broth with a rich cheese flavor. Discard the rind after cooking and proceed with the recipe.*

Risotto with Parmigiano-Reggiano Cheese

Although there are just a handful of ingredients in this deceptively simple preparation (sometimes called *risotto bianco* or white risotto), a few simple techniques draw out the most flavor from these humble ingredients: Simmering the stock with the Parmigiano rind creates a more flavorful broth. Toasting the rice before adding the liquid gives the final dish a deep, nutty flavor. And finishing the rice with a generous amount of freshly grated cheese creates a double dose of richness. With these basic steps, this recipe becomes a template that puts any risotto within your reach.

6 cups chicken stock (page 174)

Rind from Parmigiano-Reggiano cheese (optional)

1 tablespoon extra virgin olive oil

4 tablespoons (½ stick) unsalted butter

2 cups minced white onion (1 large onion)

2 cloves garlic, finely chopped

Kosher salt

2 cups Arborio rice

½ cup dry white wine (such as sauvignon blanc or pinot grigio)

2 cups freshly grated Parmigiano-Reggiano cheese (about 8 ounces), plus more for serving

Freshly ground black pepper

2 tablespoons finely chopped fresh flat-leaf parsley (optional)

❶ Warm the stock. In a saucepan, heat the chicken stock with the Parmigiano rind (if using) to simmering on medium. Turn off the heat.

❷ Sweat the onions and garlic. While the stock comes to a simmer, in a large, high-sided saucepan, heat the olive oil and 2 tablespoons of the butter on medium. Add the onion and garlic and season with ¼ teaspoon salt. Cook, stirring occasionally, for 5 to 7 minutes, until softened and fragrant but not browned.

❸ Toast the rice. Add the rice and cook, stirring frequently, for 4 to 6 minutes, until lightly toasted and fragrant. Add the wine and cook, stirring occasionally, for 1 to 2 minutes, until absorbed.

❹ Add the stock. Add 2 cups of the stock and cook, stirring frequently, for 4 to 6 minutes, until most of the liquid has been absorbed. Repeat with the remaining 4 cups stock, adding the stock 2 cups at a time and stirring until most of the liquid is absorbed before each addition, for 10 to 15 minutes total. (The rice should be al dente and the risotto creamy and thickened. Depending on the age and source of the rice, you may have some leftover stock.)

❺ Finish the risotto. Remove from the heat. Add the Parmigiano and the remaining 2 tablespoons butter. Stir constantly for 30 seconds to 1 minute, until thoroughly combined. Season with salt and pepper. Transfer to a serving dish. Top with more Parmigiano and the parsley, and serve.

Pea & Pancetta Risotto
with Mint

This recipe shows how easy it is to transform your basic "white risotto" into many other risottos with the addition of seasonal vegetables and flavor-packed elements like pancetta. In this recipe, the sweet flavor and tender-crisp texture of English peas play beautifully against browned, peppery bits of pancetta. Be careful not to overcook the peas. Briefly blanching them and then stirring them into the risotto at the end of cooking is the best way to maintain their delicate taste and vibrant hue; the same method works well for other green vegetables like asparagus.

6 cups chicken stock (page 174)

Kosher salt

1 pound fresh English peas, shelled (about 1¼ cups)

4 tablespoons (½ stick) unsalted butter

¼ pound pancetta, finely chopped

2 cups minced white onion (1 large onion)

2 cups Arborio rice

½ cup dry white wine (such as sauvignon blanc or pinot grigio)

¼ cup crème fraîche

Freshly ground black pepper

1 tablespoon fresh mint leaves, finely chopped

½ cup freshly grated Parmigiano-Reggiano cheese

2 tablespoons Pecorino Romano cheese, plus more for serving

❶ Warm the stock and cook the peas. In a saucepan, heat the chicken stock to simmering on medium. Turn off the heat. Fill a large bowl with ice water. Heat a large pot of generously salted water to boiling on high. Add the peas and cook for 3 to 4 minutes, until bright green and slightly tender. Drain thoroughly and transfer to the bowl of ice water; let stand until cool. Drain thoroughly again and pat dry with paper towels.

❷ Cook the pancetta. In a large, high-sided saucepan on medium-low, melt 2 tablespoons of the butter. Add the pancetta and cook, stirring occasionally, for 6 to 8 minutes, until browned and crispy. Place a small fine-mesh strainer over a bowl. Transfer the pancetta to the strainer, leaving any browned bits (fond) in the pan. Let stand for 30 seconds to 1 minute, until most of the fat has drained off; set aside the fat and the pancetta separately.

❸ Sweat the onion. Return 2 tablespoons of the pancetta fat to the fond; heat on medium until hot. Add the onion and season with ¼ teaspoon salt. Cook, stirring occasionally, for 4 to 6 minutes, until softened and fragrant but not browned.

❹ Toast the rice. Add the rice and cook, stirring frequently, for 4 to 6 minutes, until lightly toasted and fragrant. Add the wine and cook, stirring occasionally, for 1 to 2 minutes, until absorbed.

❺ Add the stock. Add 2 cups of the stock and cook, stirring frequently, for 4 to 6 minutes, until most of the liquid has been absorbed. Repeat with the remaining 4 cups stock, adding the stock 2 cups at a time and stirring until most of the liquid is absorbed before each addition, for 10 to 15 minutes total. (The rice should be al dente and the risotto creamy and thickened. Depending on the age and source of the rice, you may have some leftover stock.)

6 Finish the risotto. Add the pancetta and peas. Cook, stirring constantly, for 1 to 2 minutes, until warmed through. Stir in the crème fraîche and the remaining 2 tablespoons butter; season with salt and pepper. Cook, stirring constantly, for 30 seconds to 1 minute, until thoroughly combined. Remove from the heat. Stir in the mint, Parmigiano, and pecorino, until thoroughly combined. Transfer to a serving dish, top with more pecorino, and serve.

Wild Mushroom Risotto

Porcini are highly prized mushrooms named after the Italian word for "piglets" (which could refer to their stubby, fat stems). Though fresh porcini are wonderful themselves (albeit harder to find), dried porcini have their own allure, as the drying process concentrates their earthy flavor. Using both dried porcini and fresh wild mushrooms creates layers of interest in a dish brimming with deep, nuanced flavors. Adding other liquids besides stock is a great way to create depth of flavor and echo the key ingredients in risotto. Here, the soaking liquid from the dried porcini creates a quick mushroom broth that adds even more mushroom flavor to the risotto.

1 cup dried porcini mushrooms (about 2 ounces)

2 cups hot water

6 cups chicken stock (page 174)

6 tablespoons (¾ stick) unsalted butter

½ pound fresh wild mushrooms (such as yellow oyster, maitake, or king trumpet), cleaned, trimmed, and cut into bite-size pieces

1 clove garlic, peeled and lightly crushed

1 large sprig rosemary

1 sprig thyme

Kosher salt and freshly ground black pepper

2 tablespoons dry Marsala wine

Extra virgin olive oil

1 cup minced shallots (about 2 large shallots)

2 cups Arborio rice

½ cup dry white wine (such as sauvignon blanc or pinot grigio)

¼ cup crème fraîche

½ cup freshly grated Parmigiano-Reggiano cheese

❶ Soak the porcini. In a medium bowl, combine the dried porcini and hot water. Let stand for at least 10 minutes. Transfer the porcini to a cutting board, leaving the soaking water in the bowl. Set the soaking water aside. Coarsely chop the porcini.

❷ Warm the stock and start the fresh mushrooms. In a saucepan, heat the chicken stock to simmering on medium. Turn off the heat. In a large, high-sided saucepan on medium, melt 4 tablespoons of the butter until it begins to foam. Add the wild mushrooms. Cook, stirring occasionally, for 2 to 4 minutes, until lightly browned and softened. Add the garlic, rosemary, and thyme and cook, stirring occasionally, for 5 to 7 minutes, until fragrant and the mushrooms have deeply browned.

❸ Finish the mushrooms. Add the porcini and season with 1¼ teaspoons salt and ¼ teaspoon pepper. Cook, stirring occasionally, for 1 to 2 minutes, until thoroughly combined. Add the Marsala and cook, stirring occasionally, for 30 seconds to 1 minute, until the liquid has been absorbed. Add the reserved porcini water, strained to remove grit, if necessary. Cook, stirring occasionally, for 11 to 13 minutes, until the liquid is almost entirely evaporated. Carefully remove and discard the thyme, rosemary, and garlic.

COOK'S *tip*

GRIT-FREE: *Dried mushrooms can harbor grit. If you feel any in the soaking liquid, strain it through a paper towel–lined fine-mesh strainer.*

RECIPE CONTINUES

④ Sweat the shallots and toast the rice. In a large, high-sided saucepan, heat 2 tablespoons olive oil and the remaining 2 tablespoons of the butter on medium-low until the butter is melted. Add the shallots and season with ½ teaspoon salt. Cook, stirring occasionally, for 2 to 4 minutes, until softened and fragrant but not browned. Add the rice and cook, stirring frequently, for 4 to 6 minutes, until lightly toasted and fragrant. Add the white wine and cook, stirring occasionally, for 30 seconds to 1 minute, until absorbed.

⑤ Add the stock. Add 2 cups of the stock and cook, stirring frequently, for 6 to 8 minutes, until most of the liquid has been absorbed. Repeat with the remaining 4 cups stock, adding the stock 2 cups at a time and stirring until most of the liquid is absorbed before each addition, for 12 to 16 minutes total. (The rice should be al dente and the risotto creamy and thickened. Depending on the age and source of the rice, you may have some leftover stock.)

⑥ Finish the risotto. Add the mushrooms and cook, stirring constantly, for 30 seconds to 1 minute, until warmed through. Stir in the crème fraîche and cook, stirring occasionally, for 30 seconds to 1 minute, until thoroughly combined. Remove from the heat and stir in the Parmigiano. Season with salt and pepper. Transfer to a serving dish and serve.

Beet & Barley Risotto

Traditional risotto is made with short- or medium-grain rice such as Arborio or carnaroli, but the same method can be used to create similar results with other flavorful grains like barley and farro. In this recipe, beets (the bulb, stems, and leaves) join forces with barley to create a striking ruby-red risotto. As with rice, the barley is toasted in the pan until puffed to coax out the grain's nutty quality. Barley won't give off starch the same way as rice, but the beets will help make it creamy. A garnish of ricotta salata—you could also use crumbled goat cheese—balances the sweet and earthy flavors with a creamy, salty edge.

2 red or yellow beets (about 1½ pounds total), or 1½ pounds baby beets, stems and leaves reserved

Extra virgin olive oil

Kosher salt

10 cups chicken stock (page 174)

2 tablespoons unsalted butter

1 cup minced yellow onion (about 1 medium onion)

2 cloves garlic, minced

2 cups pearled barley

½ cup dry white wine (such as sauvignon blanc or pinot grigio)

¼ cup crème fraîche

2 teaspoons red wine vinegar

Freshly ground black pepper

¼ pound ricotta salata cheese, grated

❶ Prepare the beets. Preheat the oven to 425°F. Rinse the stems and greens (leaves) thoroughly. Thinly slice the stems and coarsely chop the leaves, keeping them separate. Trim off the stem ends of the bulbs; thoroughly scrub the bulbs under cold water.

❷ Roast and grate the beets. Arrange the beet bulbs in a small baking dish. Add enough water to come halfway up the sides of the beets. Drizzle with olive oil and season generously with salt. Cover the baking dish with aluminum foil and tightly seal. Roast for 1 hour, or until tender when pierced with a fork. When cool enough to handle, but still warm, use a paper towel and your fingers to gently rub the skin off the beets; discard the skins. Use a box grater to coarsely grate the beets. Set aside.

❸ Cook the beet greens. While the beets are roasting, heat a pot of salted water to boiling on high. Add the chopped beet greens (leaves) and cook for 4 to 6 minutes, until softened. Transfer to a fine-mesh strainer to drain; use a spoon to press down on the greens to release as much liquid as possible. Set aside.

COOK'S tip

BEETS: *Feel free to use yellow beets instead of red—their flavor is slightly milder, and the risotto won't have a bright red color. If baby beets are in season and available at the local market, use them. They are smaller and tend to be sweeter than their mature counterparts. Since they're smaller, they'll roast faster, so start checking for doneness after 30 minutes of roasting. Their greens are also more tender, so they'll need to be blanched for only 2 to 3 minutes.*

RECIPE CONTINUES

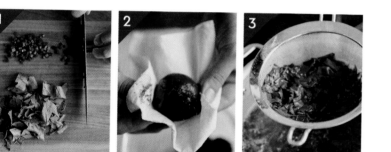

4 Warm the stock and sweat the aromatics. In a saucepan, heat the chicken stock to simmering on medium. Turn off the heat. In a large, high-sided saucepan, heat 2 tablespoons olive oil and 1 tablespoon of the butter on medium-low until the butter is melted. Add the onion, garlic, and beet stems and season with salt. Cook, stirring occasionally, for 3 to 5 minutes, until softened and fragrant but not browned.

5 Toast the barley. Add the barley. Cook, stirring occasionally, for 4 to 6 minutes, until the barley starts to puff slightly. Add the wine and cook, stirring frequently, for 30 seconds to 1 minute, until absorbed. Season with salt and stir to combine.

6 Add the stock. Add 2 cups of the stock and cook, stirring frequently, for 8 to 10 minutes, until most of the liquid has been absorbed. Repeat with the remaining 8 cups stock, adding the stock 2 cups at a time and stirring until most of the liquid is absorbed before each addition, for 22 to 28 minutes total. (The barley should be al dente and the risotto creamy and thickened. Depending on the age and source of the barley, you may have some leftover stock.)

7 Finish the risotto. Add the grated beets and cook, stirring frequently, for 2 to 3 minutes, until well combined. Add the beet greens and season with salt. Cook, stirring frequently, for 30 seconds to 1 minute, until warmed through. Add the crème fraîche, the remaining 1 tablespoon butter, and the vinegar. Cook, stirring constantly, for 2 to 3 minutes, until thoroughly combined and thickened. Remove from the heat. Season with salt and pepper. Transfer to a serving dish, top with the cheese, and serve.

Farrotto

with Roasted Squash

Hailing from the Veneto region of Italy, *farrotto* is a risotto-style dish made with farro, an ancient strain of hard wheat that has a nutty flavor and chewy bite. The technique—sautéing the grains with aromatics and adding warm cooking liquid at intervals while continuously stirring—breaks down the starches to mimic risotto's comforting consistency, but the whole grain results in a heartier character. Roasted butternut squash provides a creamy, hearty backdrop for this *farrotto*, but you can substitute other favorite winter squashes such as kabocha.

1 butternut squash (about 2 pounds)

4 cloves garlic: 2 cloves peeled and lightly crushed, 2 cloves minced

3 tablespoons thinly sliced sage leaves

Extra virgin olive oil

Kosher salt and freshly ground black pepper

8 cups vegetable stock (page 175)

¼ cup (½ stick) unsalted butter

1 cup minced yellow onion (about 1 medium onion)

2 cups semi-pearled farro

¼ cup dry Marsala wine

¼ cup dry white wine (such as sauvignon blanc or pinot grigio)

¼ cup heavy cream

2 tablespoons finely chopped fresh rosemary leaves

¼ teaspoon freshly grated nutmeg

½ cup freshly grated Parmigiano-Reggiano cheese

❶ Roast and mash the squash. Preheat the oven to 425°F. Cut off and discard the squash ends. Use a vegetable peeler to peel the squash. Cut apart the neck and bulb. Halve the bulb lengthwise; scoop out and discard the pulp and seeds, then medium-dice all the flesh. In a large bowl, combine the squash, the 2 crushed garlic cloves, and 1 tablespoon of the sage; drizzle with 2 tablespoons olive oil and season with 1 teaspoon salt and ¼ teaspoon pepper. Toss to coat. Transfer to a sheet pan and spread out in a single, even layer. Roast for about 45 minutes, until golden brown and tender when pierced with a fork. Remove from the oven. Transfer the squash and garlic to a large bowl and mash with a fork until smooth.

❷ Warm the stock and sweat the onion. In a saucepan, heat the vegetable stock to simmering on medium. Turn off the heat. In a large, high-sided saucepan, heat 2 tablespoons olive oil and the butter on medium-low until the butter is melted. Add the minced garlic and onion and season with ¼ teaspoon salt. Cook, stirring occasionally, for 5 to 7 minutes, until softened and fragrant but not browned.

❸ Toast the farro. Add the farro and cook, stirring frequently, for 4 to 6 minutes, until lightly toasted and fragrant. Add the Marsala and white wine. Cook, stirring occasionally, for 1 to 2 minutes, until absorbed. Season with 1 teaspoon salt.

❹ Add the stock. Add 2 cups of the stock and cook, stirring frequently, for 8 to 10 minutes, until most of the liquid has been absorbed. Repeat with the remaining 6 cups stock, adding the stock 2 cups at a time and stirring until most of the liquid is absorbed before each addition, for 20 to 25 minutes total. (The farro should be al dente and the risotto creamy and thickened.)

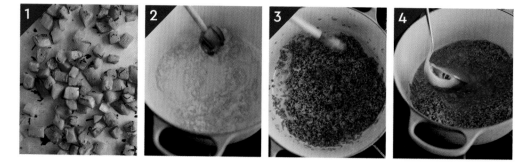

⑤ Finish the farrotto. Add the squash and cook, stirring frequently, for 2 to 4 minutes, until well combined. Add the cream, the remaining 2 tablespoons sage, the rosemary, and nutmeg. Season with salt and pepper. Cook, stirring frequently, for 1 to 2 minutes, until thoroughly combined. Remove from the heat and stir in the Parmigiano. Transfer to a serving dish and serve.

Risotto-Style Tubetti

with Saffron

Risotto is for more than just rice—small shapes of pasta like tubetti or ditalini can also be prepared using a risotto method that allows the noodles to absorb more flavor. This recipe is a take on one of the very first risotto recipes, *risotto alla milanese*, a very simple and elegant dish of rice, aromatics, broth, saffron, butter, and cheese. In this recipe, one of our chefs' oldest and most favorite preparations that we like to think of as fancy macaroni and cheese, tubetti are getting the same treatment. The pasta is sautéed with onions and saffron until it toasts and turns golden. Then, as with risotto, warm stock is added in increments, allowing the pasta to absorb the rich liquid while it's cooking.

5 cups chicken stock (page 174)

¼ cup extra virgin olive oil

1 cup minced yellow onion (about 1 medium onion)

Kosher salt

2 cups small tubetti pasta

½ teaspoon saffron threads

2 tablespoons unsalted butter

¼ cup freshly grated Parmigiano-Reggiano cheese, plus more for garnish

❶ Warm the stock and sweat the onion. In a saucepan, heat the chicken stock to simmering on medium. Turn off the heat. While the stock comes to a simmer, in a large, high-sided saucepan, heat the olive oil on medium until hot. Add the onion and season with 1 teaspoon salt. Cook, stirring occasionally, for 3 to 4 minutes, until softened and translucent but not browned.

❷ Toast the pasta. Add the pasta and cook, stirring occasionally, for 5 to 6 minutes, until golden. Add the saffron and cook, stirring frequently, for 30 to 45 seconds, until fragrant.

❸ Add the stock. Add 1½ cups of the stock and cook, stirring frequently, for 5 to 6 minutes, until all the liquid has been absorbed. Repeat with the remaining stock, adding 1 to 1½ cups at a time and stirring until most of the liquid is absorbed before each addition, for 15 to 20 minutes total. The pasta should be al dente, and a little liquid will remain.

❹ Finish the tubetti. Reduce the heat to low and stir in the butter. Remove from the heat and stir in the ¼ cup cheese. Transfer to a serving dish, top with more cheese, and serve.

13
Pasta

To us, handmade pasta is an incredible thing. It is made from the most humble ingredients (flour, water, eggs), and with work from your own two hands, it creates such universally loved dishes.

Making pasta by hand from scratch is much less complicated than people think. Great pasta is about simple ingredients and not overcomplicating it. It's important to buy the best quality of every ingredient, from olive oil to eggs and tomatoes. You won't need a large quantity of any one ingredient, but when they're all sourced from the best places, the entire dish will be more memorable.

The process is tactile and manual, which is precisely what makes it so satisfying. The time it takes to transform those ingredients into noodles by kneading and rolling the dough can be relaxing, meditative, or fun, especially in the company of family, friends, and a glass of wine. Although some chefs can spend a lifetime perfecting their fresh pasta, the beauty of it is that even if you start as a beginner, as long as you understand the very basics, your pasta is going to be delicious.

In this chapter, we focus on classics and beloved pasta dishes that anyone can prepare. After mastering a few foundational recipes (basic tomato sauce, basil pesto, fresh egg pasta), you'll be ready to move on to a rich many-layered lasagna made with Bolognese and béchamel sauces, homemade ravioli with cheese or pork filling, and vibrant vegetable purées.

Tools to Have on Hand

- Pasta machine
- Pasta cutter

PASTA EQUIPMENT

Old-fashioned hand-cranked Italian-made machines make it easy to create thin, delicate sheets of pasta. Basic models that include two pasta rollers (one for solid sheets and the other for cut sheets) will work well. Some machines have optional attachments that roll, stuff, and crimp dough to make ravioli. Use our suggestions as a guide, but note that the thickness setting on pasta machines will be slightly different with every machine. If you have a stand mixer, a pasta roller attachment is a handy addition that makes the process even easier. To create crimped edges on your noodles or ravioli, use a high-quality brass pasta cutter.

Keys to Success

1. Start with the best ingredients. Pasta is made with just two ingredients, so seek out high-quality, all-purpose flour or imported Italian flour (see page 299), and the best, freshest eggs for deeply colored yolks that make the most appetizing pasta. San Marzano tomatoes from Italy have the brightest, sweetest tomato flavor. Use freshly grated real Parmigiano-Reggiano cheese (save the rinds for risotto and soups).

It's worth seeking out an Italian market or a retailer with an extensive selection of imported oils, cheeses, and cured meats. Use the freshest vegetables and herbs that you can find. These dishes are built on simple flavors, so each ingredient has to shine.

2. Knead the pasta dough well and let it rest. This process develops the gluten in the flour, which gives the pasta texture. If the dough is too crumbly or wet, it will be hard to roll out. When you're rolling out the dough, use a light hand with flour; a fine dusting will prevent sticking, but too much flour will dry out the dough.

3. Boil mindfully. Cook pasta in generously salted, rapidly boiling water just until it's *al dente* (with a slight bite). The water should be salty and taste "like the sea." Save a cup or so of the starchy pasta water to use when tossing the pasta in the sauce—the starch in the water helps the sauce cling to the pasta.

4. Sauce the right way. A good way to gauge the right amount of sauce for a bowl? You should have enough left over that you can clean the bowl with one heel of bread. Don't oversauce; this will mask the flavor of the beautiful pasta you've just prepared.

5. Finish with care and with flavor. Fresh noodles have a delicate texture, so toss them carefully before serving. Finish the pasta dish with a fat like grated cheese or a pat of butter to maximize flavor.

Basil Pesto
(page 313)

Bolognese Sauce
(page 315)

Vegetable Sauce
(page 314)

Basic Tomato
Sauce
(page 312)

Fresh Egg Pasta

Makes 14 ounces pasta dough,
about 10 (12-inch) sheets

You'll find fresh pasta all over Italy, but regionally it's made quite differently. At its most basic, there's an invisible dividing line across the country through Rome. Northern Italy makes pasta using flour and eggs, much like the recipe here, while the southern area of the country uses durum wheat and water (sometimes with the addition of olive oil and milk). Making fresh pasta by hand requires a bit of learning and patience, but it teaches you how to use your senses (especially touch), which will help you in all parts of cooking.

- 2 cups "00" flour or high-quality all-purpose flour, plus more for dusting
- 1 large egg, at room temperature
- 4 large egg yolks, at room temperature
- 2 tablespoons water
- Semolina flour or fine cornmeal, for dusting

❶ Make the dough. Place the flour in a mound on a clean, dry work surface. Use your hands to make a well in the center. Place the whole egg, egg yolks, and water in a small bowl. Use a fork to beat until smooth. Pour into the flour well. Use the same fork to gently and slowly incorporate the flour into the eggs, until fully combined. The mixture will look slightly crumbly, but will fully come together once you start kneading.

❷ Knead the dough. Knead the dough with your hands for 14 to 16 minutes, until it is smooth, elastic, and very tight. It should be firm, but spring back slightly when you press it with your finger. Wrap tightly in plastic wrap and let stand at room temperature for at least 30 minutes or up to 1 hour. (If not using right away, store wrapped in plastic wrap in the refrigerator for up to 24 hours. Let stand for 30 minutes to 1 hour at room temperature before rolling.)

COOK'S
tip

KNEADING: *Softer doughs may be easier to knead, but they will be sticky and difficult to pass through the pasta machine. A drier, "tighter" dough takes more effort to knead, but it will prevent your sheets from sticking together later. Kneading the dough for the amount of time specified helps it develop gluten, which creates a springier, more toothsome texture when the pasta is cooked. Halfway through the kneading process, you may get tired, but keep going and your hard work will pay off when you roll out the dough with ease.*

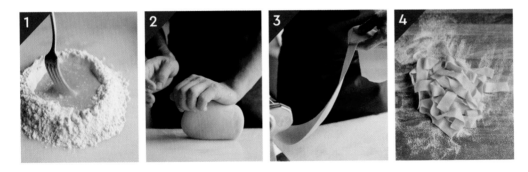

3 Roll out the dough. Sprinkle a large sheet pan with semolina flour. Divide the dough in half. (Keep the second piece of dough wrapped in the plastic wrap while working with the first.) On a floured work surface, shape and flatten the first portion into a square and sprinkle lightly with "00" flour. Using a pasta machine and starting on the thickest setting, slowly pass the dough through. Continue rolling the dough through the machine, using progressively thinner settings as you go.

After the first few passes, to laminate the dough, fold the left and right thirds of the dough over the middle, overlapping them to make a tri-fold (it will look like a rectangle with squared corners). Roll the dough and repeat the tri-fold. Roll the dough again, then fold it in half to make a bi-fold (like a book). Continue rolling the dough until you can almost see through it, but it's not so thin that it breaks; depending on the machine, this may be the second-thinnest setting (or thicker, if you prefer). If the pasta gets too long as you roll, cut it in half and continue rolling. Transfer the pasta sheet to the sheet pan, lightly sprinkling overlapping layers with semolina flour to prevent sticking. Repeat with the remaining portion of dough.

COOK'S
tip

LAMINATING: *Once you begin to roll the dough, the process of folding it in on itself (in tri-folds or bi-folds) and rerolling is called "laminating" the dough. This ensures a better, smoother pasta texture.*

4 Cut the dough. Lightly dust a cutting board with semolina flour. Cut the dough into 12-inch-long sheets. Leave the sheets uncut for lasagna or ravioli, or fold the sheets into quarters (in a zigzag or accordion fold) and cut into strips of the desired width: $\frac{1}{4}$ inch for tagliarini, $\frac{1}{2}$ to $\frac{3}{4}$ inch for tagliatelle, 1 inch for pappardelle. Gently pull the strips apart into long noodles and sprinkle with semolina flour to prevent sticking. If not using immediately, dust with additional semolina flour and store in a sealed container in the refrigerator for up to 2 days.

ITALIAN MILLED FLOUR

In Italy, flour is categorized by how finely it's ground and how much of the bran and germ of the wheat has been removed: The Italian grading system is 2 (the coarsest), 1, 0, or 00. Type 00 (sometimes called "doppio zero") is prized for pasta because it's exceptionally fine-textured and yields a smooth, supple dough that's easy to work with. Examples of this flour include Napoli Antimo Caputo "00" and King Arthur Flour's Italian-Style Flour (both available online). However, you can also use high-quality all-purpose flour.

Green Pasta

Working puréed leafy greens into pasta dough creates noodles with a vibrant color and a subtle flavor that echoes the greens used. You can use a variety of greens, such as turnips, spinach, watercress, radish greens, or carrot tops, as well as spicier greens, like mustard, arugula, or mizuna. To allow the pasta's flavor to shine, it's best to pair green pasta with a simple tomato sauce or a spicy arrabbiata sauce.

1 bunch (¼ to ½ pound) greens with stems (such as turnip greens, watercress, arugula, or spinach)

2 cups "00" flour or high-quality all-purpose flour, plus more for dusting

2 large egg yolks, at room temperature

Semolina flour or fine cornmeal, for dusting

❶ Make the purée. Thoroughly wash and dry the greens, making sure all the sand and dirt are cleaned off. Coarsely chop the greens, including the stems. Working in batches if necessary, transfer the greens and stems to a tabletop blender. Blend until very smooth, adding a few tablespoons water, if necessary. With the blender turned off, use a spatula to scrape down the sides as needed. No visible green pieces should remain.

❷ Make the dough. Place the flour in a mound on a clean, dry work surface. Use your hands to make a well in the center. Add 6 tablespoons of the purée and the egg yolks to the well. Use a fork to mix the purée and egg yolks. Use the same fork and a bench scraper to gently and slowly incorporate the flour into the eggs and purée, until fully combined.

❸ Knead the dough. Knead the dough with your hands for 2 to 3 minutes, until just combined. If the dough gets too hard to knead, let it rest for 3 to 4 minutes before continuing. Continue kneading for 1 minute more. The dough will look slightly crumbly at this point, not completely smooth, but will hold together well when formed into a ball. Wrap tightly in plastic wrap and let stand at room temperature for 30 minutes to 1 hour.

❹ Roll out the dough. Sprinkle a large sheet pan with semolina flour. Divide the dough in half. (Keep the second piece of dough wrapped in the plastic wrap while working with the first.) On a floured work surface, shape and flatten the first half into a square and sprinkle lightly with "00" flour. Using a pasta machine and starting on the thickest setting, slowly pass the dough through. Continue rolling the dough through the machine, using progressively thinner settings as you go.

After the first few passes, to "laminate" the dough, fold the left and right thirds of the dough over the middle, overlapping them to make a tri-fold (it will look like a rectangle with squared corners).

Roll the dough and repeat the tri-fold. Roll the dough again, then fold it in half to make a bi-fold (like a book). Continue rolling the dough until thin; depending on the pasta machine, this may be the third-thinnest setting (or thicker, if you prefer). If the pasta gets too long as you roll, cut it in half and continue rolling. Transfer the pasta sheet to the sheet pan, lightly sprinkling overlapping layers with semolina flour to prevent sticking. Repeat with the remaining portion of dough.

❺ Cut the dough. Lightly dust a cutting board with semolina flour. Cut the dough into 12-inch-long sheets. Leave the sheets uncut for ravioli, or fold the sheets into quarters (in a zigzag or accordion fold) and cut into strips of the desired width: ¼ inch for tagliarini, ½ to ¾ inch for tagliatelle, 1 inch for pappardelle. Gently pull the strips apart into long noodles and sprinkle with semolina flour to prevent sticking. If not using immediately, dust with additional semolina flour and store in a sealed container in the refrigerator for up to 2 days.

Ravioli

Once you have the fillings prepared and the pasta cranked out, it's easy and fun to transform the two components into homemade ravioli to serve with Basic Tomato Sauce (page 312) or our vibrant Vegetable Sauce (page 314). Start with the easy cutout circle shape, then progress to more whimsical variations. Before you know it, you'll be inviting friends over for a bowl of "little bellies" or "bishops' hats."

2 large eggs

2 tablespoons water

Semolina flour or fine cornmeal, for dusting

10 (5 by 10-inch) sheets Fresh Egg Pasta (page 298)

1 cup Cheese Filling (page 311) or Pork Filling (page 310)

Kosher salt

❶ Cut the pasta circles. Place the eggs and water in a dish; beat until smooth to make an egg wash. Sprinkle a large sheet pan with semolina flour. Lay out the pasta sheets on a clean, dry work surface and use a 2½-inch ring mold to cut out circles.

❷ Form the ravioli. Spoon 1 teaspoon filling into the center of half the circles. Use a pastry brush or your finger to lightly brush the edges of the pasta around the filling with the egg wash. Place the remaining pasta circles on top of the circles with the filling. Press around the edges to form a tight seal with the egg wash. Place the ravioli on the sheet pan in a single layer. Transfer to the refrigerator and chill for 10 minutes. (If not cooking right away, refrigerate uncovered for up to 1 day.)

❸ Finish the ravioli. Heat a large pot of salted water to boiling on high. Add the ravioli and cook for 45 seconds to 1 minute, until al dente. Sauce as desired (see page 313).

RECIPE CONTINUES

FILLED PASTA SHAPE VARIATIONS

Panzerotti ("Little Bellies")

Use a 2½-inch ring mold to cut the 12-inch pasta sheets into circles. Spoon 1 teaspoon filling into the center of each circle. Use a pastry brush or your finger to lightly brush the edges of the pasta with egg wash. Fold the circle in half and press around the edges to form a tight seal. Cook and serve as directed.

Cappellacci ("Bishops' Hats")

1 Cut the pasta sheets into 6 by 6-inch squares. Cut diagonally into triangles. Spoon 1 teaspoon filling just off center of each triangle. Use a pastry brush or your finger to lightly brush the edges of the pasta with the egg wash.
2 Fold the triangles in half and press around the edges to form a tight seal. **3** Brush a bottom corner of each triangle with egg wash; bring the two bottom corners together, slightly overlapping; and press to seal. Cook and serve as directed.

Filled Squares

1 Place the cheese filling in a pastry bag with a round tip or in a resealable plastic bag with a bottom corner snipped off. Using the 12-inch pasta sheets, 2 inches from one of the long edges, pipe a straight line of filling the length of the dough, leaving a 1-inch border at either end. **2** Use a pastry brush or your finger to lightly brush with egg wash the long edge of the dough on both sides of the filling. Fold one long edge over the filling; press to seal both sides of the filling. Press down on one short side to seal. Press down on the dough every 1½ inches to seal and create the ravioli shape. **3** Use a pastry cutter to cut into squares along the seals. Cook and serve as directed.

Agnolotti

1 Place the cheese filling in a pastry bag with a round tip or a resealable plastic bag with a bottom corner snipped off. Using the 12-inch pasta sheets, about ½ inch from the long edge closest to you, pipe a straight line of filling along the length of the dough, leaving about ½ inch uncovered at either end. Use a pastry brush or your finger to lightly brush the dough along the filling with egg wash. **2** Fold the dough over and slightly under the filling. Press down on one short end to seal. **3** Use the handle of a wooden spoon to press down on the dough every inch to seal.
4 Use a fluted pastry cutter to cut away the length of excess dough, ⅛ inch beyond the filling, then cut into agnolotti along the seals. Cook and serve as directed.

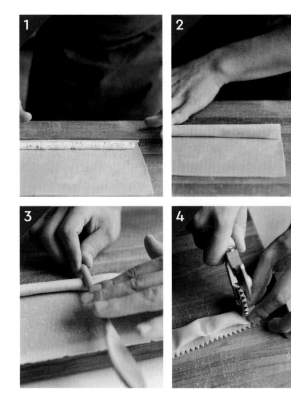

PORK FILLING

Makes about 2 cups

Rich, savory, and redolent of garlic, herbs, Parmigiano-Reggiano cheese, and a touch of nutmeg, this recipe creates the ultimate meat filling for fresh delicate pasta—just top with a simple tomato sauce. Allow the filling to cool completely, or even chill it, before using it to fill any stuffed pasta.

2 tablespoons unsalted butter

1 pound ground pork

Kosher salt and freshly ground black pepper

1 onion, finely chopped

2 cloves garlic, minced

¼ teaspoon freshly grated nutmeg

2 teaspoons finely chopped fresh sage leaves

¼ cup finely chopped flat-leaf parsley

½ cup dry white wine (such as sauvignon blanc or pinot grigio)

2 cups water

1 cup heavy cream

¼ cup freshly grated Parmigiano-Reggiano cheese

1 Render the pork. In a sauté pan on medium, melt the butter. Add the pork and season with salt and pepper. Cook, using a wooden spoon to break up the meat, for 5 to 6 minutes, until lightly browned and fine in texture. Season with salt and pepper. Use a slotted spoon to transfer the pork to a plate, leaving the fat behind.

2 Cook the aromatics. Heat the fat over medium-high until hot. Add the onion and garlic and season lightly with salt and pepper. Cook, stirring occasionally, for 2 to 3 minutes, until fragrant and beginning to soften.

3 Start the filling. Return the pork to the pan and add the nutmeg. Cook for 30 seconds to 1 minute, until fragrant. Add the sage and parsley and cook, stirring frequently, for 30 seconds to 1 minute, until thoroughly combined. Add the wine and season lightly with salt and pepper. Cook, stirring occasionally, for 4 to 5 minutes, until the wine has almost completely evaporated. Add the water and bring to a simmer. Cook, stirring occasionally, for 22 to 24 minutes, until the water has cooked off.

4 Finish the filling. Add the cream and cook, stirring occasionally, for 7 to 8 minutes, until the liquid is reduced and thickened and the pork is glazed in sauce. Stir in the Parmigiano. Remove from the heat. Season with salt and pepper. Cool completely or chill before using to fill pasta. Store in a sealed container in the refrigerator for up to 5 days or freeze for up to 1 month.

CHEESE FILLING

Makes 2¼ cups

This is our basic cheese filling for our stuffed pastas, but the flavor is anything but ordinary. The mixture is made from a blend of creamy ricotta cheese and salty Pecorino Romano (a hard sheep's milk cheese that dates back to ancient Rome), and seasoned with garlic, parsley, and a splash of olive oil. The recipe is also flexible—feel free to substitute another herb (such as oregano, chives, or thyme) for the parsley, or add finely grated lemon zest or a pinch of crushed red pepper flakes.

2 cups ricotta cheese

½ cup freshly grated Pecorino Romano cheese

2 cloves garlic, minced or finely grated into a paste

¼ cup finely chopped fresh flat-leaf parsley

2 tablespoons extra virgin olive oil

Kosher salt and freshly ground black pepper

In a large mixing bowl, combine the ricotta, pecorino, garlic, parsley, and olive oil. Stir to thoroughly combine. Season with salt and pepper. Use to fill pasta as needed. Store in a sealed container, with plastic wrap pressed against the surface of the filling, in the refrigerator for up to 3 days or in the freezer for up to 1 month.

BASIC TOMATO SAUCE

Makes 5 cups

Our favorite *sugo di pomodoro* (classic tomato sauce) begins with the right tomatoes. We love the bright flavor of canned San Marzano tomatoes, a widely available variety of plum tomato named after a region near Naples. A high-sided saucepan will contain splatters and keep the kitchen clean. For the best flavor, you'll want to gently sauté the aromatics to coax out their sweetness, but don't brown them—this will give the sauce a toasted flavor that won't let the tomatoes shine.

3 tablespoons extra virgin olive oil

3 cloves garlic, finely chopped

1 onion, small diced

Kosher salt and freshly ground black pepper

2 (28-ounce) cans whole San Marzano tomatoes

❶ Cook the aromatics. In a large, high-sided saucepan or soup pot, heat the olive oil on medium until hot. Add the garlic and onion. Season with 1 teaspoon salt and a sprinkle of black pepper. Cook, stirring occasionally, for 11 to 13 minutes, until softened but not browned.

❷ Crush the tomatoes. While the aromatics are cooking, place the tomatoes in a large bowl. Use your hands or a wooden spoon to break the tomatoes into smaller pieces.

❸ Cook the sauce. Add the tomatoes to the aromatics. Cook for 40 to 45 minutes, until the sauce is thickened and slightly sweet.

❹ Mill the sauce. Set a food mill fitted with the coarsest plate over a large bowl. Transfer the sauce to the food mill and process directly into the bowl. Alternatively, transfer the sauce to a food processor and pulse to the desired consistency, or serve as is for a more rustic consistency. Use immediately, store in the refrigerator in sealed containers for up to 3 days, or freeze for up to 1 month.

BASIL PESTO

Makes 2 cups

Whether it's tossed with hot pasta, slathered on bread, or stirred into mayonnaise to create a delicious sandwich spread, basil pesto is the essence of fresh summer flavor. It's also a snap to prepare, since it requires no cooking and just a few ingredients. Toasted nuts, Parmigiano-Reggiano cheese, and olive oil provide a satisfying richness, while garlic gives a savory punch. Pesto comes from the Liguria region of Italy, and its name comes from the word *pestare*, meaning to pound or smash, which refers to the traditional way of making pesto by hand with a mortar and pestle. When using a food processor, as we do in this recipe, pulse only briefly to combine at each addition—too much pulsing will make the olive oil taste bitter (the blades break up the bitter molecules) and heat the basil.

½ cup pine nuts, lightly toasted

2 cloves garlic, finely grated into a paste

2 loosely packed cups fresh basil leaves

¾ cup high-quality extra virgin olive oil

1 cup freshly grated Parmigiano-Reggiano cheese (about 4 ounces)

Kosher salt and freshly ground black pepper

In a food processor, combine the pine nuts, garlic, basil, and ¼ cup of the olive oil; pulse briefly. Add the remaining ½ cup olive oil and pulse until thoroughly combined. Add the cheese and pulse briefly. Transfer to a bowl. Season with salt and pepper. Store in a sealed container or divided into ice cube molds, with plastic wrap pressed against the surface of the pesto, in the refrigerator for up to 1 week or in the freezer for up to 1 month.

COOK'S tip

MORE PESTO IDEAS: *This is our classic version of pesto alla Genovese, but feel free to experiment beyond the traditional. Instead of, or in addition to, basil, try spinach or arugula. Instead of pine nuts, try other nuts, such as walnuts, pistachios, or almonds. Instead of Parmigiano-Reggiano, try sharp Pecorino Romano.*

How to SAUCE ANY PASTA

1. Use a hot pan. Instead of topping cooked pasta with sauce in your serving bowl, sauce pasta in a hot pan to bring the elements together. For one person, use about ⅓ cup pasta sauce (tomato, Bolognese, or vegetable purée) to ¼ pound pasta. In a sauté pan, heat the pasta sauce of your choice on medium.

2. Pay attention to timing. Cook the pasta in salted boiling water right before you need it so it's hot when it goes into the pan. For fresh pastas in particular, the cook times are very short (30 seconds to 1 minute), so you can even cook the pasta as the sauce heats.

3. Use the pasta water. Always reserve some of the pasta cooking water before draining—you'll need it to finish the pasta and create a thicker, cohesive consistency.

Add the hot, cooked pasta or ravioli to the sauce in the pan along with the reserved pasta cooking water (start with 1 tablespoon per person). Cook, stirring gently, for 1 to 2 minutes, until thoroughly coated. Add additional pasta water if needed.

4. Finish the pasta with flavor. For a richer consistency, stir in a small amount of butter (1 tablespoon unsalted butter per person). Remove the pan from the heat and stir in freshly grated Parmigiano-Reggiano cheese to finish. If you have only pre-grated cheese, use the cheese as a topping only. Transfer the pasta to serving bowls and top with a drizzle of olive oil and additional Parmigiano, if desired.

VEGETABLE SAUCE

Makes about 2 cups
(enough for about 1 pound of pasta)

Creamy vegetable purées offer countless possibilities for saucing any number of pastas; they work particularly well with stuffed pastas like ravioli (page 302) and agnolotti (page 307). Here we offer our basic method using corn, along with leek and zucchini variations. The vegetables are gently cooked down to capture the essence of their flavor, finished with a splash of cream and a bit of butter, then blended into a silky sauce. Feel free to follow this basic guideline to create your own purée with whatever is in season, such as root vegetables or fennel.

CORN PURÉE

4 tablespoons (½ stick) unsalted butter

1 small white onion, small diced

1 clove garlic, coarsely chopped

Kosher salt and freshly ground black pepper

2 cups fresh corn kernels (cut from about 4 ears)

1 cup water

2 tablespoons heavy cream

❶ Cook the vegetables. In a large sauté pan or saucepan, melt 2 tablespoons of the butter on medium. Add the onion and garlic and season with salt and pepper. Cover and cook, stirring occasionally, for 11 to 13 minutes, until fragrant. Add the corn and 1 tablespoon butter. Cover and cook for 15 to 18 minutes, until the corn begins to soften and stick to the pan. Add the water and scrape the bottom of the pan. Cook, uncovered, for 15 to 18 minutes, while stirring occasionally until the corn is soft and the liquid is reduced in volume by three-quarters. Add the cream and cook for 1 minute, until combined. Remove from the heat. Let cool slightly before blending.

❷ Make the purée. In a high-powered blender, combine the vegetables, any remaining liquid in the pan, and the remaining 1 tablespoon butter. Blend until smooth. Season with salt and pepper. Use immediately or store in a sealed container in the refrigerator for up to 5 days or freeze for up to 1 month. Whisk well after thawing and reheating.

Variations

To make the purée with leeks, use 2 large thinly sliced leeks instead of the corn and onion; proceed with the recipe as directed. For a zucchini purée, replace the corn with 1½ pounds thinly sliced zucchini and eliminate the water. Proceed with the recipe as directed, but blend the zucchini mixture with 1 loosely packed cup of basil leaves.

COOK'S
tip

STIRRING: *When the vegetables are sweating with the lid on, stir them only occasionally. Lifting the lid too often will release too much steam, which you need to sweat the vegetables—otherwise, they'll dry out.*

BOLOGNESE SAUCE

Makes 5 cups

Named after the city of Bologna, where it originated, *ragù alla Bolognese* is the most iconic meat-based sauce in Italy. Dense with aromatic vegetables and rich with pork and beef, this deeply flavored sauce simmers for three hours until the meat is completely tender. It's a good idea to check the pot from time to time as the meat simmers to ensure that there's enough liquid. If the mixture appears too dry, add a small amount of water. A final addition of fresh marjoram brightens the long-simmered flavors; feel free to use oregano or parsley instead. Because this sauce is a time investment, consider doubling the recipe and freezing half of it for another occasion—you'll be happy to pull it out on a blustery evening to sauce rigatoni.

3 tablespoons unsalted butter

1 large white onion, small diced

2 cloves garlic, minced

2 carrots, peeled and small diced

2 stalks celery, small diced

Kosher salt and freshly ground black pepper

½ pound ground pork

1 pound ground beef (80% lean)

1 cup whole milk

⅛ teaspoon freshly grated nutmeg

¼ teaspoon crushed red pepper flakes

¼ cup finely chopped fresh flat-leaf parsley

1 cup dry white wine (such as sauvignon blanc or pinot grigio)

1 (28-ounce) can whole San Marzano tomatoes, crushed by hand, liquid reserved

1 cup water, plus more if needed

1 tablespoon finely chopped fresh marjoram

❶ Cook the aromatics. In a Dutch oven, melt the butter on medium. Add the onion, garlic, carrots, and celery and season with salt and pepper. Cook, stirring occasionally, for 16 to 18 minutes, until the onion begins to soften.

❷ Render the meat. Add the pork and beef and season with salt and pepper. Cook, using a wooden spoon to break up the meat, for 8 to 10 minutes, until the meat is very lightly browned and cooked through.

❸ Add the liquids. Add the milk and increase the heat to medium-high. Cook for 7 to 8 minutes, until the milk has evaporated. Add the nutmeg, red pepper flakes, and parsley. Season with salt and pepper. Cook, stirring frequently, for 30 seconds to 1 minute, until thoroughly combined. Add the wine. Cook, stirring occasionally, for 9 to 10 minutes, until the liquid is reduced in volume by three-quarters.

❹ Simmer the sauce. Add the tomatoes, including their liquid, and season with salt and pepper. Bring to a simmer. Add the 1 cup water and return to a simmer. Reduce the heat to medium-low. Cover and cook for 3 hours, or until the meat is completely tender. Check the sauce about every 30 minutes and stir the bottom of the pot to prevent sticking. If the sauce needs more water, particularly in the last hour, add ¼ cup at a time.

❺ Finish the sauce. Uncover the pot and increase the heat to medium-high. Stir in the marjoram and cook for 18 to 20 minutes, until the remaining liquid is almost completely cooked off. Season with salt and pepper. Let cool before using or storing. Store in a sealed container in the refrigerator for up to 5 days or freeze for up to 1 month.

Pasta alla Gricia

A number of classic Roman pasta dishes rely on the essential method of emulsifying the starch in the pasta water to create a creamy, cohesive sauce, including *pasta alla gricia*, *pasta all'amatriciana*, and *cacio e pepe*. They all focus on a few simple, staple ingredients; for *pasta alla gricia*, they're guanciale, black pepper, and freshly grated pecorino and Parmigiano cheese. From there, add crushed red pepper flakes and omit the Parmigiano to make *pasta all'amatriciana*. Include only the cheese, black pepper, and butter to make *cacio e pepe*.

It's important to cook the guanciale slowly—starting with a cold pan helps—so that the meat doesn't burn before it properly crisps and the fat is rendered from it.

Kosher salt

2½ ounces guanciale or pancetta, cut into ¼-inch-thick, 1½-inch-long pieces

1 medium onion or 4 scallions, thinly sliced

½ pound Fresh Egg Pasta (page 298), cut into tagliatelle or pappardelle

1 tablespoon unsalted butter

¼ teaspoon freshly ground black pepper

1 tablespoon freshly grated Parmigiano-Reggiano cheese

2 tablespoons freshly grated Pecorino Romano cheese

❶ Render the guanciale. Heat a large pot of salted water to boiling on high. Place the guanciale in a cold sauté pan and turn on the heat to medium-high. Cook, stirring occasionally, for 9 to 10 minutes, until the fat has rendered and the guanciale starts to turn golden brown. Use a slotted spoon to transfer the guanciale to a small bowl. Pour the rendered fat into a separate bowl, leaving any browned bits (fond) in the pan.

❷ Cook the onion. Return 2 teaspoons of the rendered fat to the pan and heat on medium until hot. Add the onion. Cook, stirring occasionally to scrape the fond from the bottom of the pan, for 8 to 10 minutes, until softened and fragrant.

❸ Cook the pasta. Add the pasta to the boiling water. Cook for 30 seconds, until al dente. Reserving ½ cup of the pasta cooking water, drain thoroughly.

❹ Finish the pasta. Add the pasta, guanciale, butter, black pepper, and ¼ cup of the pasta cooking water to the onion. Cook, stirring gently, for 1 to 2 minutes, until thoroughly coated. If the sauce seems dry, gradually add the remaining pasta cooking water to reach the desired consistency. Stir in the Parmigiano. Cook, stirring gently, for 1 to 2 minutes, until melted and combined. Divide the pasta between two bowls. Top with the pecorino and serve.

COOK'S
tip

GUANCIALE: *Guanciale is a cured, unsmoked Italian pork product made from pork jowl. Buy it in ¼-inch-thick slices from specialty Italian groceries. Pancetta may be used as a substitute.*

Lasagna

The word "lasagna" actually has Greek origins, stemming from the word *laganon*, a flat sheet of pasta that was one of the earliest known forms of pasta. The layers in lasagna are crucial, but as with most pasta dishes, the ingredients can change slightly depending on the region or even family history. This recipe melds classic components: sheets of fresh egg pasta, creamy béchamel sauce, rich Bolognese sauce, and Parmigiano-Reggiano cheese.

One of the five "mother sauces" of French cooking, béchamel is a thick, white sauce that forms the base of creamy soups, casseroles, gratins, white gravy, and macaroni and cheese (though once you add cheese to a béchamel, it's technically a Mornay sauce). The key to a deeply flavored béchamel is allowing the flour to cook with the butter for a few minutes until it loses its raw flavor.

BÉCHAMEL SAUCE

- 6 tablespoons (¾ stick) unsalted butter
- 6 tablespoons all-purpose flour
- 4 cups whole milk
- Pinch of freshly grated nutmeg
- Kosher salt and freshly ground black pepper

LASAGNA

- 10 (4½ by 12-inch) sheets Fresh Egg Pasta (page 298)
- 5 cups Bolognese Sauce (page 315), at room temperature
- 2 cups freshly grated Parmigiano-Reggiano cheese (about 8 ounces)

❶ Make the béchamel. In a small pot over medium heat, melt the butter. Add the flour and cook, whisking constantly, for 1 to 2 minutes, until golden and thoroughly combined. Add the milk and cook, whisking constantly at first and then occasionally, for 11 to 13 minutes, until thickened. Whisk in the nutmeg. Season with salt and pepper. Remove from the heat and let cool to room temperature.

❷ Assemble the lasagna. Preheat the oven to 375°F. Spread ½ cup béchamel sauce evenly across the bottom of a 9 by 13-inch baking dish. Cover with 2 pasta sheets, side by side. Spread ½ cup béchamel onto the pasta, followed by 1 cup Bolognese. Season with salt and pepper. Repeat layering the pasta, béchamel, and Bolognese four more times; season alternate layers with salt and pepper. Evenly sprinkle the top layer of Bolognese with the Parmigiano.

❸ Bake the lasagna. Bake the lasagna for 30 to 35 minutes, until hot, bubbling, and golden brown. Remove from the oven and let stand for at least 15 minutes before serving.

14
Pizza

Pizza is an iconic food with very humble beginnings.

Pizza started as street food in eighteenth-century Naples, where a softer crust baked in a wood-fired oven was perfected. At its simplest, pizza began as flatbreads with toppings that were eaten by the poorest Neapolitan communities for breakfast, lunch, or dinner. As food for the lower class, it was often looked down upon, and so its popularity actually did not spread to the rest of Italy until after World War II, when it soon became the pride of all Italians, regardless of class or region. Italians brought their beloved specialty to America, where immigrants started their pizzerias in cities such as New York, New Haven, and Boston. From there, its popularity only grew and Italian American–style pizzas evolved. Pizza soon became a fast food to be franchised, and it was those franchises (along with Italian immigrants) that brought pizza to the rest of the world.

The recipes in this chapter honor that tradition of Neapolitan-style pies and calzones, but we also showcase another crowd-pleasing favorite of today, the Chicago-style deep-dish pizza. Like handmade fresh pasta, homemade pizza is not as intimidating as it may seem. Learning the basics of handling the dough will give you confidence not only with pizzas but with other yeast-based breads. When you plan on making pizza at home, set yourself up for success by making only pizza. In other words, have the salad and any other sides ready to go so you can focus on timing and enjoy yourself with family and friends. Prepare a range of favorite toppings and have them cut up and ready in bowls so people can mix and match from pizza to pizza. Remember that even an imperfect pizza (a little lopsided here, a little too thick there) will still taste delicious. Pizza night—even if it's only you and a loved one—should feel like a party, so most importantly, have fun!

Tools to Have on Hand

- Pizza stone
- Pizza peel

PIZZA TOOLS

Pizza stones simulate brick-oven baking by retaining heat and keeping the oven temperature steady. An unglazed stone pulls moisture from the outer surface of the dough to enhance the crisp texture. With a long handle and beveled edge that easily slides under a cooked crust, a pizza peel is the traditional tool for placing pizza, calzones, and breads in a fiery oven. If you don't have one, you can use the back of a sheet pan dusted with cornmeal or a sheet pan with no rims.

Keys to Success

1. Start with the best ingredients. As with pasta, the simplicity of great pizza requires all ingredients to shine. Look for unbleached flour and use high-quality aged cheeses (Parmigiano-Reggiano, Pecorino Romano) and grate them yourself. Always rely on fresh—never frozen—vegetables. Canned San Marzano tomatoes create pizza sauce with the brightest, sweetest flavor.

2. Keep organized. Pizza making is fast moving and all about timing, so have the ingredients prepped (herbs cleaned, cheese sliced) and at room temperature before you begin stretching dough.

3. Don't oversauce. Too much sauce will make a sloppy pizza—a thin layer will suffice. Similarly, you don't want to weigh the pizza down with too many toppings; a scattering of two or three is plenty.

4. Preheat the oven and stone. To ensure a crispy crust that cooks in minutes, make sure the oven and pizza stone are sufficiently preheated and very hot. We recommend heating them for an hour before baking.

5. Pause before slicing. The pizza might look enticing right out of the oven, but cutting into it right away will cause the toppings to slide right off (and burn the roof of your mouth). Let it cool on a wire rack for a minute or two; it will be easier to slice and eat.

BASIC PIZZA DOUGH

**Makes about 2 pounds dough,
enough for 4 (11-inch) pizzas or 4 calzones**

This is our go-to dough for crispy pies, bubbling deep-dish pizzas, and calzones. Like any dough, this one calls for some kneading—you'll know it's right if it bounces back when you push it. This dough makes a light and crackly crust, but one of our favorite variations uses a mix of rye flour (½ cup rye flour and 3½ cups all-purpose flour instead of 4 cups all-purpose flour). The rye flour makes the dough heartier, with more "tooth."

This dough takes more than a day to make, so plan ahead. If you're not making four pizzas, double-wrap leftover balls of dough in plastic wrap so you'll be armed for future pizza or calzone cravings. Refrigerate the dough for up to 12 hours or freeze for up to 2 weeks. Thaw frozen dough overnight in the refrigerator before using, and always let the dough come to room temperature before attempting to stretch it.

1¼ teaspoons active dry yeast

1½ cups warm water (90°F)

4 cups all-purpose flour, plus more for dusting

1 teaspoon kosher salt

½ teaspoon sugar

1 tablespoon extra virgin olive oil

Canola oil, for greasing the bowl and pan

❶ **Make the dough.** In a bowl or measuring cup, sprinkle the yeast into the water and let stand for 6 to 8 minutes, until foamy. In the bowl of a stand mixer fitted with the dough hook attachment, place the flour, salt, sugar, and olive oil; mix on low speed for 30 seconds to 1 minute, until combined. Gradually add the yeast-water mixture. Increase the speed to medium and mix for 6 to 8 minutes, until fully incorporated and a stiff dough has formed, stopping the mixer and scraping down the sides and bottom of the bowl as needed. Be careful not to overwork the dough. Lightly flour a clean, dry work surface. Transfer the dough to the prepared surface and knead for 2 to 3 minutes, until smooth.

❷ **Proof the dough.** Lightly oil the inside of a large bowl with canola oil. Place the dough in the bowl and brush the top with more oil. Cover with plastic wrap and refrigerate for at least 24 hours and up to 36 hours.

❸ **Divide the dough.** Lightly oil a sheet pan. Lightly dust a clean, dry work surface with flour. Turn out the dough onto the surface and use a knife or bench scraper to cut the dough into four equal pieces.

❹ **Form the dough balls.** Working with one piece at a time, roll the dough and tuck the edges under. Pinch and twist the edges together to form a ball. Gently roll the pinched side of the dough against the work surface with a cupped hand until smooth; place on the sheet pan. Repeat with the remaining pieces of dough. Cover the pan loosely with plastic wrap to prevent the dough from drying out. Let stand at room temperature for 1 to 2 hours to proof again. Proceed with the pizza or calzone recipe.

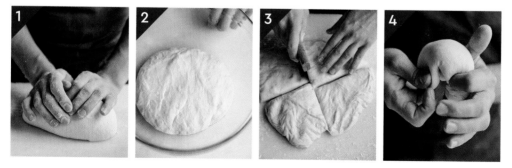

BASIC PIZZA SAUCE

Makes about 3 cups

When it comes to pizza, they don't mess around in Naples. A classic Neapolitan pie is made with San Marzano tomatoes and mozzarella, if there's cheese involved at all. In other words, the sauce is all about the bright acidity of the tomatoes, seasoned with nothing but salt and pepper. As with any recipe of few ingredients, quality is key—seek out imported San Marzano tomatoes.

1 (28-ounce) can crushed tomatoes (preferably San Marzano)

1¾ teaspoons kosher salt

½ teaspoon freshly ground black pepper

❶ Process the tomatoes. Set a fine-mesh strainer over a bowl and drain the tomatoes. Set a food mill fitted with the finest plate over a large bowl. Transfer the tomatoes to the food mill and process directly into the bowl, using a spatula to gently push on any tomato pieces that remain and to scrape from the underside of the plate.

❷ Season the sauce. Season with the salt and pepper; stir to combine. Store in the refrigerator in a sealed container for up to 1 week or freeze for up to 1 month.

PIZZA DOUGH TIPS

1. A "stiff dough" will make an impression but bounce back when you press your finger into it. The dough will be smooth on the outside but still pliable.

2. An "overworked dough" will be too firm and tight—when you try to knead it, it will feel like it's cracking.

3. When you proof the dough in the refrigerator, the position matters. Don't place it next to the refrigerator fan, as it will become too cold and prevent the dough from proofing.

4. Don't overhandle the dough—if you need more flour on your hands to make it easier, that's okay.

5. Adjust to the weather, if needed. If the room is very dry (like in the middle of winter), warm up the room a little when working with the dough. If it's very humid, make sure to have some extra flour on hand.

6. Make the dough work for you. As a novice, if you need to add a little extra flour so it's easier to work with, go for it.

Pizza Margherita

Legend has it that this famous recipe is named after the Italian queen Margherita. When she visited Naples with the king, this was the pizza that she enjoyed the most. The owner of the pizza shop was so pleased that he named it after her in her honor. Crowned with the colors of the Italian flag—green from basil, white from mozzarella, red from tomato sauce—pizza Margherita is a beautiful thing: a purist's thin-crust pie that's all about the perfect balance of toppings and lightly charred, chewy crust. A last-minute hit of Parmigiano-Reggiano cheese finishes the pizza with a salty edge, and a drizzle of olive oil and a sprinkle of flaky sea salt draw all the elements into focus.

COOK'S
tip

HOME OVENS: *To mimic the heat of a pizza oven, our at-home method uses a combination of a very hot oven, preheated for 1 hour, and the direct high heat of the oven's broil setting. If you have an undercarriage broiler (the heating element in a compartment underneath the oven), position the oven rack and pizza stone on the lowest level. Preheat the oven to 550°F (or the highest temperature on your oven; do not broil) for 1 hour and bake the pizza on the stone for 8 minutes.*

Semolina flour or fine cornmeal, for dusting

Basic Pizza Dough (page 324), at room temperature

All-purpose flour, for dusting

1 cup Basic Pizza Sauce (page 325)

1 small bunch basil

1½ pounds fresh mozzarella cheese, medium diced (about 3 cups)

¼ cup freshly grated Parmigiano-Reggiano cheese

Flaky sea salt, for garnish

Extra virgin olive oil, for garnish

❶ Prepare the dough. One hour before cooking, position an oven rack on the highest level. Place a pizza stone on the rack. Preheat the oven to 550°F (or the highest temperature for the oven). Dust a pizza peel with a few tablespoons of semolina flour. Dust the pizza dough, your hands, and a clean, dry work surface with all-purpose flour. Use a bench scraper to gently lift a ball of dough onto the work surface; lightly dust the dough with all-purpose flour.

❷ Shape the dough. Push the dough from the center outward and stretch into a circle 10 to 12 inches in diameter. If desired, stretch the dough by gently rotating it on your knuckles and outstretched fingers. If the dough springs back, let it rest for 5 to 10 minutes before attempting to stretch again.

❸ Build the pizza. Place the stretched dough on the peel. Give the peel a little shake; the dough should slide. If not, remove the dough and dust the peel with more semolina flour. Use a spoon to evenly spread ¼ cup sauce onto the dough, leaving a 1-inch border of crust. Top with 6 basil leaves and ¾ cup of the mozzarella.

❹ Bake and serve the pizza. Switch the oven to the broil setting. Gently slide the pizza from the peel onto the stone and bake for 5 minutes, until the crust is browned and the cheese is melted. Use a spatula or tongs to slide the pizza off the stone and onto a sheet pan. Sprinkle with 1 tablespoon of the Parmigiano, a small pinch of sea salt, and a drizzle of olive oil. Transfer the pizza to a wire rack and let stand for 2 minutes to cool slightly before serving. Cut into slices and serve immediately. Repeat with the remaining dough and toppings.

Variation: Pizza Bianca
To make a "white pie" or *pizza bianca,* eliminate the tomato sauce and top with dollops of fresh ricotta cheese and 1 tablespoon finely grated garlic instead. Sprinkle with pecorino cheese in addition to the Parmigiano-Reggiano cheese.

RECIPE CONTINUES

Pizza Bianca
(page 326)

PIZZA TOPPINGS

Building pizzas with favorite toppings is fun—we encourage you to be creative with your combinations. Following a few tips will help you achieve the best results. First, don't weigh down the pizza, especially when cooking a thin-crust pizza such as Pizza Margherita (page 326).

Two to three well-chosen toppings will be plenty. The top of the pizza will be exposed to the most heat—layer cooked toppings on the bottom so they won't burn (sautéed spinach, wild mushrooms, roasted red peppers, browned Italian sausage) and uncooked toppings on the top (thinly sliced red onion, brussels sprout leaves).

Neapolitan-Style Cheese Calzones

with Basil

Another brilliant import from Naples, calzones are folded pizzas that encase any number of fillings, including cured meats, cheeses, and sautéed greens. The calzone (the word translates to "pants leg," referring to its shape) probably came about because it's perfect for eating on the go: No knife or fork is needed to dig in. Our calzone is stuffed with a blend of four cheeses (mozzarella, ricotta, provolone, and Parmigiano-Reggiano)—a popular filling that you'll find in Naples. This is a thinner-style calzone that creates a crispier crust, setting it apart from heftier versions you'll typically find at pizzerias. There's no tomato in the filling, but these half-moons benefit from the sweet acidity of tomato sauce, so serve it on the side, for dipping.

1 pound fresh mozzarella cheese, medium diced (2 cups)

1 cup ricotta cheese

1 cup freshly grated Parmigiano-Reggiano cheese (about 4 ounces), plus more for garnish

½ cup shredded provolone cheese

1 teaspoon finely grated lemon zest

3 cloves garlic, finely grated into a paste

½ loosely packed cup fresh basil leaves, thinly sliced

2 tablespoons finely chopped fresh flat-leaf parsley leaves

Kosher salt and freshly ground black pepper

1 large egg

1 tablespoon water

Extra virgin olive oil

All-purpose flour, for dusting

Basic Pizza Dough (page 324), at room temperature

Flaky sea salt, for garnish

2 cups Basic Pizza Sauce (page 325), warmed, for serving

❶ Mix the filling. Preheat the oven to 475°F. In a large bowl, combine the mozzarella, ricotta, Parmigiano, provolone, lemon zest, garlic, basil, and parsley. Season with salt and pepper.

❷ Roll out the dough. Place the egg and water in a dish; beat until smooth. Brush 2 large sheet pans with olive oil. Generously dust a clean, dry work surface with flour. Working with 1 ball at a time, dust the dough with flour. Use a rolling pin to roll the dough into an 8- to 10-inch round.

❸ Fill the calzones. Place ½ cup of the filling across the bottom half of the dough round, slightly closer to the center. Use a pastry brush or your finger to lightly brush the edge of the dough with the egg wash.

❹ Form the calzones. Lift the other half of the dough and fold it over the filling. Use a fork to crimp the edges to seal. Transfer the calzone to a sheet pan. Repeat with the remaining dough and filling, spacing the calzones a few inches apart.

❺ Bake and serve the calzones. Brush the top of each calzone with olive oil. Bake for 14 to 16 minutes, until golden brown and cooked through. Let cool for 5 minutes on the sheet pan. Use a spatula to transfer the calzones to a serving plate. Drizzle the calzones with olive oil and sprinkle with sea salt and Parmigiano. Serve with the pizza sauce on the side.

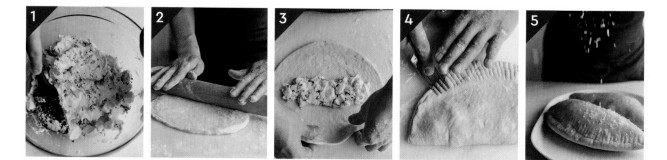

Rosemary Focaccia

Makes 1 (18 by 13-inch) loaf

Speckled with fresh rosemary and flaky salt, focaccia is a flatbread whose name traces back to the ancient Roman word for hearth (in some ways, it's the original pizza). A generous amount of olive oil drizzled on the sheet pan and over the indentations that top the dough gives the bread its characteristic rich flavor and a texture that's both crisp and chewy. In this recipe, a small amount of whole wheat flour gives the focaccia added flavor and a slightly sturdier structure. The best thing about focaccia is that you can top it any number of ways before baking: with sliced red onion, olives, or tomatoes and basil. Our favorite topping, however, is grapes—a specialty of Tuscany that celebrates the grape harvest.

1 tablespoon sugar

1¾ cups warm water (about 90°F)

2¾ teaspoons active dry yeast

4½ cups all-purpose flour, plus more for smoothness and kneading

½ cup whole wheat flour

4 teaspoons kosher salt

Extra virgin olive oil

¼ loosely packed cup whole fresh rosemary leaves

Coarse sea salt, for sprinkling

❶ **Make the dough.** In a bowl or measuring cup, stir the sugar into the water. Sprinkle in the yeast and let stand for 10 to 12 minutes, until foamy. In the bowl of a stand mixer fitted with the dough hook attachment, combine the 4½ cups all-purpose flour, whole wheat flour, salt, ½ cup olive oil, and the yeast-water mixture. Mix on medium-low speed for 3 minutes or until the dough begins to come together, stopping the mixer and scraping down the sides and bottom of the bowl as needed. Mix the dough for 6 minutes more or until smooth. If the dough still feels tacky, add all-purpose flour 1 teaspoon at a time and mix to incorporate until the dough is smooth.

❷ **Proof the dough.** Lightly oil a large bowl with olive oil. Generously dust your hands and a clean, dry work surface with all-purpose flour. Turn out the dough onto the surface and gently knead for 2 minutes. Shape the dough into a ball and transfer to the prepared bowl. Brush the top of

the dough with olive oil. Cover with plastic wrap and let stand in a warm place for 1 to 2 hours, until doubled in volume.

❸ **Shape the dough.** Coat an 18 by 13-inch rimmed sheet pan with ¼ cup olive oil. Turn out the dough onto the sheet pan. Press the dough from the center toward the corners of the pan until it is fully and evenly stretched across the pan.

❹ **Proof the dough again.** Move the dough to a warm place and let stand for 1 hour. While the dough is proofing, preheat the oven to 425°F.

❺ **Bake the focaccia.** Gently stretch the dough again to the edges of the pan and press with your fingertips to create indentations all over the dough. Drizzle ¼ cup olive oil over the top. Sprinkle with the rosemary and generously top with sea salt. Bake for 25 to 30 minutes, until golden brown and crispy on top. Transfer to a wire rack and let cool slightly before transferring to a cutting board to slice and serve.

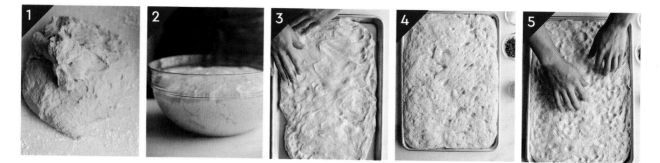

Deep-Dish Pizza

Whereas the hallmark of a great traditional Italian pizza is a thin, crispy crust, the pride of Chicago is deep-dish pizza. As the name suggests, it's a thicker, heartier affair with layers of meat, cheese, and sauce—a knife and fork are welcome. A generous drizzle of olive oil in the bottom of the pan helps create a crust with a focaccia-like chew.

NOTE: *When making the pizza dough for this recipe, portion the dough into two pieces (1 pound each) instead of four. Proceed with the dough recipe as directed, proofing the dough overnight and then again for 2 hours at room temperature.*

2 tablespoons extra virgin olive oil

1 pound Basic Pizza Dough (page 324; see Note below), at room temperature

¾ cup shredded Parmigiano-Reggiano cheese

2 cups Basic Pizza Sauce (page 325)

12 to 15 basil leaves

¼ pound thin slices salami or pepperoni

¾ pound fresh mozzarella, thinly sliced

❶ **Prepare the pizza pan.** Preheat the oven to 450°F. Brush the bottom and sides of a 12-inch deep-dish pizza pan or heavy cast-iron skillet with the olive oil.

❷ **Form the crust.** Use your hands to flatten the dough into the pan. Push the dough down and outward, working slowly from the center toward the edges. Push the dough halfway up the edges, while keeping an even, flat bottom. (If the dough springs back, let it rest for 5 to 10 minutes before attempting to stretch again.) Poke the dough all over with a fork.

❸ **Build the pizza.** Sprinkle the bottom of the pizza with ¼ cup of the Parmigiano. Spread 1 cup of the tomato sauce evenly over the cheese. Top with the basil, salami, and mozzarella. Evenly spread the remaining 1 cup tomato sauce over the mozzarella. Top with the remaining ½ cup Parmigiano.

❹ **Bake and serve the pizza.** Bake the pizza for 32 to 35 minutes, until the crust is browned and the sauce and cheese are bubbling. Transfer the pan to a wire rack and let stand for 5 to 10 minutes to cool slightly. Remove the pizza from the pan and transfer to the wire rack to cool further before serving. Cut into wedges and serve.

15
Desserts

Whether you're making a perfectly flaky pie crust or keeping it classic with chocolate chip cookies, baking is a craft, but it doesn't have to be intimidating.

Once you master the basic concepts, you'll see them pop up time and again in recipes. That's why in this chapter we start with a foundation of simple, straightforward techniques and accessible ingredients to create desserts that are our versions of time-honored classics.

All the recipes rely on learning key techniques, like creaming butter with sugar or cutting it into flour, which lead to a huge variety of baked goods. Baking is often described as an exact science, and while that's true, plenty of preparations—biscuits and pie crust come to mind—require a certain amount of feel and practice that comes from rolling up your sleeves and doing it. Don't underestimate the importance of getting your hands flour-dusted—they're the most important tools in baking, and understanding how to feel the right consistency of dough is the first step to creating amazing desserts.

Baking shows you how just flour, sugar, butter, and eggs can come together in so many different ways. Cookies get crispy on the outside and soft and chewy on the inside, while cakes rise to create the perfect light crumb texture. Plus, there's no better scent than warm sugar and vanilla or chocolate wafting through the kitchen. The satisfaction of pulling a freshly baked dessert out of the oven will make all the time and effort you put into preparing it worthwhile. Though making desserts is a skilled craft, you should still feel free to experiment to a certain extent and be creative once you've got the basics down. Desserts don't stop with baking, however. We'll also teach you techniques for both classic custards (panna cotta, lemon curd) and seasonal fruit (macerated fruit, granita) that will round out your repertoire.

Tools to Have on Hand

Baking requires its own set of tools and equipment. Here are a few essentials.

- Baking pans and sheet pans
- Food processor
- Offset spatulas
- Oven thermometer
- Parchment paper
- Rolling pin
- Silicone spatula
- Stand mixer
- Wire cooling racks

Keys to Success

1. Start with the best ingredients. Seek out high-quality all-purpose flour for baking. Unless something else is specified, you'll want to use unsalted butter for these recipes. Fresh, free-range eggs tend to have the richest color and flavor. Use organic citrus fruits when you need citrus zest, because they won't carry pesticide residue. When it comes to fruit-based desserts, always go for what's in season, and taste the fruit first. For the best flavor, use the freshest spices available, and check expiration dates for chocolate.

2. Measure with care. When it comes to baking, it's important to measure the ingredients precisely; small changes can affect the end product in a big way.

3. Use ingredients at the right temperature. Pay attention when ingredients are called for at certain temperatures (room temperature, chilled, and so on). In general, eggs should be used at room temperature, not straight-out-of-the-refrigerator cold. However, eggs are more easily separated into yolks and whites when cold; separate them cold, then let stand until they reach room temperature. Take the butter out of the refrigerator 15 minutes before you need it and let it soften at room temperature. If the pie crust or cookie dough feels too soft when you're working with it, stop and chill it in the refrigerator before proceeding.

4. Mix mindfully. Watch batters and doughs carefully as you mix. If you undermix, the ingredients won't be properly incorporated or creamed; if you overmix, the batter or dough could get too warm or tough.

MEASURING DRY INGREDIENTS

Bakers have different styles of measuring dry ingredients; our preferred way is to spoon the dry ingredient into the measuring cup and use a straightedge (like a butter knife) to level off the top, scraping away the overflowing ingredient. If the dry ingredient is slightly packed, like flour in its bag, lightly fluff it before scooping. For the easiest cleanup, scoop and scrape the flour over a piece of parchment paper to catch any excess. Once everything's measured, simply lift the sides of the parchment and pour the extra flour back into the bag of flour.

5. Keep an eye on the timing. Baked goods experience carryover cooking when they're removed from the oven. That's why we bake some items, such as cookies, just until they're set but still a little soft: they'll continue to firm up as they cool. Overbaking cookies and cakes will lead to dry, crumbly results.

6. Cool in the pan on a wire rack. Don't be tempted to dive into your baked goods right out of the oven. In general, set the baking pan on a wire rack to let the baked goods cool and firm up slightly, and then transfer the baked goods directly to the wire rack to finish cooling. Leaving them in the pan for the entire cooling process will transfer too much residual heat from the hot pan to the baked goods, overcooking them.

Chocolate Chip Cookies

This star of the American cookie jar (and the partner in crime to a cold glass of milk) is a classic example of a simple "drop dough" recipe: The dough is scooped in rounded tablespoons and dropped onto a sheet pan. Chocolate chip cookies came about in the 1930s when they were invented by the owner of the Toll House Inn in Massachusetts (until then, chocolate was usually melted before being mixed into the dough). It was only after their huge success that semisweet chocolate chips were packaged and sold by Nestlé (with the famous recipe on its packaging, of course).

2¼ cups all-purpose flour

¾ teaspoon baking soda

1¼ teaspoons kosher salt

½ cup granulated sugar

1 packed cup light brown sugar

1 cup (2 sticks) unsalted butter, at room temperature

2 large eggs, at room temperature

1½ teaspoons pure vanilla extract

2 cups semisweet chocolate chips

❶ **Mix the dry ingredients.** In a large bowl, whisk together the flour, baking soda, and salt.

❷ **Cream the butter.** In the bowl of a stand mixer fitted with the paddle attachment, combine the granulated sugar, brown sugar, and butter. Beat on medium-high speed for 3 to 4 minutes, until light and fluffy. Reduce the speed to medium and add the eggs one at a time, waiting until the first is incorporated before adding the second. Add the vanilla. Beat for 3 to 4 minutes, until light and fluffy. Scrape down the sides and bottom of the bowl as needed.

❸ **Finish and chill the dough.** Turn off the mixer and add the flour mixture; mix on low until thoroughly incorporated, for 30 seconds to 1 minute, scraping down the sides of the bowl as needed. Turn off the mixer and add the chocolate chips; mix on low until just incorporated. Transfer the mixture to a large bowl and cover tightly with plastic wrap. (Alternatively, store in a sealed plastic container.) Transfer to the refrigerator and chill for at least 2 hours or up to 24 hours.

❹ **Form the cookies.** Preheat the oven to 350°F. Line two large sheet pans with parchment paper. Working in batches, scoop the dough into portions of 1 rounded tablespoon each with a cookie scooper and drop the balls on the sheet pans 2 inches apart. Alternatively, use your hands to roll into balls or use two spoons to scoop and drop. (If not all of the dough fits on two sheet pans, work in batches and reuse the sheet pans once they've cooled.)

❺ **Bake the cookies.** Bake one sheet pan of cookies at a time, for 12 minutes, rotating after 8 minutes, or until golden brown and just set. Remove from the oven and place the pan on a wire cooling rack. Let the cookies cool on the sheet pan for 2 minutes, then transfer the cookies to the wire rack to cool before serving. Repeat with the remaining cookie dough.

Sugar Cookies

A beloved family affair during the holidays, when they're typically decorated with icing, colored sugar, and sprinkles, sugar cookies are the classic example of rolled-and-cut dough. Chilling the dough after mixing serves two functions: it allows the flour to relax and hydrate (resulting in a more tender texture) and makes the dough much easier to roll out. For the best results, chill the dough at least 2 hours, although you can also refrigerate it overnight; if you chill it overnight, let it sit at room temperature for 30 minutes before rolling so it can soften slightly. This recipe creates tender vanilla-scented cookies for any occasion worth celebrating. In fact, your biggest challenge might be deciding which shape of cookie cutter to use.

2½ cups all-purpose flour, plus more for dusting

1 teaspoon kosher salt

½ teaspoon baking powder

¾ cup (1½ sticks) unsalted butter, at room temperature

1 cup granulated sugar

1 teaspoon pure vanilla extract

1 large egg, at room temperature

❶ Start the dough. In a bowl, combine the 2½ cups flour, salt, and baking powder. Whisk to combine. In the bowl of a stand mixer fitted with the paddle attachment, combine the butter, sugar, and vanilla. Beat on medium speed for about 45 seconds, until a light paste forms. Stop the mixer and scrape down the bottom and sides of the bowl. Add the egg and beat on medium speed for about 45 seconds, until incorporated.

❷ Add the dry ingredients. Stop the mixer and add the flour mixture. Mix on low speed until just incorporated. Once the dough forms, stop the mixer (overmixing can cause the cookies to become tough).

❸ Portion and chill the dough. Transfer the dough to a clean, dry work surface. Pat the dough into a disk and wrap tightly with plastic wrap. Transfer to the refrigerator and chill for at least 2 hours or up to 24 hours.

❹ Roll and cut the cookies. Remove the dough from the refrigerator. Preheat the oven to 375°F. Line 2 large sheet pans with parchment paper. Lightly dust a clean, dry work surface and rolling pin with flour. Cut the dough in half. Roll one portion of dough to ⅛ inch thick. Use cookie cutters to cut out desired shapes; place them 1 inch apart on the sheet pans. Repeat with the remaining dough, rerolling the scraps if needed. If the dough becomes too soft, chill in the refrigerator for 10 to 15 minutes before rolling again.

❺ Bake and cool the cookies. Bake for 10 to 12 minutes for 2- to 3-inch cookies, switching and rotating the pans halfway through, until the edges just begin to brown. If the cookie cutters are larger, increase the baking time slightly by 1 to 2 minutes, depending on the size of the cookie; if they're smaller, decrease the baking time slightly. Remove the pans from the oven and place on wire cooling racks. Let the cookies cool on the sheet pans for 2 minutes. Transfer the cookies directly to the wire rack to cool completely before serving.

Classic Shortbread Cookies

While other cookie dough varieties are dropped or rolled, butter-rich shortbread is traditionally sliced into wedges or thin rectangles. The high ratio of butter to flour creates a crumbly dough that barely holds together—the secret to shortbread's delicate, melt-in-your-mouth texture. Chilling the dough beforehand solidifies the butter, which helps the cookies hold their shape better while baking. After they've cooled, store in airtight containers to retain their crispness. Serve these delicate cookies dipped in Lemon Curd (page 357) and with steaming mugs of tea.

¾ cup (1½ sticks) unsalted butter, at room temperature

½ cup granulated sugar, plus 1 tablespoon for sprinkling

2 teaspoons pure vanilla extract

½ teaspoon kosher salt

2 cups all-purpose flour, plus more for dusting

Lemon Curd (page 357), for serving (optional)

❶ **Make the dough.** In the bowl of a stand mixer fitted with the paddle attachment, combine the butter, sugar, vanilla, and salt. Beat on medium-low speed for about 45 seconds, until a thick paste forms. Stop the mixer and scrape down the sides and bottom of the bowl. Add the 2 cups flour. Mix on low speed until a dough just comes together (it will look crumbly; if overmixed, the cookies can become tough).

❷ **Chill the dough.** Transfer the dough to a clean, dry work surface and pat into a rectangle. Wrap with plastic wrap and chill for 1 hour or up to 24 hours.

❸ **Cut the cookies.** Preheat the oven to 325°F. Line 2 large sheet pans with parchment paper. Generously dust a clean, dry work surface with flour. Using a rolling pin, roll the chilled dough into a ½-inch-thick rectangle (if the dough starts to crack around the edges, let stand for 5 minutes before continuing to roll, and/or pinch together with your fingers). Use a paring knife to trim and straighten the edges of the dough. Cut the dough into 16 rectangles.

❹ **Prick the cookies.** Arrange the cookies 2 inches apart on the prepared sheet pans. Use the tines of a fork to prick rows on the tops of the cookies. Lightly sprinkle each cookie with granulated sugar.

❺ **Bake the cookies.** Bake, rotating and switching the pans halfway through, for 16 to 18 minutes, until golden brown. Transfer the cookies directly to a wire rack and cool completely before serving with the lemon curd on the side.

COOK'S *tip*

SIMPLE STIR-INS: *This is a basic shortbread recipe that's all about a classic buttery flavor, but you can add interest with other flavorings such as citrus zest, ground white pepper, finely chopped fresh herbs, or lavender. Add any of these flavorings along with the vanilla.*

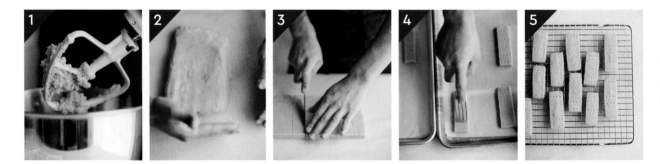

Lemon Curd
(page 357)

Pound Cake

with Sugar Glaze

So named because they were traditionally made with a pound each of four ingredients—flour, butter, eggs, and sugar—pound cakes are beloved for their rich, buttery flavor (often enhanced with vanilla and citrus zest) and dense, tender crumb. These days, recipe variations run the gamut, but a generous ratio of butter and eggs (along with bit of milk, cream, or sour cream) to flour still defines a cake that's easy to love and eat any time of day. Pound cakes are typically baked in a loaf or Bundt pan, and can be simply embellished with a dusting of powdered sugar, a light glaze (page 351), whipped cream, ice cream, lime or lemon curd (page 357), or fresh fruit preserves.

1 cup (2 sticks) unsalted butter, at room temperature, **plus more for greasing**

2 cups all-purpose flour, **plus more for the pan**

1 teaspoon baking powder

½ teaspoon kosher salt

1 cup granulated sugar

1 teaspoon finely grated lemon zest

4 large eggs, at room temperature

1 teaspoon pure vanilla extract

½ cup sour cream

⅓ cup Sugar Glaze (page 351; optional)

❶ Prepare the pan. Preheat the oven to 325°F. Lightly grease the bottom and sides of a 9 by 5-inch loaf pan with butter. Line the bottom of the pan with a piece of parchment paper. Lightly grease the parchment and coat the pan with flour; invert the pan and tap to remove any excess flour. In a bowl, whisk together the 2 cups flour, baking powder, and salt.

❷ Start the batter. In the bowl of a stand mixer fitted with the paddle attachment, combine the 1 cup butter, sugar, and lemon zest. Cream the mixture on medium-low speed for 3 minutes (it will turn pale yellow and become very fluffy). Add the eggs, one at a time, allowing each egg to incorporate before adding the next. After the last egg has been added, stop the mixer and scrape down the bottom and sides of the bowl. Add the vanilla. Mix for 30 seconds at medium-low speed, until just combined.

❸ Finish the batter. Stop the mixer. Add the flour mixture and sour cream. Mix on low speed until just combined, about 30 seconds. Pour the batter into the loaf pan and smooth the surface with a spatula.

❹ Bake the cake. Bake for 55 to 60 minutes, rotating the pan halfway through, until golden brown. (A cake tester or toothpick inserted into the center of the cake should come out clean.) Remove from the oven and place on a wire cooling rack. Let the cake cool in its pan for 10 minutes. Turn the cake out onto the wire rack. Remove and discard the parchment.

❺ Glaze the cake. Let the cake cool completely before spooning the glaze over it. Let it stand for 30 minutes for the glaze to set, then serve. If not serving immediately, wrap in plastic wrap.

Classic Yellow Cake

with Chocolate Buttercream Frosting

Meet your new go-to recipe for birthdays and any other special occasions that call for a pretty layer cake. This celebratory cake gets its familiar color and tender, moist crumb from the rich eggs and extra yolks in its batter. While the cake bakes, whip up the chocolate buttercream (page 351), but make sure the cake cools completely before you lavish it with frosting.

1 cup (2 sticks) unsalted butter, at room temperature, plus more for greasing the pans

3 cups all-purpose flour, plus more for the pans

2 teaspoons baking powder

1 teaspoon baking soda

1 teaspoon kosher salt

1¾ cups granulated sugar

3 large eggs, at room temperature

2 large egg yolks, at room temperature

2 teaspoons pure vanilla extract

1¼ cups buttermilk

Chocolate Buttercream Frosting (page 351)

❶ Preheat the oven and prepare the pans. Preheat the oven to 350°F. Lightly grease the inside of two 9-inch round cake pans. Cover the bottom of each pan with a parchment paper circle. Lightly grease the parchment and flour the inside of the pans. Invert the pans and tap gently to remove any excess flour.

❷ Start the batter. In a medium bowl, whisk together the 3 cups flour, baking powder, baking soda, and salt. In the bowl of a stand mixer fitted with the paddle attachment, combine the sugar and the 1 cup butter. Beat the mixture for 4 minutes on medium-high speed, stopping the mixer halfway through to scrape down the sides and bottom of the bowl (the butter and sugar will be very fluffy and pale yellow).

❸ Add the eggs and vanilla. With the mixer running, add the eggs and egg yolks one at a time. Allow each egg to fully incorporate before adding the next. After the last egg yolk is added, stop the mixer and scrape down the sides and bottom of the bowl. Add the vanilla and mix for 30 seconds on medium-high speed, until just combined.

❹ Add the dry ingredients and buttermilk. Reduce the mixer speed to low. Add one-third of the flour mixture (about 1 cup). Once mixed, add one-third of the buttermilk. Repeat the process, alternating between the remaining flour and the remaining buttermilk. After you've added the last of the buttermilk, mix the batter for about 30 seconds, until smooth. Divide the batter evenly between the prepared pans. Smooth the batter with a spatula. Gently tap the pan against the counter to remove any air bubbles.

❺ Bake the cake. Bake for 33 to 37 minutes, until golden brown. (A cake tester or toothpick inserted in the center of the cake should come out clean.) Place the pans on wire racks and let the cakes cool in the pans for 10 minutes. Turn the cakes out onto the wire racks. Remove and discard the parchment circles. Cool completely before icing with the frosting.

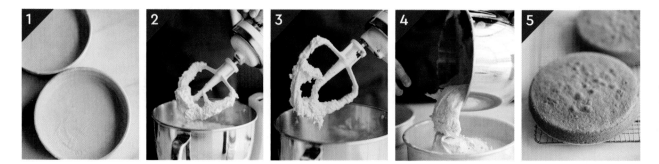

How to FROST A CAKE

1 Use a serrated bread knife to even out the rounded top of each cake layer.

2 Place one cake layer on the cake stand, cut side up. Cut four strips of waxed paper and slide them all around the edge of the cake. Use an offset spatula to spread a ¼-inch-thick layer of frosting on top of the cake.

3 Add the second layer, cut side down.

4 Apply a thin layer of frosting over the top and sides of the cake. Transfer to the refrigerator to dry for 15 minutes. (This is the "crumb coat"—a foundational layer of frosting that traps the crumbs.)

5 Apply the final layer of frosting all over the cake.

6 Carefully slide out the waxed paper strips and discard.

CHOCOLATE BUTTERCREAM FROSTING

Makes about 4 cups, enough to frost 1 (9-inch) two-layer cake

With a fluffy, spreadable texture and rich, buttery flavor, classic buttercream is the quintessential recipe for birthday cake frosting and creamy fillings. Sifting the dry ingredients is an essential step to ensure a perfectly smooth—not gritty—texture.

1 cup (2 sticks) unsalted butter, softened

4 cups confectioners' sugar, sifted

¾ cup unsweetened cocoa powder (natural or Dutch-processed), sifted

¼ teaspoon kosher salt

⅓ cup whole milk

1 teaspoon pure vanilla extract

In the bowl of a stand mixer fitted with the paddle attachment, combine the butter, confectioners' sugar, cocoa powder, and salt. Turn the mixer to low speed. Add the milk in a slow, steady stream. Add the vanilla and increase the speed to medium. Mix until smooth and fluffy, about 1 minute. Use immediately or store in the refrigerator in a sealed container for up to 1 week. (Allow the frosting to come to room temperature and stir it before using it on a cake.)

SUGAR GLAZE

Makes about ¾ cup (enough for 2 pound cakes)

A simple sugar glaze can coat pound cakes, Bundt cakes, cinnamon rolls, or scones with a light layer of sweetness. This version, with a touch of vanilla, uses milk, resulting in a creamy glaze.

¼ cup (½ stick) unsalted butter, melted

2 cups confectioners' sugar

¼ cup whole milk

1¼ teaspoons pure vanilla extract

¼ teaspoon kosher salt

In a bowl, whisk together the butter, sugar, milk, vanilla, and salt until smooth. Use immediately or store in the refrigerator in a sealed container for up to 1 week. Bring to room temperature and stir well before using.

Variation
For a citrus version, replace the milk with ¼ cup freshly squeezed citrus juice of your choice, such as orange, lemon, or lime, and add 1 tablespoon finely grated zest of the same fruit.

Olive Oil Cake

Using olive oil instead of butter in cakes and other baked goods is common in Italy and other countries along the Mediterranean. Olive oil has a very long culinary history, and its use represented a dividing line between northern Europe, where butter was plentiful; and southern Europe, where olive trees could grow. Unlike canola and other neutral-tasting oils, extra virgin olive oil adds personality—it infuses a cake with its own distinctive flavor nuances (for example, peppery, fruity, herbaceous). This is a simple, delicious cake perfect for dessert, but light enough for breakfast too—the way it's often enjoyed in Italy.

1⅓ cups high-quality extra virgin olive oil, plus more for greasing the pan

¾ cup all-purpose flour, plus more for the pan

3 tablespoons cornstarch

1 teaspoon baking powder

½ teaspoon kosher salt

1 cup granulated sugar

Grated zest of 1 lemon

Grated zest of ½ navel orange

4 large eggs, at room temperature

1½ teaspoons pure vanilla extract

1 cup crème fraîche, for serving (optional)

❶ Prepare the pan. Preheat the oven to 325°F. Lightly brush the inside of a 9-inch round cake pan with olive oil. Line the bottom of the pan with a parchment paper circle and brush with more olive oil. Lightly flour the pan and parchment circle, tapping to remove any excess.

❷ Mix the dry ingredients. In a medium bowl, whisk together the ¾ cup flour, cornstarch, baking powder, and salt.

❸ Make the citrus sugar. Detach the bowl from a stand mixer fitted with the paddle attachment. In the bowl, combine the sugar and the lemon and orange zests. Rub together with your fingers until evenly distributed and fragrant. Reattach the bowl to the stand mixer.

❹ Mix the batter. On low speed, stream the 1⅓ cups oil into the citrus sugar; mix for 1 to 2 minutes, until combined. Increase the speed to medium. Add the eggs one at a time, beating for 20 to 30 seconds after each addition, until incorporated. Add the vanilla and mix until incorporated. Reduce the speed to low and add the dry ingredients, one-third at a time, stopping and scraping down the sides and bottom of the bowl between additions. After the last addition, mix for 1 to 2 minutes, until just incorporated. Pour the batter into the pan. Smooth the batter with a spatula.

❺ Bake the cake. Bake for 45 to 50 minutes, until the top springs back when lightly pressed. (A cake tester or toothpick inserted into the center of the cake should come out clean.) Remove the pan from the oven and place on a wire cooling rack. Let the cake cool in the pan for 15 minutes. Turn the cake out onto the wire rack. Remove and discard the parchment circle. Let cool completely before serving with the crème fraîche.

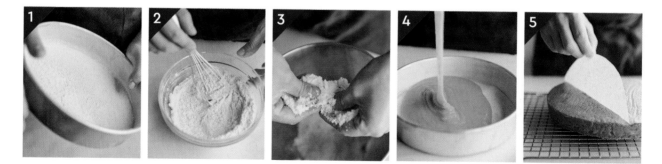

Flourless Chocolate Cake

Makes 1 (9-inch) cake

This fudgey, truffle-like chocolate cake is essentially an aerated custard, created when whipped egg whites are folded into an enriched bittersweet chocolate syrup. Garnishing the cake with a sprinkle of flaky sea salt is the perfect way to counterbalance sweetness and enhance the bittersweet chocolate. To ensure gentle, even cooking, the cake is cooked in a *bain-marie* (water bath), a method used to bake cheesecakes as well. Filling the pan with water only after it's on the oven rack keeps you from having to carry a pan full of sloshing hot water to the oven.

½ cup (1 stick) unsalted butter, at room temperature, plus more for greasing the pan

1 cup superfine sugar

7 tablespoons water

12 ounces bittersweet chocolate (68 to 75% cacao), coarsely chopped

5 large eggs: 2 whole eggs, 3 eggs separated into whites and yolks, at room temperature

½ teaspoon kosher salt

¼ teaspoon cream of tartar

Flaky sea salt, for garnish

Confectioners' sugar, for garnish

❶ Prepare the pan. Preheat the oven to 325°F. Wrap the bottom and sides of a 9-inch springform cake pan with heavy-duty foil, making sure there are no tears (this is to prevent water from leaking into the pan). Grease the inside of the pan with butter and line the bottom with a parchment paper circle. Grease the parchment with more butter.

❷ Make the syrup. In a small saucepan, combine ¾ cup of the superfine sugar with the water and bring to a simmer on medium-high. Cook, whisking occasionally, for 2 to 3 minutes, until the sugar is fully dissolved. Remove from the heat and let cool slightly.

❸ Melt the chocolate. Fill a medium pot halfway with water and bring to a simmer on medium-high. Reduce the heat to medium. Combine the chocolate and the ½ cup butter in a large heatproof glass or stainless steel bowl and set it on the rim of the pot, over (not touching) the water. Cook, stirring frequently, for 4 to 5 minutes, until the chocolate has completely melted. Whisk in the 3 egg yolks one at a time, whisking constantly until thoroughly incorporated and thickened (if the chocolate is too hot, you risk scrambling the eggs). Whisk in the kosher salt, then the syrup. Remove from the heat and set aside to cool slightly.

❹ Whip the eggs and sugar. In the bowl of a stand mixer fitted with the whisk attachment, whip the 2 whole eggs, the 3 egg whites, cream of tartar, and the remaining ¼ cup sugar on high speed for about 4 minutes, until thick and quadrupled in volume (the mixture will fall off the whisk in thick ribbons).

RECIPE CONTINUES

5 **Make the batter.** Remove the bowl from the stand mixer. Working in batches, use a rubber spatula to gradually and gently fold the whipped egg mixture into the chocolate, rotating the bowl after each fold and scraping the bottom of the bowl. Make sure to fold gently or the egg mixture will deflate too much. Mix until fully incorporated. Pour the batter into the cake pan.

6 **Prepare the bain-marie.** Set a folded kitchen towel in the bottom of a roasting pan and set the cake pan on top of the towel. Transfer the roasting pan to the oven. Using a kettle or pitcher, carefully fill the roasting pan with hot tap water one-third of the way up the side of the cake pan.

7 **Bake the cake.** Bake for 40 to 45 minutes, or until the center is set. Carefully remove the roasting pan from the oven and let the cake cool in the water bath. Remove the cake from the water bath and unmold. Transfer to a plate and loosely cover with plastic wrap. Transfer to the refrigerator and chill for 2 hours or up to 24 hours. Just before serving, sprinkle with flaky salt and a light dusting of confectioners' sugar.

DOUBLE BOILERS

Double boilers are used when you want gentle, steady, indirect heat. Although you can buy pots with a double boiler insert, it's easy to set up your own by placing a heatproof bowl on top of a simmering pot of water. Choose a large or medium bowl depending on how much of the ingredient you'll be heating inside it. Glass or stainless steel bowls work best, but note that the thicker glass bowls take more time to heat up. Choose the right size saucepan to go with the bowl—the rim should fit snugly all around the bowl, allowing no steam to escape, and the bowl should not touch the water. If the pot is too wide, the bowl may sit too low; if it's too small, you won't have a secure setup or enough surface area for heating.

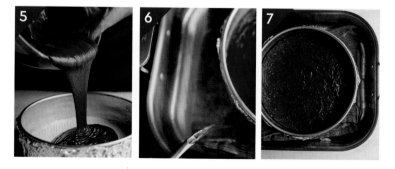

Lemon Curd

With a thick, creamy texture and bright, sunny flavor, lemon curd is a luxurious treat. Rubbing the sugar with the finely grated zest releases the lemon's essential oils and infuses them into the sugar. Don't worry when the mixture looks broken after whisking in the eggs; it will combine into a smooth, glossy curd once it's cooked. Lemon curd will keep for up to a week in the refrigerator, so it's great to make ahead. Try it served with scones, toasted Pound Cake (page 346), Classic Shortbread Cookies (page 344), or fresh fruit, or used as a filling for tarts and cakes.

1½ cups granulated sugar

2 tablespoons finely grated lemon zest

½ cup (1 stick) unsalted butter, at room temperature

¼ teaspoon kosher salt

3 large eggs, at room temperature

2 large egg yolks, at room temperature

½ cup freshly squeezed lemon juice (about 4 lemons)

1 Make the lemon sugar. Place the sugar and lemon zest in a small bowl. Use your fingers to rub them together until well blended and fragrant.

2 Cream the butter and sugar. In the bowl of a stand mixer fitted with the paddle attachment, combine the butter, lemon sugar, and salt. Beat for 2 minutes on medium-high speed, until light and fluffy.

3 Add the eggs and lemon juice. Add the eggs and egg yolks, one at a time, allowing each to fully incorporate before adding the next. Add the lemon juice in a slow and steady stream (the mixture will look curdled; this is normal).

4 Cook the curd. Transfer the mixture to a medium heavy-bottomed saucepan. Cook, whisking constantly, for 15 to 20 minutes on low, until thickened and the marks of the whisk leave a trail; an instant-read thermometer inserted in the curd should register 170°F. Transfer the curd to a heatproof bowl and place a sheet of plastic wrap directly on the curd to prevent a skin from forming. Refrigerate to cool. Transfer to a sealed container and store in the refrigerator for up to 1 week.

Variation: Lime Curd
Substitute equal amounts of lime juice and zest for the lemon.

COOK'S tip

LEMONS: *Before zesting the lemons, wash them under warm water to remove any wax coating or pesticide that may be on the rind. It's easier to grate the zest before you squeeze the lemons for juice.*

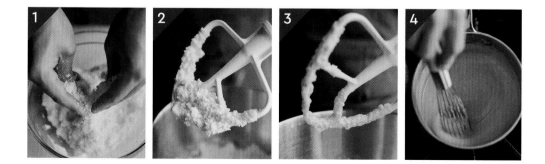

Panna Cotta

Translating to "cooked cream," *panna cotta* is a beloved Italian dessert in which sweetened cream is thickened with gelatin and then chilled in a mold or ramekin. The cream is often flavored with vanilla, coffee, or rum, but it can be infused with just about any flavor that strikes your fancy (see variations).

For a perfectly creamy texture throughout, it's essential to stir and cool the cream before chilling—otherwise the gelatin will sink to the bottom of the ramekin; cooling also allows the flavoring to permeate every bite.

Note that this dessert needs to be refrigerated overnight to set up, so plan accordingly. After chilling, the panna cotta can be unmolded and garnished with fruit, fresh herbs, or chocolate sauce for a fancier presentation, or served straight from its ramekin. This panna cotta can be made up to 5 days ahead and stored in the refrigerator wrapped in plastic wrap.

3 tablespoons cool water
¼ ounce (1 packet) powdered gelatin
1 quart heavy cream
½ cup granulated sugar
⅛ teaspoon kosher salt
1 vanilla bean, split, seeds scraped, pod reserved

❶ **Bloom the gelatin.** Place the water in a small bowl and gently stir in the gelatin; let stand for 5 minutes (it will thicken and look like applesauce).

❷ **Make the base.** In a heavy-bottomed saucepan on medium-low, bring the cream, sugar, salt, vanilla seeds, and vanilla bean pod to a simmer, whisking occasionally. Once simmering, remove from the heat. Add the bloomed gelatin. Whisk constantly for 1 to 2 minutes, until the gelatin is melted and fully incorporated.

❸ **Cool the base.** Fill a large bowl with ice and water. Place a fine-mesh strainer over a medium heatproof bowl. Strain the cream through the strainer. Set the bowl in the ice

bath and cool, stirring with a rubber spatula every 5 minutes, until an instant-read thermometer inserted in the cream registers 60°F.

❹ **Pour the panna cotta.** Evenly divide the cream among 6 (6-ounce) ramekins. (Use a spatula to scrape down the sides of the bowl to ensure that all of the cream is used.) Gently wrap each ramekin with plastic wrap and refrigerate for 12 to 16 hours.

❺ **Unmold the panna cotta.** The next day, carefully run an offset spatula or paring knife along the edge of the ramekins. Fill a bowl with warm water. Hold each ramekin base in the warm water for 5 seconds. Invert each panna cotta onto a plate and serve.

Variations

Add further flavorings in step 2 after the cream comes to a simmer. Cover, remove from the heat, and let stand for 15 minutes. Uncover, return to a simmer, and proceed with adding the gelatin mixture. Suggested flavorings include strips of orange or lemon zest, lavender, bay leaves, lemongrass, or a cinnamon stick.

Apple Crisp

Crisps are an easy-to-assemble, old-fashioned pleasure that we never tire of. The perfect crisp is all about the balance of tender fruit and an oat-flecked crumble topping. To give ours a nutty crunch, we grind a generous amount of almonds with the flour and seasonings. Bourbon-plumped golden raisins set this recipe apart (if you'd like, use apple cider instead of bourbon). We're using apples here, but crisps can be made with any seasonal fruit that you like (stone fruit, berries). To us, a scoop of vanilla ice cream with your crisp is pretty much a necessity.

½ cup golden raisins

¼ cup boiling water

¼ cup bourbon (or apple cider)

7 large tart-sweet apples (such as Honeycrisp, about 3½ pounds), cored, quartered, then cut into 1-inch pieces

¼ cup granulated sugar

½ teaspoon kosher salt

2 teaspoons pure vanilla extract

1 teaspoon ground cinnamon

¼ teaspoon grated nutmeg

Zest and juice of 1 lemon

½ cup all-purpose flour

TOPPING

1½ cups packed light brown sugar

1½ cups whole raw almonds

¾ cup all-purpose flour

¼ teaspoon kosher salt

¾ cup (1½ sticks) unsalted butter, melted

½ cup old-fashioned oats

1 Prepare the bourbon-soaked raisins. Preheat the oven to 375°F. Place the raisins in a small heatproof bowl. Add enough boiling water (about ¼ cup) to just cover the raisins. Stir in the bourbon. Let stand for 10 minutes to plump the raisins.

2 Make the apple filling. Place the apples in a large bowl. Add the raisins (including the soaking liquid), sugar, salt, vanilla, cinnamon, nutmeg, lemon zest and juice, and flour; toss until well combined. Transfer to a 3-quart baking dish.

3 Make the crisp topping. Place the brown sugar, almonds, flour, and salt in a food processor; process until the almonds are finely chopped. Transfer to a large bowl. Add the melted butter; mix with a fork until well combined (the consistency should be like wet sand). Fold in the oats until evenly combined.

4 Bake the crisp. Evenly sprinkle the topping over the apples. Bake the crisp for 50 to 55 minutes, or until the apples are tender and the mixture is bubbling around the edges (if the crisp is browning too quickly, tent with foil and continue baking). Let cool for about 15 minutes before serving.

Macerated Summer Berries

In their peak season, ripe, juicy summer berries need little adornment. However, macerating them in a bit of sugar and perhaps a complementary liqueur—amaretto and Cointreau are good options—coaxes out the berries' juices and enhances their natural sweetness. This technique transforms a simple bowl of berries (or stone fruits, such as peaches, nectarines, and apricots) into a truly memorable summer dessert, especially when they're finished with a touch of fresh basil and homemade whipped cream.

1 pound mixed summer berries (such as blueberries, blackberries, strawberries, and/or raspberries)

3 tablespoons granulated sugar

1 tablespoon confectioners' sugar

½ teaspoon kosher salt

Grated zest of 1 lemon

1 tablespoon freshly squeezed lemon juice

1 teaspoon amaretto or other liqueur (optional)

6 large fresh basil leaves, plus extra for garnish

2 cups unsweetened whipped cream (see Cook's Tip)

❶ Prepare the berries. In a colander or fine-mesh strainer, rinse the berries in small batches so as not to bruise them. Lay them out on paper towels to dry. Hull the strawberries and halve them if they're large. Combine all the berries in a nonreactive bowl with the granulated and confectioners' sugars, salt, lemon zest, lemon juice, and amaretto. Use a wooden spoon or spatula to gently mix, then cover with plastic wrap and refrigerate for 1 hour.

❷ Finish the berries. Remove the berries from the refrigerator. Transfer ¾ cup berries to a small bowl and coarsely mash with a fork. Stir the mashed berries back into the whole berries to combine. Thinly slice the 6 basil leaves and stir into the berries. Transfer the berries to a serving dish and garnish with extra whole basil leaves. Serve with the whipped cream on the side.

COOK'S
tip

HOMEMADE WHIPPED CREAM: *To make your own whipped cream, pour 1 cup heavy cream into a large bowl. Freeze for 10 minutes until cold but not frozen. Whisk vigorously and constantly until soft peaks form (the cream will cling to the whisk and form a peak at the tip).*

Strawberry-Mint Granita

Granita is a frozen dessert made from sugar, water, and puréed fruit—there's no better friend on a sweltering summer afternoon. Granita originated in Sicily, but these days it's available all over Italy in various forms. Depending on where and how it's made, the texture can range from fine to coarse. Scraping the slushy mixture with a fork, as we do here, creates ice crystals with a coarse but fluffy consistency. This recipe is written for peak season strawberries, but you can use the same fruit-sugar-water ratio for any fruit that's in season (such as cherries, nectarines, peaches, or blackberries). Granitas can be savory too (think celery granita on heirloom tomatoes), so feel free to experiment.

1 cup water

⅔ cup granulated sugar

¼ teaspoon kosher salt

1 sprig mint, plus extra leaves for garnish

1 pound strawberries, hulled

2 teaspoons freshly squeezed lemon juice

❶ Make the sugar syrup.
In a small pot, combine the water, sugar, salt, and mint sprig; heat on medium-low until hot. Simmer for 4 to 5 minutes, until fragrant. Remove from the heat and let stand for 5 minutes to cool slightly. Carefully remove and discard the mint sprig.

❷ Purée and add the strawberries. Place the strawberries and lemon juice in a food processor and process until smooth. Slowly whisk the purée into the syrup until thoroughly combined.

❸ Freeze the granita. Pour the granita base into a 9 by 13-inch baking dish. Freeze for about 25 minutes, until you see flaky icy crystals forming around the edges. Use a fork to scrape the ice crystals toward the center. Return the pan to the freezer. Repeat the process, scraping every 20 to 30 minutes, until the granita is frozen and fluffy, about 4 hours total. Serve immediately.

BASIC PIE CRUST

Makes 2 (9-inch) crusts

Consider this basic, easy-to-assemble crust your go-to foundation for any seasonal pie, tart, crostata, or galette that strikes your fancy. Note that the recipe contains two fats: butter for a rich flavor, and a bit of vegetable shortening to create a light, flaky texture.

This recipe makes two pie crusts, enough for a double-crust pie like our Peach Lattice Pie (page 374). If you need only one crust for a recipe, such as the Strawberry Crostata (page 368) or Late Summer Blueberry Pie (page 370), refrigerate the second crust for up to 2 days or wrap in several layers of plastic wrap and freeze for up to 1 month; thaw in the refrigerator overnight before using.

A food processor makes the process quick, but feel free to make the pie crust by hand, the old-fashioned way, if you don't have a processor at home. To do this, whisk together the dry ingredients in a bowl. Add the pieces of butter and shortening and cut them into the flour with a pastry cutter, or rub them in with your fingertips. Add the water, stir together with a wooden spoon, and proceed with the recipe as directed.

3 cups all-purpose flour, plus more for dusting

2 tablespoons granulated sugar

1½ teaspoons kosher salt

14 tablespoons (1¾ sticks) unsalted butter, cold and small diced

4 tablespoons solid vegetable shortening, cold and small diced

6 tablespoons cold water, plus more if needed

❶ Mix the dough. In a food processor fitted with the steel blade, briefly pulse the 3 cups flour, sugar, and salt to combine. Add the butter and shortening. Pulse until no large pieces of butter remain (none larger than a small pea); the mixture will look like coarse meal. Sprinkle with the water, 2 tablespoons at a time; briefly pulse between additions at 2-second intervals until the dough just begins to come together. Be careful not to overprocess; the dough will look crumbly. The dough should hold together when squeezed in your hand. If the dough feels dry or sandy, add 1 to 2 more tablespoons of water, 1 tablespoon at a time.

❷ Refrigerate the dough. Lightly dust your hands and a clean, dry work surface with flour. Transfer the dough to the work surface. Use your hands to gather the dough together. Divide the dough in half and shape into two 5-inch disks. Wrap each disk tightly in plastic wrap. Refrigerate for 2 hours or up to 24 hours before using. If not using immediately, freeze for up to 1 month.

COOK'S tip

DOUGH CONSISTENCY: *It's easy to add too much water to a pie dough when making it in a food processor because the water gets trapped at the edge of the bowl where the blade does not reach. To assess the amount of moisture in the dough, give it a squeeze with your hands or even turn it out into a bowl first. The pie dough will look crumbly, but once you combine it on the work surface with your hands, it will come together.*

Strawberry Crostata

When fresh fruit is in season and bursting with flavor, the less you do to it the better. We love crostatas because they're a very easy way to make the most of seasonal fruit, whether it's blueberries, peaches, or—as here—strawberries. For this crostata filling, a small amount of sugar and lemon brightens the strawberry flavors, and cornstarch thickens the juices and creates a syrup while the crostata bakes. A few grinds of black pepper add a subtle heat that complements the sweetness. Don't worry about being too perfect with folding the dough—the beauty of crostatas is that they're a bit rustic, but nevertheless delicious.

All-purpose flour, for dusting

1 unbaked pie crust (Basic Pie Crust, page 366), chilled

1 pound strawberries, hulled and cut into ¼-inch-thick slices

3 tablespoons granulated sugar

1 tablespoon cornstarch

Finely grated zest of 1 lemon

⅛ teaspoon kosher salt

Pinch of freshly ground black pepper

1 large egg

1 tablespoon water

2 teaspoons turbinado sugar

❶ Roll out the crust. Remove the disk of dough from the refrigerator and let stand at room temperature for 15 minutes to soften slightly. Line a sheet pan with parchment paper. Generously dust a clean, dry work surface and rolling pin with flour. Unwrap the dough and place it on the work surface. Use the rolling pin to evenly roll the dough from the center to the edges into a 12-inch circle. Carefully wrap the dough around the rolling pin and transfer to the sheet pan. Transfer to the refrigerator to chill for 10 to 15 minutes. While the crust is chilling, preheat the oven to 425°F.

❷ Make the filling. In a large bowl, combine the strawberries, granulated sugar, cornstarch, lemon zest, salt, and pepper. Toss to thoroughly coat the berries.

❸ Form the crostata. Remove the crust from the refrigerator. Drain the filling through a fine-mesh strainer; discard the juices. Mound the filling slightly in the center of the crust, leaving a 1½- to 2-inch border. Working your way around the edge, fold the crust up and slightly over the filling, gently pleating as you go.

❹ Bake the crostata. In a small bowl, whisk together the egg and water until smooth. Use a pastry brush to lightly brush the crust with the egg wash. Sprinkle the turbinado sugar all over the crust. Bake for 25 to 30 minutes, until the crust is golden brown and cooked through. Let cool on the pan for 15 to 20 minutes before serving.

COOK'S
tip

CROSTATA FOLDING: *If you're having trouble folding the dough up over the fruit filling, use the parchment paper to help you by lifting and folding the edge of the paper with the dough as you work your way around.*

Late Summer Blueberry Pie

This is not your average blueberry pie. The filling uses a mix of cooked and fresh fruit, so it has the jammy consistency of a baked blueberry filling along with the juicy bursts of fresh berries. That filling is then poured into a fully baked crust that was blind baked. "Blind baking" a pie crust means prebaking it either partially or completely before adding the pie filling. You most often blind bake crusts for open-faced pies when the filling doesn't need to be baked as long as the crust (or doesn't need baking at all, like this one). This process helps keep the bottom crust flaky and not soggy. Serve slices of this pie with whipped cream, vanilla ice cream or gelato, or a dollop of lightly sweetened mascarpone on warm summer evenings.

1 unbaked pie crust (Basic Pie Crust, page 366), chilled

All-purpose flour, for dusting

⅔ cup granulated sugar

½ teaspoon kosher salt

2 tablespoons cornstarch

Grated zest of 1 lemon

3 tablespoons freshly squeezed lemon juice

½ teaspoon ground cinnamon

6 cups fresh blueberries

¼ cup cold water, plus 1 tablespoon

1 large egg

❶ Roll out the crust. Remove the disk of dough from the refrigerator and let stand at room temperature for 10 to 15 minutes to soften very slightly. Generously dust a clean, dry work surface and rolling pin with flour. Unwrap the dough and place it on the work surface. Use the rolling pin to evenly roll the dough from the center to the edges into a 13-inch circle. Carefully wrap the dough around the rolling pin and transfer to a 9-inch pie dish; the edges will hang over. Gently press the dough into the dish. Use kitchen shears or a paring knife to trim the dough that hangs over the rim of the dish to about ½ inch. Crimp the edges as desired. Use a fork to prick all over the dough. Transfer to the refrigerator and chill for 30 minutes.

❷ Start the filling. While the crust is chilling, preheat the oven to 425°F. In a small bowl, combine the sugar, salt, cornstarch, lemon zest, lemon juice, and cinnamon. In a saucepan, combine 2 cups of the blueberries and ¼ cup water. Cover and bring to a boil on high. Stir in the sugar mixture and cook, stirring constantly, for 3 to 4 minutes, until thickened. Transfer to a bowl and let cool completely, stirring occasionally. Stir the remaining 4 cups blueberries into the cooked blueberry mixture. Cover with plastic wrap and set aside.

RECIPE CONTINUES

❸ Blind bake the crust. Remove the crust from the refrigerator. Line with parchment paper and fill with pie weights or dried beans. Place the pie dish on a sheet pan and bake for 16 to 17 minutes, until beginning to brown. Remove from the oven and carefully remove the pie weights and parchment.

❹ Finish baking the crust. In a small bowl, whisk together the egg and the 1 tablespoon water until smooth. Use a pastry brush to lightly brush the crust with the egg wash; return to the oven and bake for 10 minutes, until golden brown. Remove from the oven and let cool on a wire rack for 10 minutes.

❺ Assemble the pie. Pour the filling into the crust, slightly mounding it in the center. Refrigerate for 30 minutes to 2 hours, until the filling firms up slightly, before serving.

COOK'S
tip

PIE WEIGHTS: *Adding pie weights to the crust keeps the sides from shrinking and the bottom from bubbling up while the crust blind bakes. You can buy ceramic pie weights or use dried beans.*

CRIMPING PIE CRUSTS

Crimping your pie crust adds a decorative element to your pies, but also serves the functional purpose of keeping the crust from slipping into the pan as it bakes and contracts. One of the simplest ways to crimp a pie crust is with the tines of fork. For a scalloped pattern, use the edge of two spoons (one larger, one smaller). For a wavy pattern, use your knuckles or thumb and index finger. Regardless of the pattern you choose, when you trim the dough after pressing it into the pie dish, always leave enough overhang (dough hanging over the edge). Roll the excess under itself to create a thick crust that will be easy to crimp.

5

Peach Lattice Pie

A woven crosshatch of pastry over a bubbling fruit filling—also known as a lattice-topped pie—is a classic dessert as delightful to behold as it is to eat. Double-crust pies like this one have fillings that take longer to cook, so the crust is usually unbaked when filled (no blind baking needed). This also allows for the dough of the top crust to be crimped nicely to the unbaked bottom crust. Lattice patterns may take a little practice to master, but remember that even an imperfect-looking pie is going to taste really good. The following recipe makes the most of ripe, juicy peaches, but you can use this method for any number of fruit pies.

2 unbaked pie crusts (Basic Pie Crust, page 366), chilled

All-purpose flour, for dusting

¾ cup granulated sugar

¼ cup packed light brown sugar

¼ cup cornstarch

¼ teaspoon ground cinnamon

½ teaspoon freshly grated nutmeg

½ teaspoon kosher salt

3½ pounds medium to large peaches (ripe but firm), peeled, pitted, and thinly sliced

Grated zest and juice of 1 lemon

2 tablespoons unsalted butter, chilled and cut into small pieces

1 large egg

1 tablespoon water

1 tablespoon turbinado sugar

❶ Roll out the bottom crust. Remove one chilled disk of dough from the refrigerator and let stand at room temperature for 15 minutes to soften very slightly. Dust a clean, dry work surface and rolling pin with flour. Unwrap the dough and place it on the work surface. Use the rolling pin to evenly roll the dough from the center to the edges into a 13-inch circle. Carefully wrap the dough around the rolling pin and transfer to a 9-inch pie dish (the edges will hang over). Gently press the dough into the dish. Use kitchen shears or a paring knife to trim the dough that hangs over the side of the dish to about ½ inch. Use a fork to prick the dough all over. Transfer to the refrigerator and chill for 30 minutes. While the crust is chilling, position the oven rack at the lowest level and preheat the oven to 425°F.

❷ Make the filling. In a small bowl, use a fork to stir together the granulated sugar, brown sugar, cornstarch, cinnamon, nutmeg, and salt. In a large bowl, gently toss the peaches with the lemon zest and juice. Add the sugar mixture and toss gently until well combined. Let stand for 20 to 30 minutes to soften.

❸ Fill the pie. Remove the remaining disk of dough from the refrigerator and let stand at room temperature for 10 to 15 minutes to soften very slightly. Remove the bottom pie crust from the refrigerator. Use a slotted spoon to evenly layer the filling in the bottom crust, leaving any liquid in the bowl. Dot the top of the peaches with the butter. In a small bowl, whisk together the egg and water until smooth. Use a pastry brush to lightly brush the edge of the dough with some of the egg wash.

❹ Make the lattice top. Generously dust a clean, dry work surface and rolling pin with flour. Unwrap the dough disk and place it on the work surface. Use the rolling pin to evenly roll the dough from the center to the edges into a 13-inch circle. With a knife or a fluted pastry cutter, cut into ½-inch-wide strips. In an overlapping pattern, start with the longest pieces in the center of the pie and carefully lay and weave the strips of dough into a lattice pattern on top of the filling. Use kitchen shears or a paring knife to trim the strips of dough that hang over the side of the dish equal to the bottom crust. Gently press the outer edges of the dough together and fold up over the lattice edge. Crimp as desired.

❺ Finish the top and bake the pie. Use a pastry brush to lightly brush the lattice with the remaining egg wash. Lightly sprinkle the turbinado sugar all over the lattice. Place the pie dish on a sheet pan and bake on the bottom rack for 20 minutes. After 20 minutes, loosely tent with foil and bake for an additional 40 to 45 minutes, until the crust is deep golden brown and the filling is bubbling. Transfer to a wire cooling rack and let cool for 2 to 3 hours (the filling will thicken) before serving.

**Late Summer
Blueberry Pie**
(page 370)

Strawberry Crostata
(page 368)

Peach Lattice Pie
(page 374)

Acknowledgments

The **Blue Apron Culinary Team** consists of all the chefs, recipe writers, editors, and test kitchen managers and associates who worked tirelessly to create this cookbook, but especially: co-founder Matthew Wadiak, whose passion shaped the entire culinary program for five years; Chris Sorensen, the team's fearless leader; John Adler, who led on recipe testing and development with the recipe writers, including Lisa Appleton, Leila Clifford, Judi Peña, and Alex Saggiomo; colleagues Tim Kemp, Claire King, Lili Dagan, Sarah Comerford, and Lauren Bernstein; and Jenn Sit, who managed this cookbook's creation.

We'd like to give our most sincere thanks to:

Co-founders Matt Salzberg and Ilia Papas, for their leadership and their continued support for the cookbooks

Harper Wave, including publisher Karen Rinaldi and editor Hannah Robinson, who believed in our publishing program and led us through the process with patience

Kathryn Bain, for her creative direction, along with the entire photography team, including John Kernick, Simon Andrews, Kaitlyn DuRoss, Alex Leonard, Janine Desiderio, Rizwan Alvi, and Sophia Pappas, whose prodigious talents created the photographs that grace this book

Our literary agent, Janis Donnaud, who is always our champion

Laura Palese, for her beautiful design, and Paula Disbrowe, who helped bring this content to life

The entire leadership team, including Jared Cluff and Rani Yadav, who work to share Blue Apron's mission and story with the world

The thousands of Blue Apron employees who work so hard every day to make that mission a reality

Bill Niman, Alice Waters, and the countless farmers, vendors, and producers who inspire us to be better chefs and build a better food system for generations to come

All the chefs we've ever learned from, who taught us with great patience and passion

Last, but certainly not least, to the Blue Apron home chefs around the country: Thank you for inspiring us and making our jobs worthwhile. We do this for you.

Index

(Page references in *italics* refer to illustrations.)